# UNDEFEATED

## JIM THORPE AND THE CARLISLE INDIAN SCHOOL FOOTBALL TEAM

# UNDEFEATED

## JIM THORPE AND THE CARLISLE INDIAN SCHOOL FOOTBALL TEAM

## Steve Sheinkin

SQUARE
FISH

ROARING BROOK PRESS    *New York*

SQUARE
FISH

An imprint of Macmillan Publishing Group, LLC
175 Fifth Avenue, New York, NY 10010
mackids.com

Our books may be purchased in bulk for promotional, educational, or business use.
Please contact your local bookseller or the Macmillan Corporate and Premium Sales Department
at (800) 221-7945 ext. 5442 or by email at MacmillanSpecialMarkets@macmillan.com.

Library of Congress Cataloging-in-Publication Data
Names: Sheinkin, Steve, author.
Title: Undefeated : Jim Thorpe and the Carlisle Indian School football team
    football team / Steve Sheinkin.
Description: New York, New York : Roaring Brook Press, 2017.
Identifiers: LCCN 2016009083 (print) | LCCN 2016034829 (ebook) |
    ISBN 978-1-250-29447-0 (paperback) | ISBN 978-1-5964-3955-9 (ebook)
Subjects: LCSH: United States Indian School (Carlisle, Pa.)—Football—
    Juvenile literature. | Thorpe, Jim, 1887–1953—Juvenile literature. | Warner,
    Glenn S. (Glenn Scobey), 1871–1954—Juvenile literature. | BISAC: JUVENILE
    NONFICTION / Biography & Autobiography / Sports & Recreation. |
    JUVENILE NONFICTION / People & Places / United States / Native American. |
    JUVENILE NONFICTION / History / United States / 20th Century.
Classification: LCC GV958.U33 S54 2017 (print) | LCC GV958.U33 (ebook) |
    DDC 796.332/630974843—dc23
LC record available at https://lccn.loc.gov/2016009083

Originally published in the United States by Roaring Brook Press
First Square Fish edition, 2019
Square Fish logo designed by Filomena Tuosto

1   3   5   7   9   10   8   6   4   2

AR: 6.8 / LEXILE: 980L

For David

# Contents

**J**im Thorpe looked ridiculous and he knew it—like a scarecrow dressed for football, he'd later say. The borrowed pants barely reached his knees. The grass-stained jersey hung loose on his lanky frame. The cleats were coming apart.

He walked out to Indian Field anyway.

Football practice had already begun, and about thirty athletes in their teens and early twenties were loosening up. The head coach, Pop Warner, stood watching. Warner was a big man with a square block of a head, a whistle on a string around his neck, a cigarette dangling from the corner of his mouth. He saw the scarecrow coming.

"What do you think you're doing out here?"

"I want to play football," Thorpe said.

The players stopped and looked. A few laughed.

Warner was not laughing. "I'm only going to tell you once, Jim. Go back to the locker room and take that uniform off! You're my most valuable track man, and I don't want you to get hurt playing football."

Thorpe had expected as much from Warner, who also coached the track team. At nineteen, Thorpe owned pretty much every running and jumping record at the Carlisle Indian Industrial School. Just under six feet tall, muscular but thin, he was built for speed—but he loved football, too.

And besides, he despised being told there was something he couldn't do.

"I want to play *football*," he said again.

Jim Thorpe's jaw-dropping tryout earned him this better-fitting uniform—but Coach Warner still thought he was too skinny for football.

Again, Warner told Jim to take a hike. With less than two weeks to get his team ready for the 1907 college football season, the coach had no time for nonsense.

But Thorpe would not leave the field.

"All right," Warner finally grunted. "If this is what you want, go out there and give my varsity boys a little tackling practice." He tossed Thorpe a football. "And believe me, that's *all* you'll be to them."

Thorpe caught the ball and held it, running his fingers over the leather and laces of a store-bought football for the first time in his life. He tucked the ball under his arm, walked to one of the chalk goal lines, turned, and studied the field.

There in front of him was the famous Carlisle School football team, a diverse group of Native Americans from all over the country. There was the team he'd been hearing about, dreaming about, since he was a kid.

The players were spread out on the grass, maybe five feet between each man. There was no chance for a runner to get very far. That was the point. This was a tackling exercise.

Warner shouted for Thorpe to begin.

He started forward. The first few defenders got low and grabbed for his legs. Thorpe spun free and continued. Another group dove at him. He lifted his knees high and churned through outstretched arms. Picking up his pace, he faked out the next few tacklers; then, with a bit of open field around him, he turned on his sprinter's speed and was gone.

The cigarette fell from the corner of Pop Warner's open mouth.

After crossing the goal line, Thorpe circled back to the coach. A huge grin on his face, he tossed Warner the football.

"I gave them some good practice, right, Pop?"

Warner's coaching assistant was smiling too. "You're supposed to let them tackle you, Jim," he said.

The man was kidding, but Thorpe thought he was being laughed at. His smile vanished. He said, "Nobody's going to tackle Jim."

Warner's square face flushed raw-beef red. He slammed the ball back into Thorpe's chest.

"Well, let's see if you can do it again, kid!"

And to his team he yelled, "Get mean out there! Smack him down! Hit him down so hard he doesn't get up! Who does he think he is? This isn't a track meet! This is football! *Hit! Hit! Hit!*"

Pop lit a new cigarette. Thorpe walked back to the goal line.

And then he ran through the whole team again.

He twisted through tackles and shoved defenders out of the way, faking some guys out and flat-out blowing by others. It was a combination of power, agility, and speed Pop Warner had never seen in one player—and never would again.

Thorpe jogged back to Warner. No grin this time. He tossed the coach the ball.

"Sorry, Pop," he said. "Nobody's going to tackle Jim."

**FIRST**

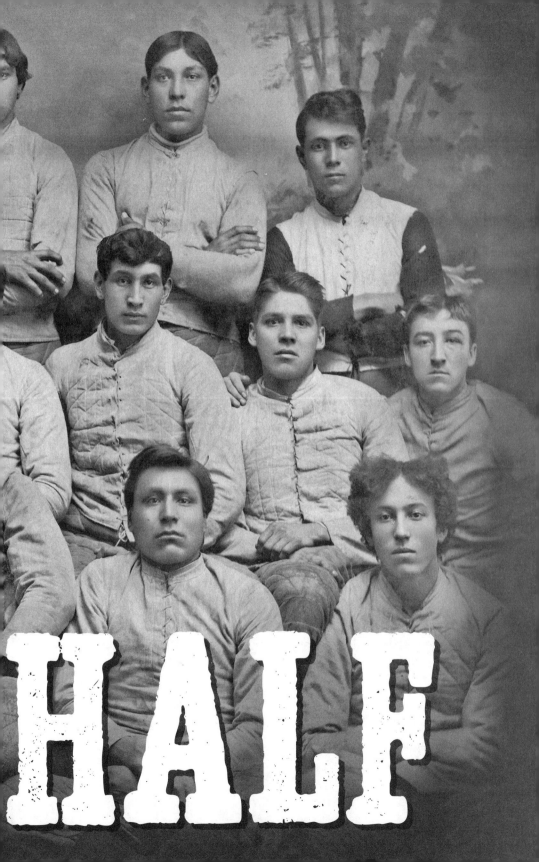

**Y**es, Jim Thorpe made the team.

And for a brief and magical span of years, the Carlisle Indian Industrial School had the best football team in the country. Carlisle was the fastest team anyone had ever seen, the most creative, the most fun to watch. They traveled anywhere and took on anyone, playing all their toughest games on the road. The team drew crowds in train stations, hotel lobbies, and especially football stadiums—Carlisle's 1911 showdown with powerhouse Harvard University drew more fans than the opening game of that year's World Series. Carlisle had the game's most innovative coach in Pop Warner, and, in Jim Thorpe, the greatest star the sport had ever seen.

None of it was easy.

After a lifetime in the sport, Warner would say, "No college player I ever saw had the natural aptitude for football possessed by Jim Thorpe." But what the coach called "natural aptitude" was really something richer, a mix of outrageous athletic talent and a force of will hard-earned from a childhood that would have broken most boys.

The challenges began early. Jim's father, an enormous man named Hiram, saw to that.

As a toddler, Jim liked to splash around in the shallow water near the bank of the North Canadian River, which ran behind his family's cabin in Oklahoma. One day Hiram strode into the river in his boots, grabbed the kid, hauled him out to the deep water, and dropped him into the current. Hiram then waded back to the bank and watched.

Jim raised his head above the water. It was forty yards to the riverbank. It looked like a mile.

He managed to dog-paddle to shore and collapsed on dry land.

Hiram stood over his three-year-old boy and said, "Don't be afraid of the water, son, and it won't be afraid of you."

◄❖►

Hiram Thorpe pushed his son hard, and their clashes of will would only intensify as Jim grew older.

Charlotte Vieux was born in Kansas, but moved to Oklahoma with her family when she was twelve. The Potawatomi, like the people of many other nations, were removed from their land several times by the US government.

And Jim really didn't seem to fear anything, or anyone. Not even his father.

Hiram Thorpe, son of a Sac and Fox Indian mother and an Irish father, stood six foot three, 235 pounds. He walked around armed with a pistol, bullets in his belt, wearing a black cowboy hat. No one messed with Jim's mother, either. Charlotte Vieux, daughter of a Potawatomi Indian woman who'd married a French-Canadian trader, was described by friends as pretty, tall, and big-boned, about two hundred pounds, with exceptionally strong hands.

Hiram had already had two marriages and fathered five children when he and Charlotte married in 1882. They settled on Sac and Fox land in what was called "Indian Territory," which covered most of what is now Oklahoma.

The shameful history behind Indian Territory is not the subject of this story, but it's important to know—it shaped the world Jim Thorpe and the other Carlisle School students would grow up in. In 1830, with the passage of the Indian Removal Act, the US government made it official policy to force Native Americans off their lands in order to open the land to white settlers. President Andrew Jackson explained the objective in bluntly racist language. Native Americans were surrounded by what Jackson called "a superior race" and needed to get out of the way. "They must necessarily yield to the force of circumstances," he said, "and ere long disappear."

The government set aside Indian Territory as a place to send the displaced nations, whether they agreed to go or not. In what became known as the Trail of Tears, to cite the most infamous example, US soldiers marched more than fifteen thousand Cherokee men, women, and children 1,200 miles from Georgia to Indian Territory. An estimated four thousand people died of disease, cold, and starvation before the nightmare journey ended.

Over the following decades, the US government forced the people of more than sixty different American Indian nations—including the Sac and Fox, originally from the western Great Lakes region—to leave their traditional land and resettle in Indian Territory. Different nations were assigned different areas of land, or reservations. By treaty, the reservation land belonged permanently to the Indians. Then the government changed the rules again.

Pressured by land-hungry settlers, Congress passed the General Allotment Act in 1887, stating that Native American families would be "given" 160-acre plots. The remaining land in Indian Territory would be stripped from Indian control and opened up to new settlers.

Charlotte and Hiram Thorpe were granted a piece of decent grazing land on the banks of the North Canadian River. They built a cabin of cottonwood and hickory, and it was there, in 1888, that Charlotte gave birth to twin boys, James and Charles—Jim and Charlie, as they came to be known. Jim would later explain that his mother, following Potawatomi custom, also gave her sons names inspired by something experienced right after childbirth. Through the window near her bed, Charlotte watched the early-morning sun light the path to their cabin. She named Jim *Wathohuck*, translated as "Bright Path." Charlie's Potawatomi name has been lost to history.

Three years later, twenty thousand settlers lined the edge of what had been Sac and Fox land. A government agent fired a gun, the signal for the land rush to begin, and everyone raced in on horseback or in wagons, claiming open sections of land by driving stakes into the soil.

By nightfall, the plains around the Thorpes' farm were dotted with settlers' tents and campfires. In just a few hours, the Sac and Fox had lost nearly 80 percent of their land.

The newcomers built towns, including one called Keokuk Falls, ten miles from the Thorpe family farm. Keokuk Falls was a wild and violent place, home of the "seven deadly saloons," as locals called them. It was a place where even the pigs got drunk—a whiskey distillery near town dumped used corn mash behind the building, and hogs gorged on it and staggered down the dirt streets.

Settlers race for the best plots of land in this 1893 Oklahoma land rush. From his family's farm, Jim watched scenes like this change his world forever.

"Keokuk Falls," a stagecoach driver announced to riders as he pulled into town. "Stay for half an hour and see a man killed."

✦

"Our lives were lived out in the open, winter and summer," Jim later recalled of his childhood. "We were never in the house when we could be out of it."

It was a no-nonsense, hardworking way of life. Charlotte sewed their clothes, mixing Potawatomi designs with modern patterns she saw in

Young Jim's first hero, Ma-ka-tai-me-she-kia-kiak, Black Sparrow Hawk, or Black Hawk. Black Hawk was a member of the Thunder Clan of the Sac and Fox, the same clan as Jim Thorpe.

town. She raised chickens and planted corn, pumpkins, and beans. Hiram tended the livestock and hunted turkey and deer. The family bathed in the river, which in winter meant hacking through the ice and dunking bare bodies through the hole.

Jim's first hero was Black Hawk, the famous Sac leader who had led his people in a desperate fight to hold on to their ancestral land in the 1830s. Thousands of well-armed US soldiers and volunteers—including militia member Abraham Lincoln—overwhelmed Black Hawk's much smaller force.

Jim grew up hearing stories of Black Hawk, of his legendary feats of running and swimming and wrestling, of his pride and defiance, even in the face of defeat. Jim grew up hearing that his own father, Hiram, resembled Black Hawk not only in looks, but in athletic skill and pure strength.

And Jim knew it was true. On warm evenings, when the chores were done, Sac and Fox families gathered near the Thorpe cabin, and the men competed in jumping contests and swimming and running races. Hiram always dominated. And then, near sunset, the families formed a circle for the main event: wrestling.

For the rest of his life, Jim would tell tales of these epic tests of strength and will. Night after night, he sat in the fading light, bursting with pride as his father conquered one opponent after another.

**P**op Warner did not grow up playing football. And "Pop" was not his first nickname—before "Pop" came "Butter."

It was not a compliment.

Today Pop Warner is remembered as one of the greatest football coaches of all time, and kids all over the country play in leagues named in his honor. But as a boy in the small town of Springville, New York, Glenn Warner did not inspire visions of athletic glory.

Born in 1871, seventeen years before Jim Thorpe, Glenn was a shy kid, awkward and chubby, a boy who lived in fear of his classmates. They pelted his broad backside with beans shot through straws, and pebbles launched from slingshots. Day after day, they surrounded him as he walked home from school, chanting:

"Butter! Butter!"

One winter afternoon, when Glenn was ten, he was trudging home when one of the class bullies grabbed his hat, tossed it into a slushy puddle, and stomped on it. The other boys stood around, laughing.

In a burst of rage, Glenn pounced on the bully, knocked him down, and started pummeling him. The other kids looked on in shock.

"This battle," Warner would later recall, "showed me a new way of looking at life."

Glenn grew tall in his teen years, and started to show some interest in sports. During school recess, the boys played a game loosely based on English football, or soccer. The streets on either side of the field were goal

After "Butter" but before "Pop"—
Glenn Scobey Warner as a teenager.

lines, and the basic idea was to kick the ball past the other team's goal. "We used anything that we could for a football," Warner remembered. "Most of the time we ended up playing with a blown-up cow's bladder."

Bladders make crummy sporting goods. They're never truly round, tend to deflate—and quickly start to stink. That could be why Glenn preferred baseball. His mother cut and sewed his overalls into something like baseball pants, and he was good enough to pitch for the Springville team.

After graduating from high school, he took the entrance exam for West Point, the prestigious US Military Academy. Forty teens took the test with Warner. Four were admitted. Warner was not one of them.

At eighteen, with nothing better to do, he moved with his family to a ranch in Wichita Falls, Texas. He and his younger brother, Bill, busted their backs in the blazing sun, clearing brush, planting wheat, herding cattle. The layer of flab that had inspired Glenn's first nickname melted away.

In the summer of 1892, Warner returned to Springville to see friends.

He spent a few days at the horse track in Buffalo, where he bet all the money he'd earned in Texas. He won fifty dollars. That convinced him he was a brilliant gambler, so his new career plan was to travel from track to track, living the good life on his winnings.

It lasted a week. At the next track he went to, in Rochester, he lost nearly everything. Glenn had barely enough cash left for a one-way train ticket back to Wichita Falls.

"I soon became depressed and was forced to do some serious thinking," Warner later recalled. He didn't really want to be a rancher; he didn't know *what* he wanted to do. "I began to review my options, which were limited. I dared not write to my father and tell him that I was broke, because I would have had to explain what had happened to the money."

Glenn's father had been urging him to become a lawyer. That didn't sound very fun. But now, he realized, it presented an opportunity to escape his financial hole. He wrote to his dad, saying he'd decided to go to law school after all and asking for money to cover tuition.

A few weeks later an envelope arrived from Texas. Inside was a check for a hundred dollars.

Warner figured he had to at least give school a shot. He applied to Cornell University and was accepted.

"At the time, I considered this event to be a great misfortune," Warner would later say. "But, instead, it turned out to be about the luckiest thing that ever happened to me."

Now twenty-one, Glenn was a burly six foot two, with curly brown hair. He rode the train from Buffalo to Ithaca, in central New York, and walked around the Cornell campus, strolling pathways between grassy lawns and gray stone buildings. He wandered out to the sports field, where the football team was practicing.

Curious how the American version of this sport was played, he stood for a while and watched. He was startled to see the team captain, Carl Johanson, striding toward him.

Johanson looked Warner up and down and asked what he weighed.

"Two hundred and fifteen pounds," Warner said.

"Fine. Get on a suit right away. We need a left guard."

Warner was stunned.

"Wait a minute," he managed to say. "I don't know anything about the game at all."

"Never mind," Johanson told him. "All you've got to do is keep them from going through you and spoiling the play when we've got the ball. And when they've got the ball, knock the tar out of your man and tackle the runner. Perfectly simple."

Facing page: In the early days of football, almost every play ended in painful pileups like this. Notice how the ball-carrier's shirt is being torn off as he hands the ball to a teammate.

**T**here was more to the sport of football than Carl Johanson's brief instructions suggested.

But not *that* much more.

The first American football game between college teams was played on November 6, 1869, on the campus of Rutgers University in New Jersey. A group of twenty-five students came from nearby Princeton University to challenge the Rutgers team. The players took off their hats, jackets, and vests, and, to minimize confusion on the crowded field, the Rutgers students tied scarlet bandannas, pirate-style, over their heads.

Princeton kicked off, and the first football game was under way. It would be unrecognizable to fans today.

Basically, it was a chaotic mash-up of soccer and rugby, with all fifty athletes on the field at once. Rutgers won, 6–4. The most memorable moment was when a clump of players chasing a loose ball crashed into a fence spectators were leaning on, and the players and fans tumbled to the ground in a heap. One of the Rutgers men, George Large, took a blow to the head and came up woozy. He stayed in the game.

For the rest of his life, Large would boast that he was the first man ever injured playing American football.

The day after meeting Carl Johanson, Glenn Warner walked onto the Cornell football field for his first day of practice. The game had changed somewhat in the twenty-three years since Princeton had traveled to Rutgers—there were now eleven men per team on the field at once, for instance.

But the sport was still just loosely organized combat.

"Early-day football was anything but a parlor sport," Warner recalled, "many games being little more than free-for-all fights."

After only one practice, Warner was named starting left guard on the Cornell football team. Like everyone, he'd be on the field for every play, offense and defense. He learned on the fly.

Each play started with the teams lined up, facing each other, the ball on the ground between them. Before the play began, opposing linemen grunted at one another, spat, picked up dirt and threw it in each other's eyes. A lineman on offense snapped the ball to the quarterback, who then tossed it backward to one of the running backs lined up behind him. The man with the ball started forward, and defenders tried to knock him down. Teams could score by carrying the ball across the opponent's goal line, or by kicking it through goalposts at the goal line. The ball itself was bigger and rounder than today's ball, made for tucking under an arm or kicking, not throwing.

There was no such thing as passing; the forward pass was illegal.

Modern players memorize binders full of intricately choreographed plays. This was not the sport Warner learned. Early-day football was simple, repetitive, and—believe it or not—much *more* violent than today's game. The typical play involved the ballcarrier plunging headfirst into a tightly packed wall of defenders, while his entire team pushed and pulled him—a "mass play," as it was called. Some teams even sewed suitcase handles onto the pants of their running backs so teammates could lift and drag ballcarriers through the pile. Defenders dove for the runner's legs or leaped onto his back until he fell to the ground.

But the play still wasn't over. It wasn't over until the man with the ball quit moving. So while he squirmed and wriggled forward, more defenders piled on, and plays ended in massive, writhing mounds, inside of which guys would throw elbows and knees, scratch and bite, spit and choke, until the refs could untangle the heap.

Then, bruised and bleeding, everyone lined up and did it again.

This Winslow Homer illustration, captioned "Holiday in Camp—soldiers playing 'football,'" is only a slight exaggeration of the mayhem and violence of early-day football.

The team on offense had three plays to move the ball just five yards. Five yards got you a first down—a fresh set of three plays to gain another five—so there was no need to do anything other than plunge straight ahead, play after play. "The stronger team usually was able to smash and grind the ball downfield in short, steady gains," Warner recalled, "until they had finally crossed the goal line."

And unlike today, football players wore little or no padding.

"In fact, one who wore homemade pads was regarded as a sissy," recalled John Heisman, an early player and coach for whom the Heisman Trophy was later named. Leather helmets were optional, and considered borderline wimpy. "Hair was the only head protection we knew," Heisman said, "and in preparation for football, we would let it grow from the first of June."

Warner joined the fashion, growing out his curly locks. "This sometimes had its disadvantages," he'd later say, "for when no arm or leg presented itself, a man made his tackle by simply knotting both hands in the opponent's hair."

It was hardly enough to dampen Warner's growing enthusiasm. "After I had gotten used to having my face pushed in and my head tramped on, I began to take an interest in the game."

One day, soon after he'd joined the team, Warner made a nice play at practice, and Carl Johanson shouted, "Good work, Pop!" Johanson never explained the nickname's origin. Warner figured it had something to do with his being a couple of years older than most college freshmen.

Anyway, the name stuck. From then on, he was Pop Warner.

"Pop worked his way through school by waiting tables at a restaurant and played well enough to keep his spot at left guard." On the field, he paid special attention to the way his coach tried to get an edge using strategy—to use the word loosely. "If a player was too good-natured or easy-going," Warner explained, "the coach would tell one of his own mates to sock him in the jaw when he wasn't looking and then blame it on the other team so as to make him mad."

Pop Warner sports knee pads and "football hair"—the only padding he wore on the playing field.

*Did football really have to be like that?* Warner wondered. *Wasn't there room for a slightly more creative approach?*

He got a chance to find out during the 1894 season, his last at Cornell. The coach had to leave town right before a game with Williams College, and he put Pop in temporary charge of the Cornell club. Thrilled with the opportunity, Warner sat up all night sketching a new play.

The next day, on the practice field, he gathered his teammates around a small chalkboard and showed them how it worked. The play, Number 39 in the Cornell playbook, was inspired by the fact that defenses moved in tight packs, bringing the combined mass of players to bear on blockers and the ballcarrier. Warner explained how, with a bit of deception, they could use this to their advantage.

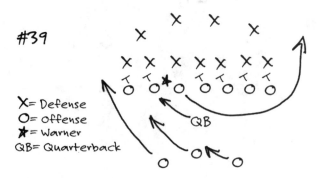

That Saturday, when the Cornell team huddled up late in a scoreless game, Warner turned to the quarterback and said, "Number 39."

The teams lined up. Warner took his usual position on the left side of the offensive line. The ball was snapped to the quarterback, who took a few steps to his left. The entire offensive line drove into the defense and plowed left, too. The quarterback lifted the ball as if he were about to pitch it to the back behind him, who was also moving left.

To the defense, it looked like yet another mass play to the left. But then the quarterback did something that sounds simple, but simply wasn't done. After faking the pitch to the left, he pivoted and handed the ball to

Pop Warner, who had peeled off from the pile of bodies and was already moving to the right.

Pop looked up. Stretching before him was a wide-open field of green.

Both arms wrapped clumsily around the ball, he rumbled toward the winning score. But in the time it took him to cover twenty-five yards, a couple of speedy defenders recovered from the deception, gave chase, and jumped on Warner's back. As Pop tumbled to earth, the ball popped loose, bounced into the air, and was recovered by a Williams player.

The game ended in a 0–0 tie.

"My first play as an interim coach proved to be a successful one," Warner would later recall, "but I put the wrong player—me—in the game to run with the ball." It was a lesson he'd never forget. No matter how good his ideas were, he was going to need to entrust them to much better athletes.

Pop Warner would find those athletes, eventually. He'd find them at a place called the Carlisle Indian Industrial School.

The Carlisle Indian Industrial School football team would one day change the way the game was played—they'd even help *save* the sport from being banned entirely.

But it took a while to get there.

In the fall of 1890, when Jim Thorpe was still a toddler in Oklahoma, and Pop Warner was a teenage ranch hand in Texas, the Carlisle School's football program got off to perhaps the least promising start in the history of American sports.

It began on a Saturday afternoon, with a group of students walking through the town of Carlisle, Pennsylvania. This was the Carlisle football team. Or, more accurately, a loosely organized club. The players had no uniforms, no coach, and only a vague understanding of the rules of the sport. They had never played against another school, but Dickinson College, near the Carlisle campus, had a team and had agreed to a game. So that's where the Carlisle students were headed.

A couple of hours later, the young men walked back through town toward campus. They were now pulling a creaky wooden cart. In the cart, wailing in agony, lay their teammate, Stacy Matlock. His foot was facing the wrong way.

The teens guided the cart through the gates of the Carlisle School and toward the superintendent's building.

"It's Stacy, sir!" one of them called up to the second story. "He's hurt!"

A tall man in a blue military uniform appeared in the window and

Left to right
**BACK ROW:** William Tivis, Comanche; Jemima Wheelock, Oneida; Dennison Wheelock, Oneida; Stacy Matlock, Pawnee; Levi Levering, Omaha; Veronica Holliday, Chippewa; Benjamin Lawry, Winnebago. **MIDDLE ROW:** George W. Means, Sioux; Howard Logan, Winnebago; George Vallier, Quapaw; William Morgan, Pawnee; Carl Leider, Crow; Percy Zadoka, Keechi; Benjamin Thomas, Pueblo. **FRONT ROW:** Lawrence Smith, Winnebago; Rosa Bourassa, Chippewa; Nellie Robertson, Sioux; Julie Bent, Cheyenne.

glared down. This was Richard Henry Pratt, a forty-nine-year-old US Army captain, founder and superintendent of the Carlisle School.

Pratt hurried out the front door and up to the cart. There was Matlock, a Pawnee Indian from Oklahoma, one of the most popular students on campus. The guys started to explain: they'd gone over to Dickinson to play football, and Matlock had been carrying the ball when—

"Football!" Pratt angrily cut in.

They pulled the cart to the school infirmary. Pratt helped lift Matlock, who howled as they carried him up the steps and into the building. They set him down on a table. The school doctor came to inspect Matlock's leg, though medical expertise was hardly required to make a diagnosis: beneath the knee, two ugly lumps poked into purple, swollen skin. Pratt and the students stayed to help. They could do little beyond giving the patient a hunk of leather to bite, and holding him down as the doctor set the broken bone.

As Matlock's face twisted with suffering, Pratt made a decision— Carlisle's first football game would also be its last.

◈

Richard Pratt (left), along with his wife and two children, with a group of prisoners of war at Fort Marion, Florida. Pratt set up classes for the prisoners at Fort Marion, and this led to his idea for a Native American boarding school.

It was not so much the injury that bothered Pratt. A career army officer and combat veteran, he'd seen far worse. But this was the second broken bone from football in a week; another student's collarbone had been snapped in a pickup game on campus. Pratt, who strived for total control over his students' lives, feared football was becoming a dangerous distraction—and not at all what he'd envisioned when he founded this school.

The Carlisle Indian Industrial School was Richard Henry Pratt's creation, his life's work.

After fighting in the Union Army during the Civil War, Captain Pratt had gone west in the late 1860s to serve in the US government's wars against Native Americans. The government had already forced Native Americans from east of the Mississippi River—including the Potawatomi and Sac and Fox ancestors of Jim Thorpe—onto reservations; now it was doing the

same to the nations of the West. Pratt was part of the effort—he was an Indian fighter, with no regrets. "I had concluded," he'd later confess, "that as an army officer I was there to deal with atrocious aborigines."

In a series of ferocious wars, US troops removed nearly all the Native American nations of the West from their lands, forcing thousands of people to resettle on reservations. At the same time, railroad crews were hammering tracks across the West, farmers were stringing barbed wire around the most fertile land, and government was paying hunters to wipe out the once-vast buffalo herds Plains Indians had depended on for food.

All of this resulted in what newspapers called the "Indian problem." Native Americans could no longer live in their traditional ways; they didn't have access to the land or resources anymore. Yet they were not part of the thriving economy of the West, either. Stuck on isolated chunks

Richard Henry Pratt poses in his military uniform in 1879, the year he founded the Carlisle Indian Industrial School.

of land settlers didn't want, they lived far from cities and industries and jobs. Indian families couldn't produce enough food in the lousy reservation soil—but if they left the reservation to hunt on land that had always been theirs, they were treated like outlaws, arrested or even shot.

So what next? That was the problem. Richard Henry Pratt had helped create it. He also believed he had the solution.

In his ten years in the West, Pratt's views had gradually changed. Working alongside Cherokee and Choctaw allies, guarding Comanche and Cheyenne prisoners of war, Pratt got to know many of them as individuals, as human beings. He'd come to see that, despite cultural differences, there was no difference between Indians and whites in terms of intelligence or ability. If Indians could no longer live in their traditional ways, Pratt decided, they should be taken into white American society instead.

Pratt's answer to the "Indian problem" was to treat Native Americans as if they were immigrants to the United States. His answer was to help young Indians—if necessary, to *force* them—to assimilate into white American culture.

The way to accomplish this, he reasoned, was with a boarding school in the East. The school would be far from the reservations of the West, so students would be cut off completely from their families and traditions. Pratt's plan was harsh, and he didn't try to sugarcoat it. "I believe in immersing the Indians in our civilization," he declared, "and when we get them under, holding them there until they are thoroughly soaked."

Wouldn't it have been possible for young Native Americans to transition to the realities of modern American life without being torn from their parents and culture? As tough as life was for most immigrants, they could at least live with their families, speak their native language at home, celebrate their religious holidays. Why should Native Americans—the only people on the continent who *weren't* immigrants—be treated so differently?

To put it bluntly, Pratt did not respect Indian culture. He seems to have genuinely believed he was helping the *people*, but he began with the bigoted conviction that white American civilization was superior to all others. The rich diversity of Native American cultures and languages, the complex relationships between nations, the thousands of years' worth of knowledge about living in this part of the world—Pratt dismissed it all as savage and worthless.

"Left in the surroundings of savagery, he grows to possess a savage language, superstition, and life," Pratt would say of Indian children. "All the Indian there is in the race should be dead," he said. "Kill the Indian in him, and save the man."

Pratt approached the government with his idea for an Indian school. He was given permission to use Carlisle Barracks, an abandoned military base in central Pennsylvania.

The next step was to somehow persuade Native American parents to trust him with their sons and daughters. In the fall of 1879, Pratt set out for the Rosebud Reservation, a Lakota reservation in the dry, hilly prairies of the Dakota Territory.

◈

A few days later, at Rosebud, an eleven-year-old boy named Ota Kte—which roughly translates to "Plenty Kill," a name his father gave him after he'd returned from a successful deer hunt—was playing outside with his cousin. They noticed, in the distance, a large group going into the council building.

They ran to the building. Ota Kte peered through the window.

Inside were many Lakota men he recognized. Standing in front of them was a tall white man in a US Army uniform.

The man was Richard Henry Pratt. An interpreter translated as Pratt made his pitch for Carlisle. He explained that he wanted to take boys and girls east, teach them English, teach them skills that would help them find jobs in a rapidly changing country.

Spotted Tail, a respected Lakota leader, stood to respond.

"The white people are all thieves and liars," he said. "We do not want our children to learn such things."

Other men in the room murmured in agreement. They had reason to be wary.

Eleven years earlier, Lakota leaders and the US government had signed a treaty establishing the Great Sioux Reservation, eighteen million acres of traditional Lakota land that were to be forever off-limits to settlers and roads. Then gold was found in the Black Hills, part of the Sioux Reservation. The government offered to buy the Black Hills; Lakota leaders declined.

The first party of students arriving at Carlisle, 1879.

Miners began sneaking onto the land. The government gave the Lakota an ultimatum: move onto smaller reservations or the army will force you to move. When the Lakota refused to leave, American soldiers rode in. The ensuing war included the famous Battle of Little Bighorn, at which General George Armstrong Custer attacked a Lakota and Cheyenne camp and was killed along with all 210 of his men. But in the long run, the Indians didn't stand a chance against the larger and better-equipped US forces. The Lakota were forced onto smaller reservations, including Rosebud.

Pratt knew the story, of course. But he had not come to discuss history.

Like it or not, Pratt explained, Indians were facing a new reality. Yes, the government had cheated them time and again. The only way to break the pattern, Pratt argued, would be to learn the white man's rules.

❖

"Do you want to go, son?" Ota Kte's father, Standing Bear, asked the boy later that day.

From what little he'd heard, Ota Kte did not particularly like the idea of Pratt's school. "At that time," he would later write, "we did not trust the white people very strongly." But he *did* like the idea of leaving home to face a challenge. "I was thinking of my father," he explained, "and how he had many times said to me, 'Son, be brave!'" For that reason alone, he decided to go.

As the sun set a few days later, Ota Kte was among eighty-two boys and girls lined up on the banks of the Missouri River. Reluctantly, seeing little hope for the future on the reservation, Spotted Tail and many other parents had agreed to send their children to Pratt's school. Families watched from the riverbank, many weeping, as the children walked up a wooden plank onto a paddle-wheel steamboat.

The paddle-wheels churned the muddy water and the boat pulled away from the land, sliding southeast with the current. The sky grew dark. Boys and girls wrapped themselves in blankets and tried to sleep. "But I could not get to sleep," Ota Kte remembered, "because I was wondering where we were going and what was to be done with us after we arrived."

# ALIEN WORLD

The next day, the children sat aboard a moving train, gazing with wonder out the window as they zipped past telegraph poles and buildings.

When the train stopped in Sioux City, Iowa, crowds of people lined up to watch Pratt's students walk from the train station to a nearby restaurant. The townspeople waved their arms and made grunting sounds—mimicking their ignorant idea of Indian behavior, Ota Kte realized. "Many of the little Indian boys and girls were afraid of the white people," he recalled. "I really did not blame them, because the whites acted so wild."

The children couldn't eat, not with strange people whooping at them. They wrapped food in their blankets and carried it back to the train.

They continued east. The cities got bigger, and the streets more crowded, and the skies thicker with the smoke of mills and factories. After two more days of travel, they arrived in Carlisle, Pennsylvania. It was midnight. Pratt led the exhausted students to the campus of the Carlisle Indian Industrial School. "I was thrust into an alien world," Ota Kte would later say of the next few days. "Into an environment as different from the one into which I was born as it is possible to imagine."

◆

Pratt's plan was to strip these kids of their Indian identities, and he started right away.

Left to right: Wounded Yellow Robe, Henry Standing Bear, and Chauncy Yellow Robe, photographed when they arrived at Carlisle in 1883.

The same three Sioux students—though Chauncy Yellow Robe now sits on the left—three years after arriving at the Carlisle School.

He took away their moccasins, blankets, and deer-hide leggings. Girls were given long gray dresses and heavy stockings. Boys were handed wool suits, itchy red long underwear, and farmers' boots. Students marched into classrooms and sat at wooden desks. In Ota Kte's class, a white woman—the teacher, he figured—was standing in front of a chalkboard, writing what appeared to be a series of meaningless squiggles.

"Do you see all these marks on the blackboard?" the teacher asked her class through an interpreter. "Well, each word is a white man's name. They are going to give each one of you one of these names by which you will hereafter be known."

The teacher motioned for a boy to come to the front of the room. She handed him a long wooden stick and gestured for him to point to one of the clumps of squiggles. There were names from the Bible, names of US presidents, though, of course, the students had no way of knowing this. Besides, these children already had names, names rich in meaning, names given to them to honor relatives or to recognize special traits or achievements.

The boy turned to the class, looking for guidance. Finally, he pointed randomly to one of the names.

The teacher wrote the name on a piece of white fabric and sewed it to his shirt. Then she erased that name from the blackboard and called on another student.

When it was Ota Kte's turn, he pointed to a name that turned out to be "Luther." From that point on, he was known as Luther Standing Bear.

An Apache student named Daklugie, who would endure this process a few years later, would never forget the pain it caused. "I've always hated that name," he said of his assigned name, Asa. "It was forced on me as though I had been an animal."

Next came the haircuts. Lakota boys traditionally wore their hair in a long braid—Pratt considered this "uncivilized." One by one, the boys were called out of class and led to a room where a barber had set up his chair and tools. The barber cut off each boy's braid, then cropped his hair close. Like many of the boys, Ota Kte felt tears fill his eyes as his hair fell to the floor.

◆◈◆

Over the next ten years, Pratt expanded the Carlisle School enrollment to about one thousand students. Ranging in age from under ten to early twenties, the students came from all over the country, representing more than seventy Native American nations. The old military barracks were refurbished, largely by the students themselves, into an attractive campus, with whitewashed buildings lining a grass-covered parade ground.

Pratt surrounded the entire campus with a seven-foot wooden fence. The idea was to keep curious tourists out—and students in.

"We keep them moving," Pratt said of his students, "and they have no time for homesickness—none for mischief—none for regret."

He was kidding himself, or else willfully ignoring reality.

The students of the Carlisle Indian Industrial School, circa 1900.

For the students, everything at Carlisle was foreign. The clothes, the climate, the food, even the sounds—clanging bells and clinking silverware—were new and jarring. Indian languages were forbidden, and teachers slapped students with extra chores, and sometimes beat them, for speaking to each other in the only language they knew. Severe violations, like running away or getting caught alone with a student of the opposite sex, would land students in the dreaded guardhouse. This dark, damp structure, with three-foot-thick stone walls, had been built during the American Revolution by German prisoners of war captured by George Washington at the Battle of Trenton. For Pratt, it became the campus prison.

By wrenching boys and girls from their families, telling them everything they knew and loved was worthless, Pratt was inflicting tremendous stress and pain. The evidence was all around. A girl named Maggie Stands Looking got so frustrated with being repeatedly corrected that she slapped a teacher. Two young women, Elizabeth Flanders and Fannie Eaglehorn, stuffed a pillowcase with paper, struck a match, and threw the flaming bundle into a closet in their dorm. The fire was quickly extinguished. Both women served eighteen months in a Pennsylvania prison.

Another of the first students, Earnest White Thunder, went on a hunger strike. Pratt tried to physically force the boy to eat, but he spat everything out and eventually starved to death.

"Boys and girls actually suffered in the flesh as well as the spirit," one school official would later say, "could not eat, would not sleep, and so prepared the way for serious trouble." Weakened bodies were especially susceptible to contagious diseases like tuberculosis, which spread quickly in crowded dorms. Six students died in the first year at Carlisle. Pratt set aside a spot on campus for a cemetery, and the number of small white gravestones would steadily grow in the years to come.

But most days at Carlisle were routine—strict, grinding, boring routine.

Pratt ran his school as a military academy, with every minute of the day accounted for. A bugler woke students at five-thirty, and they marched to exercises before breakfast. At meals, they sat on long benches in the dining hall while school staff watched over them, correcting table manners. Students spent the rest of the morning in the classroom, learning reading, writing, history, and math. Afternoons were for vocational training—which explains the "Industrial" in the school name. The boys learned carpentry, tailoring, printing, baking; girls practiced cooking, canning, sewing, child care.

Pratt watched it all. From his favorite spot on the bandstand in the middle of campus, he inspected the students' clothes, their hair, the polish on their shoes. He lectured them and urged them on.

Pratt wanted his school to be self-sufficient, which meant nearly endless work for both male and female students in workshops, kitchens, and the campus laundry.

The Carlisle campus had its own farm—and, of course, students did all the work.

"You've got to stick to it," he said again and again. "Stick to it!"

Where did football fit in with Pratt's vision? It didn't. "I was not especially pleased to encourage it," he recalled.

But many of the students loved the sport. In defiance of Pratt, they pooled their money to buy a ball, and organized games between workshops—tailors vs. blacksmiths, bakers vs. printers. Then came Carlisle's first real game, against Dickinson College, which ended with Stacy Matlock's badly broken leg.

The day after Matlock's injury, Pratt made an official announcement to the whole school: "Carlisle teams will no longer be allowed to play football against other schools."

And the story of Carlisle Indian football—one of the great underdog stories in all of American history—could easily have ended right there.

The students refused to let it.

# THE TEAM

Two years after Pratt banned football at Carlisle, about forty uniformed students gathered outside the door to the superintendent's office. They took off their caps and held them in their hands. One of the boys knocked.

Pratt called for the visitors to enter.

The students filed in and crowded around Pratt's desk. As they had planned, one of the teens, a champion on the school's speech-and-debate team, stepped forward.

"Sir," he began, "we understand your reasons for forbidding us to play football against outside schools."

He then made the case in favor of competitive football. The sport was popular at the best colleges. It was a game of strength, discipline, teamwork, perseverance. It was dangerous, but so what? "We are not afraid of injuries," the student explained. What they *were* afraid of was being denied the opportunity to compete, the chance to show what they could do.

Pratt was silent for a long moment. He was demanding a lot of these students. They were living far from home, totally cut off from families for years at a time. Maybe football could be a positive outlet for their frustration and their anger. Maybe the chance to compete against white schools had some kind of symbolic meaning for them. Maybe they just loved the game.

Maybe all of the above.

"Boys, I begin to realize that I must surrender," Pratt finally said. "I will let you take up outside football again, under two conditions."

The students cheered.

"First," Pratt said, "you will never, under any circumstances, slug."

Slugging—flat-out punching opponents when the referee wasn't looking—was a common feature of early football. A football team representing Carlisle, Pratt knew, would be facing not only that kind of violence, but also the prejudice of white fans and sportswriters. Pratt explained: "Can't you see that if you slug, people who are looking on will say, 'There, that's the Indian of it. Just see them. They are savages and you can't get it out of them.' Our white fellows may do a lot of slugging and it causes little or no remark, but you have to make a record for your race."

"All right, Captain," several of the students said. "We agree to that."

"My other condition is this," Pratt said. "That, in the course of two, three, or four years, you will develop your strength and ability to such a degree that you will whip the biggest football team in the country. What do you say to that?"

The students hesitated, and with good reason.

Professional football and the National Football League were still decades away. College football *was* football, and the sport was *totally* dominated by elite eastern universities. These schools recruited the biggest players and pounded their way to victory after victory. In the twenty-three years since the first game at Rutgers, every single national championship had been claimed by one of just four schools—Harvard, Yale, Princeton, and the University of Pennsylvania, the "Big Four," as sportswriters called them.

Carlisle, on the other hand, had a student body of fewer than one thousand. Just half the students were boys, and half of *those* were under sixteen. The would-be players had no football coach and knew very little beyond the basic rules of the game. How could they ever expect to beat a team like Harvard or Yale?

"Well, Captain," the champion debater said, "we will try."

"I don't want you to promise to try," Pratt snapped. "I want you to say that you will do it. The man who only thinks of trying to do a thing admits to himself that he may fail."

The young men looked at each other.

Their spokesman said, "Yes, sir. We will agree to that."

Step one was to learn how the game was supposed to be played.

Pratt was clueless, but a Carlisle teacher named Anna Luckenbaugh reached out to a friend of hers, Vance McCormick, a former Yale quarterback who happened to live nearby. He agreed to teach the team some football basics.

Vance McCormick, pictured here as captain of the Yale University football team, went on to become the first coach at Carlisle.

McCormick showed up in a hat and stylish suit. He walked onto a muddy field and looked over the group gathered in front of him, young men in loose canvas pants and tattered sweaters. Deciding to start with a simple demonstration, he picked up a football and tossed it down the slightly sloping field.

The watermelon-shaped ball waddled to a stop in a puddle. McCormick told the team to race for the ball, see who could dive on it first. No one moved.

Maybe, McCormick figured, the men weren't following his English. He motioned with his arms toward the loose ball. No response.

So he turned and charged toward the ball himself, diving for it and landing headfirst with a splash. He came up covered in mud, brown water dripping from the brim of his hat. He was holding the football.

That was lesson number one—you've got to *want it* more than the other guy.

The proper way to cover a loose ball, as described in a correspondence course Pop Warner would begin selling in 1912.

McCormick continued dropping by Carlisle a few afternoons a week. Most of the players were a lot smaller than the brutes he'd played with at Yale, but he liked their desire and toughness. There was potential here for a decent team.

The players stunned McCormick by telling him they had their sights set a lot higher—they wanted to play his old team, Yale.

But best, all agreed, to start small. Carlisle's first official game, played on November 11, 1893, was a scrimmage with Harrisburg High School. Carlisle won, 10–0. The following fall, the team played its first schedule of games against men their own age, college teams and athletic clubs.

Reality set in, fast.

They were mauled by Lehigh University, Navy, and Bucknell. The biggest crowd to see Carlisle that season gathered in a park in Washington, DC, for a matchup with the Columbia Athletic Club. Describing the Carlisle team as a cute little novelty act, the *Washington Post* attributed the big turnout to mere curiosity.

For a group of Assiniboine leaders from Montana, in town for talks with the government, the game had an entirely different meaning. They sat in the bleachers, cheering the visiting team with what the *Washington Times* called "obvious delight." It was an early indication that Native Americans from all over the country might one day look to this Carlisle team for hope and inspiration.

If they were any good, that is. They weren't.

In an article headlined LO, THE POOR INDIANS, the *Post* described the vicious beating Carlisle took that afternoon. The much bigger home team slugged openly, sending four Indian players staggering to the sidelines. The low point was when Carlisle's Ben American Horse, nicknamed "Flying Man" for his bold leaps over defenders, tried his trademark move—and was met with a fist to the face. Blood spurted from his broken nose before he even hit the ground.

Final Score: Columbia Athletic Club, 18, Carlisle, 0.

**B**y this point Jim Thorpe was six years old. He had still never seen a football.

He played just about everything else, though. "I was always of a restless disposition," Thorpe would say, looking back on his childhood. "I played all the games and played them hard."

Jim and Charlie were inseparable. The twin brothers rode horses and swam in the river and gorged on wild blackberries. They camped together in the woods and played a game called baseball brought west by white settlers. "We made our own balls out of whatever was handy," Thorpe recalled, "used sticks for bats, flat rocks for bases, and made up our own rules."

Their favorite sport was one of their own creation: a free-form, marathon follow-the-leader. Jim always wanted to be the leader. He'd take off running, then climb over a barn, splash through a stream, scramble up a tree, and swing from a high branch to the ground, then start running again. Everyone else—Charlie and six or eight local boys, both Indian and white—had to keep up. Or pay the price. "Any kid who failed to follow the leader in the various stunts would be put through the familiar slapping machine," Jim explained. "This consisted of scampering on hands and knees between the legs of the others in the game, assisted by a brisk paddling."

It was a lot of fun. Until school got in the way.

Both Hiram and Charlotte had learned to read and write English, and both believed their boys would need an English-based education to find

The Thorpe twins: Jim (left) and Charlie, age three.

good jobs. Hiram put the boys in his wagon and drove them to the nearby Sac and Fox Agency School, one of many new government-run boarding schools that had been inspired by the original Indian boarding school, Carlisle.

For Jim and Charlie, who were raised with a mix of Indian and white culture, the transition was not as shocking as it was for some. The Thorpe boys had learned English at home, but many students hadn't, and the school's English-only rule was enforced with beatings.

Jim and Charlie wriggled into stiff three-piece suits and black hats. Girls wore dresses and scratchy stockings. Everyone marched from class to workshop with military-style discipline. "Our lives were just one bell after another," a classmate of Jim's remembered. "We got up by bells, ate by bells, went to class by bells."

Even rare moments of free time were strictly governed. No free-form

The Sac and Fox Agency School.

follow-the-leader. No familiar games like lacrosse. Students were told they could play horseshoes. It was unclear to Jim how tossing a horseshoe at a stake in the dirt was supposed to be fun.

Charlie Thorpe was among the few who adjusted well. Teachers described him as an excellent student, "calm, even-tempered, and a natural friend to his school books."

Jim struggled from the start. He shot at flies with rubber bands when he was supposed to be reading. He was a daydreamer and "an incorrigible youngster," according to school records, "uninterested in anything except the outdoor life" and "always fidgeting to get outdoors."

Miserable and homesick, with a defiant streak inherited from his father, Jim simply walked away. He left campus and hiked twenty-three miles back to his family's farm.

Hiram was furious. He gave Jim a whipping, then loaded him into the back of his wagon. Neighbors along the road would never forget the sound of the boy howling—screaming with rage, it seemed, at the sky, at the trees above—all the way back to school.

Pop Warner was no better at sitting still.

After finishing school at Cornell, Warner put away his football gear and took a job with a law firm in Buffalo. Just as his father had always wanted, Warner wore a suit every day and earned a comfortable living in a comfortable office.

It was awful.

A few months after taking the job, Warner heard that the Iowa Agricultural College—now Iowa State University—was looking for a football coach. He sent off an application and got the job. Pop taught the Iowa boys everything he'd learned at Cornell, and in September 1895 they headed west for their first game, a matchup with an athletic club in Butte, Montana.

Warner was confident he had a good team—too confident. The saloons of Butte were packed with gamblers betting on the game, and Pop laid down $150, his entire salary for the year.

His confidence wavered when he walked out to the playing field. It was a patch of sun-dried dirt, he remembered, "bare and hard as an iron griddle." Then the game got under way, and he *really* started to worry.

The Butte club was stacked with rugged miners and former college players. Any time they made a good play, the rowdy crowd pulled out revolvers and blasted bullets into the sky, terrifying the visiting team. "If Iowa State threatened to score," Warner recalled, "the referee, a local man who had been picked by Butte AC, would make some penalty call that would cause us a setback."

In the second half, the desperate coach put himself in the game. It didn't help. "We not only lost the game but also our uniforms," Pop remembered. "Almost all of my clothes were ripped or torn by the middle of the third quarter."

Warner headed back to Iowa in rags. He was aching all over. He was utterly broke.

He was hooked.

Coaching football, Pop Warner would later say, "made the law seem pretty tame."

◆

At the Carlisle School, a twenty-year-old student named Bemus Pierce was feeling pretty restless himself.

Pierce had come to Carlisle from his family's home on a Seneca reservation in western New York. At six foot two, 225 pounds, he was a natural for the football team. Like the other guys, he was serious about this sport—serious enough to spend spare moments ripping up the school's sloping football field.

Other schools had employees for this kind of work. But if Carlisle was going to have a decent field, the players were going to have to build it themselves.

Pierce took the job of standing on the beam of a plow, using his weight to sink the blades into the soil. Six horses were hitched to the plow, urged and dragged forward by three of Pierce's teammates. After loosening the earth, the players pulled countless rocks from the dirt. They did their best to flatten the surface. They planted grass. And when the field was ready, they began to practice.

From that point on, the "football boys," as the players were called on campus, limped around blotched with bruises. And proud of it.

The team elected Bemus Pierce captain for the 1895 season. The Carlisle players had vowed to beat the best teams in the country, and that year they got their first chance, with two games against Big Four schools.

The University of Pennsylvania rolled over Carlisle, 36–0. Yale crushed them, 18–0.

Carlisle managed to win two of its last three, finishing the season a respectable 4-4, and newspapers praised the team's relentless effort. But the same papers resorted to crude stereotypes, describing Carlisle's wins as "massacres" or "scalpings."

These kinds of labels were common—and totally inaccurate.

Historians have found that Native Americans were more likely to be the *victims* of massacres and scalpings than the perpetrators. As early as 1703, leaders of the Massachusetts Bay Colony started offering settlers a bounty of $60 for every Indian scalp they brought in.

But the facts didn't matter. Over the years, newspapers and novels and paintings continuously depicted Indians as the ones who were savage and violent. So by the time Carlisle took up football, white readers accepted this sort of language without a second thought.

Team captain Bemus Pierce poses in his football sweater during Carlisle's soon-to-be legendary 1896 season.

"There was an uprising of Indians in the northern part of Manhattan Island yesterday afternoon," the *New York Times* wrote after one of Carlisle's 1895 games. "A band of eleven full-blooded warriors, with their war paint and feathers, attacked a band of men from the Young Men's Christian Association."

The players read these articles. They knew exactly what they were up against.

All the more incentive to win.

For the 1896 season, the Carlisle Indians chose team colors: dark red and gold. Bemus Pierce was again elected captain, and his younger brother Hawley—six two, 210—joined Bemus on the line. Their part-time coach, Vance McCormick, couldn't get away from work to help out, but William Hickok, another ex-Yale star, agreed to fill in.

Carlisle opened with a win over Dickinson College, then traveled to Pittsburgh and thumped an athletic club team. The team was gaining confidence, and they'd need it. In 1896, for reasons not entirely clear, the players decided they were ready to challenge not just one or two of the Big Four—they were going to take on all of them.

Princeton, Yale, Harvard, and Pennsylvania.

In a row.

All on the road.

This had never been attempted by *any* team and sounded to sportswriters like some sort of ill-advised military campaign, a football death march. It began with a train ride to New Jersey.

**E**leven young men in matching sweaters of red and gold lined up near the middle of the football field on the campus of Princeton University.

Carlisle's Jonas Metoxen stepped forward and booted the ball high into the air. As the kicking team sprinted down the field, a Princeton man caught the ball near his own goal line and his blockers formed a wedge in front of him. The group charged ahead—and the two sides slammed together at top speed.

The next few minutes went exactly as football experts had predicted. With the home crowd cheering and singing, waving black-and-orange pennants, the noticeably bigger Princeton backs picked up chunks of yardage on power runs right up the middle. The Tigers marched steadily to Carlisle's five-yard line.

"Then," as the *Philadelphia Inquirer* reported, "the unlooked for and unexpected took place."

The Princeton quarterback took the next snap, spun, and flipped the ball to his halfback. The runner bobbled the pitch, and the ball bounced free just as Artie Miller, Carlisle's right end, knifed into the backfield. Miller snatched the ball and sprinted past the thirty, the forty, the fifty, the fifty-five—the regulation field was 110 yards—and on past the fifty, the forty, the thirty. Princeton's fastest player closed on Miller, dove at him, and they landed together with a thud just over the white chalk of the goal line.

The touchdown was worth four points, and the scoring team could then try to kick the ball through the goalposts for an additional two. Bemus Pierce made the kick.

The stadium went silent as the scorekeeper hung a six beside the name of the visiting team. These were the first points Princeton had yielded that season.

Fans understood that if Carlisle managed to beat Princeton—or *any* one of the Big Four—it would be the greatest upset the sport had ever seen.

At halftime it was still 6–0. Panicked Princeton coaches spent the ten-minute break berating their players. The Tigers came out sharper in the second half, imposing their will on the smaller team, aided by vicious slugging that was not penalized.

Frustrated by the officiating—or lack of it—Bemus Pierce called time and strode to the referee. Fans looked on, expecting angry words, maybe worse.

Pierce calmly said, "You must remember that you are umpiring for both sides."

Then he walked back to his teammates.

Final score: Princeton 22, Carlisle 6.

◆◈◆

Next up was Yale at the Polo Grounds in New York City. It was a cool and sunny afternoon: football weather.

The story of Carlisle's surprisingly competitive game with Princeton had spread, and a huge crowd streamed into the stadium. Thousands more found spots on a hill rising above the open end of the arena. Fans even crowded onto the platform of a nearby elevated train to catch glimpses of the action.

Near the field, packed in among men in suits and women in enormous feather-covered hats and reporters from every big New York paper, sat Richard Henry Pratt and his daughter, Nana. Though he still didn't quite understand the rules, Pratt was starting to like football. He especially liked the attention football was bringing to his school. To Pratt, the players

# AMATEUR SPORT

*This Department went to press Friday, October 30.*

AN INDIAN MASS PLAY ON YALE TACKLE FOR FIVE YARDS GAIN.

Under date of October 24 this Department criticised the University of Pennsylvania Athletic Committee for continuing, after other universities had abandoned it as of unwholesome influence, preliminary football practice; on the "evidence thus given of viewing the game, and the preparation for it rather as a business than as a sport"; and for the thereby suggested assimilation to a professional spirit which regards victory of first importance.

We have received a letter from this committee, which, as requested, is herewith published—not that there are two sides to the preliminary-practice question, but because the work of this committee in other directions in the general effort making for healthful college sport suggests the possibility of an honest difference of opinion, and entitles them to our consideration.

Philadelphia, October 25, 1896.

Sir,—The paragraphs in this week's issue of Harper's Weekly in which you refer to us contain views which we believe are unsound, and criticisms that are unjust to Pennsylvania. With your statement that Pennsylvania is revealing a professional spirit in football we take distinct issue. It is true that the candidates for our team spent three weeks (not a month) in preliminary training at a hotel, not "hired especially for the occasion," but along with many September guests. This practice was taken openly, not covertly, as in the case, as you know, of some of the other prominent universities. Consistently with amateur sport, similar preliminary training has always been recognized and indulged in—e.g., the annual preliminary training of the Yale and Harvard crews at New London; of our own and the Columbia, Cornell, and Harvard crews, who were quartered for several weeks at the hotels near Poughkeepsie last summer; of the Yale crew who recently spent six weeks in preliminary training at Henley, as did Cornell the year before; of the Yale track team preparatory to their games with Oxford in '95; of the Cambridge track team here last summer; and of the All

the same preposition to Yale and Princeton had we expected to play football with them.

With respect to our rules of eligibility, you will know they are very strict, and have been rigidly enforced for several years, including the rule in which you call attention in this same issue as having been recently passed by another university, namely, the "one year's residence rule."

There may be ground, in spite of the above facts, for some honest difference of opinion as to the permission we have granted for three

works' preliminary practice, but talk of such action as "revealing a professional spirit" is as intemperate as in itself to do more harm to the cause of amateur sport than would on ever longer period of preliminary training. Yours truly,
J. William White,
H. Laussat Geyelin,
Jas. C. Bell,
Simon Wharton Potter.

Evidently these gentlemen do not completely understand precisely what is meant by preliminary practice. The custom upon which this Department has always directed its criticism, and will continue always to do so, is that of getting together for football drilling, several weeks before the college term opens, all candidates for the eleven and boarding and lodging them free of cost. I fail to see what difference it makes in the spirit of the proceeding whether part of a hotel or the entire caravansary is "hired

especially for the occasion," or whether the period of free board and lodging extends over six weeks or is ended at three.

The comparison in the Committee's letter of this preliminary football practice with the final work of the college crews at New London and Poughkeepsie has no point whatsoever. They are by no means parallel cases, either in spirit or in fact. Besides, the crew-work at Poughkeepsie and New London is not preliminary (except inasmuch as all training is indeed preliminary up to the very day of contest); it is the finishing work just before the race, and the men are practically all assigned to their positions. Both the Yale and the Cornell crews, and the Yale and the Cambridge track teams, had been in training several months before they went into final preparation near the scene of their approaching international struggle.

But all this is beside the question of the preliminary practice with which we have been confronted in football. Of course the life of men during preliminary football practice is "simple and wholesome"; men in training are not usually permitted indulgence in dissipations. It is not the point how much expenditure of "physical exertion" is needed by football; it is not the point that the men likely to neglect his studies for football should be taught "a part of his football lesson before his actual scholastic work

begins"; it is the point that any university should lay such stress upon the winning of their football eleven as to go beyond the usual time of preparation and breed professional instincts by lodging and boarding men for no other purpose than that they might secure that much more drilling and advantage over their rivals, and have thereby an extra chance or two of success.

This is the point in this specific case:—that Pennsylvania should persist in maintaining this preliminary prac-

YALE vs. CARLISLE INDIANS, MANHATTAN FIELD, OCTOBER 24, 1896.
Cayou, Indian Back, awaiting his Signal.

American amateur track team preparatory to their contest with the representative amateur team of England in 1895.

If "the example and experience of older and more conservative institutions" (as may say, en passant, that Pennsylvania, second only to Harvard in point of age, was founded by Franklin in 1740 are necessary, you will at once recall the above and other instances of a similar kind.

From our faculty's stand-point a limited period thus spent in preliminary training is eminently proper and beneficial. The mode of life of the young men during these three weeks was simple and wholesome; their fare was of the plainest; their work was carefully supervised with relation to their general health as much as to their football capacity. The men who were thought to be slow in their studies were encouraged to spend a part of each day with their books.

Football is a game requiring a maximum expenditure of physical exertion, and a condition of several alertness and activity which makes great demands on both the body and the mind of the player. We believe that it is unwise to allow young men to engage in it without at least so much careful preliminary attention to their bodily condition as will ensure them against unnecessary strain and injury; and we think, with all respect, that this is a matter about which you are less qualified to form an intelligent opinion than you are from our own body. We believe also that the football season makes less demand on the time and thought of an undergraduate if he has learned at least a part of his football lesson before his actual scholastic work begins. Otherwise the students are apt to be so physically fatigued as to be unfit for study, and therefore unable to maintain their class standing—a prerequisite to participation in athletics at Pennsylvania.

Our medical advisers, as well as our faculty committee, believe that the men are both safer physically and better students, as well as better football-players, for limiting rather than abolishing this preliminary practice.

We think, moreover, that the game itself as developed in this country has a value to the whole student body, as encouraging and fostering manly attributes, and justifies this slight extension of the football season as a means of promoting the scientific character of the game.

We have been in favor of a limitation of this preliminary training, which, like much else in American athletics, has tended to extremes. On February 19, 1896, we wrote to Harvard that we thought "It would be wise to limit the preliminary season for football training, and would be quite willing to act simultaneously with Harvard in the passage of a rule which should forbid the candidates for the team from assembling for that purpose, either as a body or in separate squads, for a period longer than three weeks prior to the date of the opening of the university." We added: "The climate in Philadelphia and vicinity is so intolerably hot, however, in September, that we would not deem it prudent, as far as Pennsylvania is concerned, to require the candidates to assemble till the university opens. If you will draft such a rule and send it on, our committee will join with you in coaching it." To this proposition we had a cordial assent, saying that there had been opposition to such action, but that if we would act jointly with them there would be no more trouble about it. Although, on account of preoccupation, the mutual agreement was not formally entered into, our committee proceeded to make the rule as above suggested to govern Pennsylvania. We would, of course, have made

INDIANS SCORE A TOUCH-DOWN.
Captain B. Pierce about to kick Goal.

THE INDIAN CENTRE.
Lone Wolf, Centre; B. Pierce, Right Guard; Wheelock, Left Guard; Hudson, Quarter-back.

"AMERICAN FOOTBALL."—By Walter Camp.—New and Revised Edition.—Post 8vo, Cloth, $1 25.—Harper & Brothers.

*Harper's Weekly* printed several photos from Carlisle's controversial game against Yale in New York City.

55

were traveling ambassadors for Carlisle, living proof the school was working—so long as they continued to behave like "gentlemen," that is.

It wasn't easy. As the *New York Sun* reported, the moment the Carlisle men jogged onto the field, "the crowd at once began to indulge in war whoops."

The Indian players didn't respond. They'd already learned to expect this obnoxious sort of reception.

Yale came out in dark blue, with big white Ys on the fronts of their jerseys. The Yale players averaged about six feet, nearly two hundred pounds; even with the Pierce brothers, Carlisle averaged five eight, 150. Confident Yale fans were heard offering two wagers.

First: the Indians would not score.

Second: Yale would top Princeton's total of twenty-two points.

"After the game," noted the *Sun*, "these same speculators denied having made any such offers."

William Hickok, Carlisle's volunteer coach, sent his team out for the kickoff. Then the former Yale star walked onto the field with a handkerchief in his pocket and a whistle around his neck. As was common at the time, the coach was going to serve as a referee.

A small group of Carlisle students around Pratt started to chant:

> *Hello! Hellee! Who are we?*
> *Hello! Hellee! Who are we?*
> *Hello! Hellee! Who are we?*
> *Indians! C-A-R-L-I-S-L-E!*

Early in the first half, the Carlisle men lined up at their own twenty-five, the low autumn sun shining in their eyes. Yale's bigger linemen snarled and grunted while Frank Hudson, Carlisle's 130-pound quarterback, called signals.

Hudson took the snap and pitched it to halfback Frank Cayou. Cayou wriggled through a gap in the line and burst into the open field. A Yale defender dove at him from behind. Cayou stumbled but stayed on his feet.

The fans, used to seeing short runs ending in dusty pileups, leaped to their feet and roared as Cayou tore eighty-five yards down the field. He was smiling as he crossed the goal line and, as required by rule, touched the ball down to the turf—a touchdown.

"Carlisle! Carlisle! Carlisle!" shouted the student cheering section.

Pratt turned to his daughter, grinning, and said, "That's one!"

Just three minutes into the game, the scoreboard read Carlisle 6, Yale 0.

"The Yale men looked at each other as if they were not sure what had happened," wrote the *New York World*. Team captain Fred Murphy gathered his rattled mates, shouting, "They've scored once, that means we must score three times! Now buck up and hit these fellows!"

Then Yale did its thing: power runs up the middle, with blockers literally lifting the ballcarrier and yanking him forward. Yale tied the game, then added a second touchdown before halftime.

The Yale players went into the clubhouse for rubdowns. Carlisle had no staff for such comforts; they stayed on the field.

"We will score again," Bemus Pierce told his teammates. "All we have to do is keep *them* from scoring."

"We can do it," Martin Wheelock urged.

Frank Hudson agreed. "We *will* do it."

The second half began, and Carlisle charged again and again into the stout Yale defense. They couldn't score, but neither could Yale. In the trenches, the game was only getting rougher. At one point, frustrated by relentless Carlisle blockers, Yale's Fred Murphy reared back and slugged Hawley Pierce in the face.

"The official didn't see it," reported the *New York Sun*, "although the crowd did and hissed the Yale captain."

Late in the second half, with Yale still clinging to a 12–6 lead, came the most talked-about play of the entire 1896 football season.

Carlisle was stuck in its own territory. Time was running out. Frank Hudson took the snap and flipped the ball back to the speedy Jake Jamison. The crowd saw Jamison hit the right side of the line and disappear into a wall of defenders. The play appeared to end in the predictable pile of humanity.

Until Jamison came out the other side.

Thousands of fans—not just the Carlisle section, but fans all over the stadium, fans on the hill, fans on the elevated train platform—screamed and waved pennants and threw hats into the air. Two of Yale's fastest defenders caught Jamison at the Carlisle thirty, grabbing his jersey, but he tore free and cruised over the goal line. The Carlisle students shrieked and laughed.

But the cheering quieted when fans noticed the ref, William Hickok, standing all the way back where the play had begun. He was waving his handkerchief.

"What's going on, Coach?" Bemus Pierce demanded. "What's wrong?"

"I thought they'd stopped him," the ref said.

"What? He broke away!"

"But I *thought* they had stopped him."

Both teams crowded around. Hickok explained that he thought Jamison had been tackled in the pile. He'd blown his whistle. The score-keeper had already hung a ten beside Carlisle's name. Now he changed it back to a six.

Jake Jamison ran up, panting and furious. "It was a fair run! I scored! You can't take it away!"

Hickok knew Jamison was right. He'd blown the whistle too soon. Likely an honest mistake—or had his old Yale loyalties come into play?

Fans suspected the worst. They shouted "Robbery!" as Hickok walked to the spot where the play had begun, stamped his heel into the soil, and said, "The ball is down right here."

The jeers from the stands lasted five full minutes.

"Never did New York see a more exciting football game," wrote the *New York World* of Yale's 12–6 win over Carlisle. "Never was there a greater surprise."

That was the theme on sports pages in New York and beyond—that little-known Carlisle had played a stunningly strong game with Yale and had been, intentionally or not, robbed of the tying touchdown. Some even saw history repeating itself. "Now, if we have a right to rob the Indian anywhere," a Rochester paper commented with bitter sarcasm, "we certainly have a right to cheat him out of football games."

For the players, there was no time to brood. Next Saturday Carlisle was in Boston to take on mighty Harvard. It was another hard-hitting, low-scoring, much-closer-than-anyone-expected football game. The bigger Harvard boys tried to bully Carlisle, slugging freely in the pileups. The refs allowed it.

Bemus Pierce did not.

"Mr. Donald," he said softly to Barkie Donald, the lineman opposite him, after a particularly vicious play, "you have been hitting me, and if you do it again, I shall hit you."

The next play, Donald punched Pierce even harder. Pierce said nothing.

The teams lined up again. The ball was snapped. The lines collided, and Donald felt what he would later describe as a sledgehammer to the head. "I remember charging, but that was all," he recalled. He managed to stand on wobbly knees, barely able to see the blurry outlines of other players.

"Mr. Donald," Pierce said, "you hit me one, two, three times, I hit you only once—we're square."

No argument from Donald. They were square.

Harvard won, 4–0.

The next week Carlisle traveled to Philadelphia to play the previous year's national champs, the University of Pennsylvania Quakers. The exhausted Carlisle team was pushed around all afternoon in a 21–0 loss.

Drained and aching, the Carlisle Indians walked off the field together.

That was the winter Jim Thorpe's world changed forever.

When Jim and Charlie were eight years old, measles and typhoid fever swept through the Sac and Fox Agency School in Oklahoma. A young teacher, Harriet Patrick, spent long days and nights moving from one sick child to the next. "I took care of them, giving them medicine every hour," she remembered, "but by the time that I had made the rounds, it was time to begin again."

Jim escaped serious illness, but Charlie developed a dangerous case of pneumonia. Harriet Patrick sent for the boys' parents.

Charlotte and Hiram hurried to the school and rushed into the room that was being used as a makeshift hospital. Dozens of students lay suffering in beds, hot packs on their chests, coughing ceaselessly. Patrick asked the Thorpes to keep the fire going in the stove while she got some rest. Jim joined his parents, and they sat together by Charlie's bed. At some point in the night, they all fell asleep.

At five the next morning, Patrick returned. She looked at Charlie. He was barely breathing. "I went to him and took him in my arms," she recalled. She sent for the doctor. "But the poor little fellow just lay back and died."

Jim woke to see the teacher holding Charlie's lifeless body.

Hiram and Charlotte took Jim home. Devastated by his brother's death, Jim walked into the woods. He needed to be alone—or, maybe, not quite alone. "I asked my father where he got all his strength," Jim Thorpe's son Jack would say many years later. "He said he had inherited it from his brother. When his brother passed away, he got all his strength. He just felt Charlie was with him all the time."

Jim camped in the forest. He fished and hunted, and earned money selling raccoon and skunk pelts. Charlotte and Hiram allowed it for a while. Then they dragged him back to school. Jim had always been quiet; now he was completely withdrawn. He sat in class, ignoring the teacher, lost in his own thoughts.

He ran away again in the spring, hiking those familiar twenty-three miles to his home. His father met him at the door, turned him right around, and drove him back to school. Hiram headed back home. So did Jim. "But I took a shortcut," Jim recalled, "which shortened the distance to eighteen miles, running all the way, and when he got home this time, it was I who met him at the door."

Hiram was done. He told Jim, "Now I'm going to send you so far away from home you'll never find your way back."

"**E**ver scrub before?"

Howard Gansworth shook his head no. The fifteen-year-old son of Seneca and Tuscarora parents had just arrived at Carlisle. He'd just been assigned to work with this other kid, who knew the job all too well. They dropped to the wooden floor and started scrubbing.

"You use too much water."

Gansworth watched the boy demonstrate how to rub a small area clean, wipe it dry, and move on. Together, they inched down the long corridor.

This was life at Carlisle. On top of classes, workshops, study hours, and prayer meetings, the men and boys were put to work maintaining buildings, making furniture, and running the campus farm. The women and girls cooked and cleaned and sewed and washed and ironed.

An endless cycle of work, lectures, rules—Howard Gansworth called it "the Carlisle rut."

"I wondered how I could stand the life at Carlisle," he later wrote of his first few days. "It seemed as if we were always answering roll call, always reporting to someone, always marching somewhere, always keeping step with somebody, always under an officer's charge."

And the officer watching most closely was Richard Henry Pratt.

On Gansworth's first Saturday on campus, he joined the entire student body in the chapel for the superintendent's weekly lecture. He watched Pratt step onto the stage in his long blue coat.

No fan of Carlisle at first, Howard Gansworth became a successful student and went on to graduate from Princeton University.

Pratt lifted a piece of paper and read out the names of students who had been caught smoking tobacco or speaking their native language. He made no comment—just let the names of the offenders linger in the silent room.

Then, striding to the edge of the stage, he called out, "How shall we abolish the Indian problem? Boys, girls, anyone . . . In just a sentence."

A boy shouted, "Get the Indian into civilization and citizenship!"

Other boys offered similar answers.

"What's the matter with the girls?" Pratt challenged. "Why don't they speak up?"

A girl named Martha Napawat responded. "To civilize the Indian, get him into civilization," she said. "To keep him there, let him stay."

"A little louder Martha," commanded Pratt, "so we can all hear."

She repeated the lines. But these were not her words; this was Pratt's school motto, printed at the top of the school newspaper. She was only saying what Pratt wanted to hear.

Gansworth was stunned by how thoroughly Pratt seemed to be intimidating and controlling his students.

Martha Napawat, Kiowa (left), and Nellie Robertson, Sisseton Sioux, in their Carlisle School uniforms.

It was all by design. Everywhere they turned, students were hammered by Pratt's unrelenting "kill the Indian in them" philosophy. Even the American history textbook they used was a weapon. It barely acknowledged the existence of Native Americans—and when it did, described them as "savages" and "ignorant barbarians."

One night at supper, a student named Nellie Robertson spoke a single word in Sioux to a friend. She'd been so battered by Pratt's teachings, she felt like a criminal for speaking her own language. "I could not eat my supper," she confessed to Pratt in writing, "and I could not forget that Indian word, and while I was sitting at the table the tears rolled down my cheeks."

Pratt published the letter in the school newspaper as a lesson to other students.

Some students broke the language rule—but carefully, in small groups, late at night in the dorms. "Somebody would have a coughing spell while the two had their conversation," a student named John Alonzo explained, "and then when they were finished, somebody else would cough a while and someone else could talk." Others secretly shared traditional stories and legends. "When we were in school we used to think about our own people and our own ways," one Apache student remembered.

Many students—sometimes forty or more a year—resorted to Jim Thorpe's method of resistance to Indian boarding school. They ran away.

The football team found a different way to escape Pratt's grasp—for a few days at a time, at least.

With no stadium on campus, Carlisle played all of its games in 1896 on the road. The travel was exhausting, and left the players at a disadvantage against well-rested opponents. It was worth it. In December, the team finished its season with a long trip to Chicago, where they beat the University of Wisconsin in the world's first indoor football game.

After the game, the players collapsed onto couches at their hotel and lit up cigars—a final moment of freedom before the return to campus.

The Carlisle Indians obviously had not accomplished their goal of beating one of the Big Four in 1896—in those four games they'd been outscored 59–12. But they *had* managed wins over a few good teams, and finished the season at 5-5.

Just two years before, these guys had been plowing their own practice field. They'd come an incredibly long way, and the sports world was taking note.

"Too much praise cannot be given this Indian team for its showing this year," wrote Caspar Whitney, an influential sportswriter, in *Harper's Weekly*, "for the quality of its football after but three years of the game at Carlisle, and above all for its sportsmanly conduct and clean play." They were picked on and provoked, got some lousy calls from the refs, but they kept their cool and played through it all. "I regard the conduct of these Indians," Whitney wrote, "to have had a more wholesome influence on the game than any occurrence of recent years."

And this was a sport in *dire* need of a wholesome influence.

On October 30, 1897, at a game between the universities of Virginia and Georgia, a Georgia player named Von Gammon dove into a mass of

A drawing of the University of Georgia's Von Gammon, whose shocking death in 1897 sparked loud calls for the end of football in Georgia—and beyond.

Virginia blockers. He hit the ground headfirst and wound up at the bottom of a pile of bodies.

Everyone else got up. Gammon lay on the grass. The blood drained from his face. His eyes were open, his lips quivering. A doctor ran onto the field and diagnosed a fractured skull. Gammon was lifted into a horse-drawn ambulance and rushed to a hospital. He died early the next morning.

FOOTBALL MUST GO, declared a headline in Gammon's hometown paper, the *Rome Tribune*, STOP THE DEADLY GAME.

It looked as if this might actually happen. The University of Georgia canceled the remainder of its football season, and the Georgia legislature passed a bill banning the sport entirely. Governor William Atkinson was debating whether to sign the bill into law when he got a letter from Rosalind Gammon, Von's mother. "Grant me the right," she asked, "to request that my boy's death should not be used to defeat the most cherished object of his life."

Atkinson vetoed the bill. But with each grisly injury, the national debate over football's future intensified.

DEATH ON THE FOOTBALL FIELD, screamed the headline of the *New York Herald* just two weeks after Gammon's death.

The story reported that nine boys and young men had been killed in the past year alone playing football. Descriptions of each fatal injury—mostly fractured skulls and broken necks—were given. The next day's *New York World* ran a ghoulish cartoon of a skeleton playing football. The *New York Journal* printed a front-page editorial calling for the banning of the game.

Utter nonsense, charged a young politician from New York named Theodore Roosevelt.

A Harvard graduate and football fan, Roosevelt made no apologies for his love of the sport. In what would become an increasingly heated debate in the years ahead, he would be one of football's most outspoken defenders.

One of football's first and fiercest defenders, Theodore Roosevelt. "The sports especially dear to a vigorous and manly nation are always those in which there is a certain slight element of risk," he wrote in 1893.

"I emphatically disbelieve in seeing Harvard or any other college turn out mollycoddles instead of vigorous men," Roosevelt told students at a visit to his old school. "I do not in the least object to a sport because it is rough."

The Carlisle Indians were called a lot of names. Mollycoddle was not one of them.

In 1897 the team powered its way to its first winning season, going 6-4. But against Princeton, Yale, and Pennsylvania, Carlisle was outscored 62–19 in three lopsided losses. The team seemed no closer to the goal of taking its place among the sport's elite schools.

They'd never get there, said some commentators. Repeating baseless stereotypes, writers suggested the Indians were lazy and easily discouraged, and had no hope of breaking the Big Four stranglehold.

Others made the more logical case that Carlisle was still new to the sport, and missing a key ingredient. The *Boston Globe* said it well: "Their chief shortcoming seems to be a limited knowledge of the fine points of the game."

Carlisle halfback Frank Cayou echoed the point: "We only need a little more time and coaching."

Richard Henry Pratt was no football expert, but he was beginning to get the message. What Carlisle needed was a better coach.

**J**im Thorpe rode a wagon to Guthrie, Oklahoma, then a train to Lawrence, Kansas. The three-hundred-mile journey ended with a walk beneath the stone arch entryway of the Haskell Institute.

This was Hiram Thorpe's solution to his eleven-year-old son's restless soul. Set on flat land surrounded by fields of wheat, Haskell was an Indian boarding school with a reputation for strict discipline. Like all incoming students, Jim reported to the infirmary, where his hair was cut short, soaked in kerosene to kill any lice, and parted down the middle. He was given a uniform and told the rules.

Young students at the Haskell Institute in Lawrence, Kansas.

Just as at Carlisle, each day began with reveille at five-thirty. Jim learned to dress quickly, making sure his shoes and clothes were immaculate—even brass jacket buttons had to shine. He marched in military formation to meals and classes and vocational training. At night, before bed, he stood at attention with a thousand other students as the school band played "The Star-Spangled Banner."

In free moments, Jim walked out to the athletic fields to watch the older boys practicing.

This is where he saw football for the first time.

"An Indian on the Haskell squad named Chauncey Archiquette became my idol," Thorpe remembered, "and I decided to try to emulate him." Jim and his friends made their own ball: grass shoved into a sock and tied shut. "We played in our hickory-cloth work shirts, jeans, and heavy shoes," Jim's classmate—and future Carlisle teammate—Henry Roberts described. "Sometimes we had to fatten the ball by stuffing more grass into it."

They would watch the varsity team practice, and then, when practice was over, dash onto the field for their own game. Jim was one of the smaller kids, but he was fast, hard to grab. One day Chauncey Archiquette walked over to him and took a look at the boy's "football." He asked if Jim would like a real ball. They walked to the harness shop, and Archiquette sewed together some leather scraps, stuffing the oval with rags.

He handed it to Jim. Jim held his new ball, a huge smile on his face.

And he played. He played every chance he got.

He and his friends chose teams and romped around the massive field, free—for the moment—of rules and routine, discipline and punishment.

On many nights, as the sun set and the other boys headed inside, Jim stayed alone on the field. He'd tuck the ball under his arm and take off, zigzagging past imaginary tacklers, a carefree kid again, racing Charlie across the Oklahoma plains.

◆◈◆

In Ithaca, New York, Pop Warner walked off the Cornell football field and trudged into the team's locker room. He stepped into a small equipment closet, shut the door behind him, sat down, and cried.

While Jim Thorpe was adjusting to life at Haskell, Warner had landed his dream job: head football coach at his old school. He'd opened the 1897 season with a string of wins. When Princeton came to town, he felt his club could pull off a monumental upset, a win that would propel Cornell—and Pop himself—into football's top tier.

Cornell lost, 10–0. That's when Warner headed for the privacy of the equipment closet.

Eight decades later, the great NFL coach Bill Parcells would famously say, "There is winning, and there is misery." Pop Warner saw life exactly the same way.

At Cornell, Pop mostly won. The game that stuck most vividly in his memory was played on Cornell's Percy Field on October 6, 1898. It was a warm fall day. The stands were full. The trees around the field were red and gold, and loose leaves swirled across the grass in a light breeze. Warner watched the visiting team run onto the field.

Pop had heard about this team. He knew they hadn't been playing ball for long. He knew they'd already gained a reputation for audacity, for going anywhere, playing anyone. He'd heard the players were undersized, but fast.

Now, watching the Carlisle Indians warm up, he was amazed at *how* fast.

Cornell jumped out to a lead with two quick touchdowns. Carlisle answered with two scores, both of which were called back by a referee who just happened to have been Cornell's team captain the year before. "The twelfth member of the Cornell team," Frank Hudson joked bitterly after the game.

Warner didn't disagree. "We outscored 'em," he told reporters, "but we didn't defeat 'em, if you follow me."

Warner led his team to a 10-2 record that year, but he never felt appreciated at Cornell. Wealthy alumni were constantly second-guessing his decisions. Eager assistants angled for his job. He wasn't even sure the school was going to extend his contract for the 1899 season. Pop wanted to go somewhere he could build his own program, make his own mark— somewhere he could really be the boss.

And he couldn't stop thinking about that Carlisle team he'd seen in October. Sure, the players needed help with fundamentals. But their athleticism and heart were things you just couldn't teach.

As Warner would later say, "The Indian boys appealed to my football imagination."

**P**op **Warner sat in Richard Henry Pratt's** office at the Carlisle School. He watched Pratt's face for a reaction to what he had just said. The man didn't even blink.

Warner, now twenty-eight years old, had come to interview for the position of football coach. Wanting the job badly, but hoping not to appear overeager, he'd just delivered a list of demands, including a salary of $1,200. Plus travel expenses.

If Pratt was shocked, he didn't show it. He had done his homework, asking around about the best young coaches. He already knew he wanted Warner. The salary was absurdly high—among the highest of any coach in the nation—but still, Pratt figured, it might be a sound investment. The football team was already earning positive press—imagine if they actually started *winning*. Wins would bring bigger crowds. Bigger crowds would mean more money for Carlisle, which took home a share of ticket sales. Pratt was constantly struggling to raise donations and pry cash from Congress for his school; a fresh source of income would be most welcome.

Pratt reached across his desk to offer Warner his hand.

Feeling more financially secure than he ever had, Warner married his childhood sweetheart, Tibb Lorraine Smith, and they moved together to

a small cottage on the Carlisle campus. When the 1899 school year began in September, the coach walked out to Indian Field to meet his new team.

His career at Carlisle nearly ended that same week.

"Having been coached by some rather hard-boiled gents during my days as a player," Warner later explained, "I took a fairly extensive vocabulary with me to Carlisle, and made full use of it." A polite way of saying he cursed up a storm on the practice field.

"Play @#$& football!" he'd scream.

"What in the %&*# you think you're doin'?"

Warner saw it as a way of motivating his guys. The players saw it as unnecessary and offensive. A couple of the best athletes stopped coming to practice. Every day, fewer and fewer players showed up. Warner would see the men on campus during the day; he *knew* they were still at school.

He stopped one, shouting, "You haven't been to practice in two days!"

"I'm tired of coming out to practice every day and listening to your swearing every time I make a mistake. I've had it!"

Warner hadn't realized what the problem was. "If you will come back," he said, "I will never swear at you or anyone again."

The players came back. Warner promised to tone down his language. And he did, for a while.

Finally, they got to work. While the team drilled, Pop strode the field with a whistle around his neck, smoke rising from a cigarette between his lips. He studied the players' strengths, watched for weaknesses. "I had all the prejudices of the average white," he'd later admit. "I used to read that Indians always quit if they didn't win a fight at the very outset."

That was wrong, Warner quickly realized. Dead wrong.

These guys had lost plenty, and not only on the football field. Most came from families that had endured decades of attack and upheaval. They were far from home, stuck at a school designed to erase an essential part of who they were. But here, on the field, there was fire in their eyes. They were wide open to new ideas, quick to absorb information. When Pop wanted to show the players a new play or technique, he'd gather them around and draw it on a blackboard. They only had to see it once.

The one thing that still bothered Warner was the team's lack of size.

Bemus Pierce had graduated and was coaching football at the University

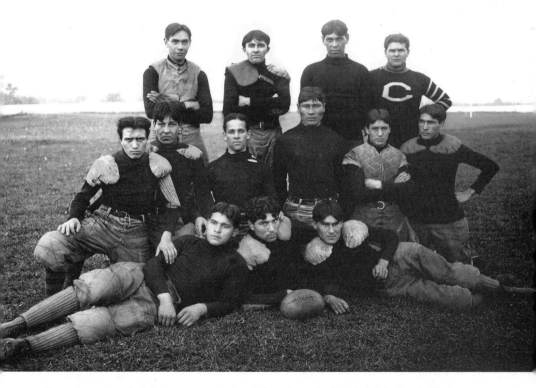

No one beyond the Carlisle campus expected much from the undersized Carlisle Indians in 1899.

75

of Buffalo. Even with Hawley Pierce still in action, the team was going to be badly outweighed by top schools. They were quick, but how much would that help? "Speed had little place in a team's offensive attack," Warner said of early-day football. "Big human mountains were sought and valued by every coach, and it didn't matter if the behemoths could navigate slowly or swiftly."

Could a team succeed without behemoths? None ever had. But that didn't mean it couldn't be done.

Frank Hudson had already figured this out.

Born in a Pueblo village in New Mexico, Hudson had been sent to Carlisle when he was just nine. He was a studious, serious boy who learned to set type in the printing shop and worked on the school newspaper. He was serious about football, too. Often referred to in articles as "the little Indian quarterback," the five-foot-five Hudson used speed and quick thinking to transform himself from bony teen into elite player.

He also saw a scoring opportunity that wasn't being used to its potential. Field goals were then worth five points, the same as touchdowns (which rule makers had just increased in value from four to five). At the time, the standard way to kick a field goal was the dropkick—the kicker literally dropped the ball on the ground in front of him, let it bounce, and kicked it as it rose. The fat ball bounced fairly predictably; the kicking part was the problem. Airborne, the ball wobbled and swerved, and field goal tries of more than thirty yards were crapshoots.

Hudson thought he could do better. Night after night, he stayed after practice, drop-kicking the ball toward—and sometimes through—the goalposts on Indian Field. On winter evenings, he practiced in the gym, aiming at goalposts he built from gymnastics bars.

Now, in his last year at Carlisle, Hudson showed the new coach that he could drop-kick consistently from forty yards out. With either foot.

Warner was not one to gush with praise. At least, not in front of his players.

"Okay, son," he told Hudson. "That will do nicely."

At home, he gushed.

"This is a new kind of team," Pop told Tibb one evening over dinner. "They're light, but they're fast and tricky. Once they get into an open field, they're like acrobats, they're so hard to knock off their feet. And proud! It's just the kind of team that I've always dreamed of coaching."

❖

With the first game of the season approaching, Warner continued shifting players around, trying different combinations on the line and in the backfield. He worked the team hard, hammering away at tackling technique, and the proper way to block bigger men. "The Indians took to it like ducks to water," Pop would later explain, "and when they blocked a man, he *stayed* blocked."

On rare occasions when a player wasn't aggressive enough for Pop's liking, he'd line up opposite the offender and demand better.

"Now get down here," he'd grunt, "and show me how it should be done."

When he challenged a Cherokee lineman named James Phillips, Phillips burst forward with such force he knocked Pop unconscious.

Everyone stopped and watched the coach. After a few moments Warner sat up. He looked at Phillips and said, "Now that's the way it's done!"

Another day at practice, Warner asked the gathered team, "When you're on defense and the other team starts a play in which they all move to your right, what do you do?"

"Slide along to the right with them," Martin Wheelock answered. "Find the ballcarrier, and dive in."

"Right. It's only natural," Warner said. "Okay, you men, line up over there."

The starters lined up on defense. Warner huddled his second-teamers on offense and described a variation of his old Number 39 play.

The offense snapped the ball. The entire line drove left, and the ballcarrier followed. Once the momentum of the play was moving in that direction, the man with the ball stopped, turned, and raced to the right. He sprinted, untouched, all the way to the goal line.

"Get the other team moving in one direction," Warner lectured, "so your ballcarrier can go the other."

Carlisle practiced it over and over. They added an additional wrinkle: the ballcarrier started, say, to his left, then, instead of reversing direction himself, he pitched the ball to a teammate who was already running to the right—a reverse, as it's now known. Warner and the team agreed to save it for just the right occasion.

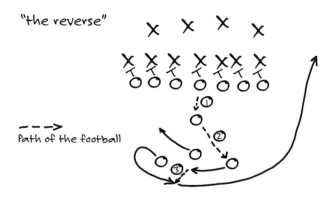

"the reverse"

Path of the football

The team cruised to a 21–0 win in the season opener against Gettysburg College. No need to get creative the following week, either, as Carlisle walloped Susquehanna University, 56–0.

Then things got serious. Next on the schedule was the first Big Four challenge of the Pop Warner era, the University of Pennsylvania. Penn had been absurdly dominant over the last five seasons, compiling a record of 67-2. They'd outscored Carlisle 112–15 in four blowout victories. They were overwhelming favorites to win easily again.

That was fine with Pop Warner. He knew Carlisle's record so far against the Big Four was 0-12. But he also knew his players were more than hungry. He knew they were starting to click as a team—and that they were a lot better than anyone beyond the Carlisle campus realized.

On the afternoon of Saturday, October 14, more than twenty thou-sand fans filled Philadelphia's Franklin Field. The Penn band played and the crowd sang and the stands surrounding the field, reported the *Philadelphia Times*, were "a varying mass of color and animation."

Somewhere in there, chanting for their school, was an island of Carlisle students, a hundred young women and men. They'd spent their savings from summer jobs on train fare, hotel rooms, and tickets to the school's first crack at a Big Four team under the new coach.

Penn set the tone early.

"Guards back, right!" Penn quarterback John Gardiner shouted in the huddle. This was their signature mass play—it would let the visitors know they were in over their heads.

Three linemen formed a human wall in front of the halfback, and three more stood behind him. Gardiner caught the snap from center, tossed the halfback the ball, and he and the bunched linemen swung forward like a wrecking ball.

Warner had prepared his men for this. The Carlisle linemen got low and dodged, letting the blockers' momentum carry them past. Then the defenders sprung at the ballcarrier's legs, bringing him down.

Penn lined up and ran the same play again. Again Carlisle tacklers dove through gaps in the mass to upend the runner, setting up a third down. The home team faced a choice. They could punt the ball to Carlisle, or they could go for it—try again to gain the needed yardage. But if they were stopped short, Carlisle would take over on offense right there.

Pennsylvania decided to punt. For fans expecting Penn to steam-roll Carlisle yet again, this was the first indication that something had changed.

This was going to be a game.

Most coaches sat on the bench during games. Not Warner. Warner paced endlessly, chain-smoking, shouting at his players, barking at the refs. He watched Carlisle run two plays that went nowhere. They punted it back to Penn.

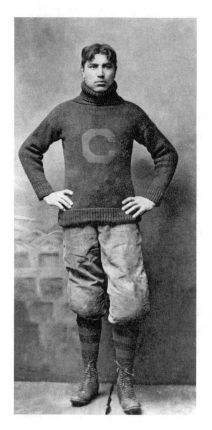

As captain of the 1899 football team, Martin Wheelock helped lead the Carlisle Indians to their best season yet.

From there, the game settled into a typical field-position battle, with lots of short runs, lots of punting back and forth. But, to the surprise of the crowd, it was Carlisle that put together the first drive. Hawley Pierce found a soft spot in Penn's defensive line and barreled through for good gains. Quarterback Frank Hudson, who called all the plays himself, mixed the up-the-middle runs with pitches to Martin Wheelock and Isaac Seneca, who sped around the edge of the defense.

The drive stalled with a third down at Penn's thirty-four-yard line. Too far for a field goal attempt, said conventional wisdom. Hudson called for a field goal attempt.

He dropped back to the forty, caught the snap, held the ball in front of him, let it fall, and swung his toe forward. The big ball rose and tumbled and was on its way down when it sailed through the goalposts.

At halftime it was Carlisle 5, Pennsylvania 0. But the Indians had taken leads on Big Four teams before; they'd never been able to hold them.

This time was different.

Penn tried to get its power game going in the second half, but couldn't. "The Indians were tearing through the line like Rough Riders in full charge," reported the *Philadelphia Times*, comparing the Carlisle team to the soldiers Theodore Roosevelt had led on a victorious charge up Cuba's San Juan Hill in the Spanish-American War the year before. On offense, Frank Hudson continued calling an unpredictable mix of runs. "First Pierce would come crashing through tackle for a good gain," wrote the *Times*, "and then Wheelock and Seneca would thunder around the end."

Frustrated, with no idea what was coming next, Penn players snapped at each other between plays. The fans seemed stunned. They had never seen a team play this fast.

Hudson sensed it—time to go for the knockout.

"This is the time for the new play," he told the team in the huddle.

It flowed like lines on Pop's chalkboard.

Hudson took the snap, and everyone started left—until he slipped the ball to Isaac Seneca, who cut it back the other way. The Carlisle fans jumped and screamed as Seneca raced forty yards before being dragged down at the Penn five. Hawley Pierce then pounded in for the touchdown, and the extra point made it Carlisle 11, Penn 0.

Penn sent in fresh players and finally put together a good drive, leading to a short field goal. But Carlisle iced the upset with a drive of its own. The setting sun was glowing red, and the moon could be seen rising in the east, as Jimmie Johnson, pushed from behind by a wall of blockers, plowed over the goal line.

Final: Carlisle 16, Penn 5.

❦

Richard Henry Pratt could hear the ruckus from his bedroom.

As soon as the team got back late Saturday night, the campus erupted—students dashed outside in their nightshirts and pulled the victorious players around in a wagon. Everyone was shouting and singing.

They'd finally done it, Pratt knew, exactly as promised. They'd finally whipped one of the big boys.

Doing it again would prove a lot harder.

After a home win over Dickinson, Carlisle went back on the road to take on the two best teams in the country that year, Harvard and Princeton. Harvard beat them, 22–10. Princeton shut them out, 12–0.

Carlisle beat everyone else on the schedule, ending the season in New York City against a strong Columbia University team. The *New York Sun* predicted "one of the most interesting football battles of the year" between evenly matched clubs. Columbia fans were confident the home team's running backs would score at least one or two touchdowns. "Hudson's wonderful goal kicking ability has not been overlooked in the calculation," the *Sun* added, "so that Columbia adherents will not be surprised if both teams score."

In fact, only one team scored.

On Thanksgiving Day, Carlisle astonished the New York crowd with what would today be called a "hurry-up" offense. Frank Hudson called plays before defenders could even get set, as Carlisle "played the fastest game seen on the gridiron this season," noted the *New York Tribune*. Carlisle's 45–0 trouncing of Columbia was a statement win, proof Carlisle now belonged among the country's top teams.

Maybe not at the *very* top with Harvard and Princeton—but close.

◆

A month later they were on the road again.

Since the Transcontinental Railroad had been completed thirty years before, plenty of people had made the three-thousand-mile trip across the United States by rail—but never to play a football game. The Carlisle Indians were the first. With national fame, and the proven ability to draw crowds, the team had been invited to play the University of California in what newspapers were billing as an "East-West Championship."

The players took schoolbooks along and tried to keep up with work as their train sped west. At station stops, they'd get out and toss around a football. "At one point along the road, where the wait was long," reported the *San Francisco Call*, "the Indians ran to the next station and boarded the train there."

During another stop on the five-day trip, Warner was sitting on a bench, watching the team run plays in a nearby field, when a man with a long gray beard walked up. He asked Warner about the guys in red sweaters.

"This is the Carlisle football team," Warner said, "and we're en route to San Francisco to play the University of California."

"Well," the old man said, "they are going a darned long way to get the hell kicked out of them."

Pop said nothing, but later noted: "As it happened, he proved a poor prophet."

On Christmas Day in San Francisco, a big crowd waved ribbons of California blue and gold as the teams ran onto the field. Frank Hudson responded to the cheers with an acrobatic series of handsprings.

The game itself was less exciting. The field was sandy and slow, and the day's only score came when the Cal center snapped the ball over the punter's head. The punter raced back and scooped it up near Cal's goal line, and was met there by Hawley Pierce, who drove him backward into a fence. Then, as now, tackling an opposing runner behind his own goal line was a safety, worth two points. The nation's first East-West football showdown ended 2–0.

CALIFORNIA VIRTUALLY TIES CARLISLE, blared the next day's *San Francisco Chronicle* headline, INDIANS SCORE TWO POINTS ON A FLUKE.

Even this blatantly biased headline was, in a way, a sign of respect. Losing to Carlisle by just two was seen as something to crow about.

Carlisle finished the 1899 season a remarkable 9-2. No team had played a tougher schedule, or played more entertaining ball, or traveled more, and it was about this time that newspapers started calling Carlisle "Nomads of the Gridiron." The team was even beginning to change the way football was played, demonstrating the untapped potential of speed and strategy.

Walter Camp, a former Yale coach and influential sportswriter, put Carlisle #4 in his annual top-ten ranking. It was the first time *any* team outside the Big Four cracked Camp's top four.

On the long trip back east, the Carlisle team stopped to visit several government-run Indian boarding schools. By 1900, more than twenty of these schools, with about twenty thousand students, had been established around the country.

At each campus, students lined up to meet the famous Carlisle Indians. The team put on football clinics, showing kids the basics of the game, while Warner stood to the side, scouting talent. He'd later pull promising players aside and make a recruiting pitch for Carlisle.

On January 12, 1900, Warner and the team stopped at the Haskell Institute in Kansas. The players, in their red turtlenecks, walked across the snow-covered campus toward rows of students standing in formation.

Pop Warner was always on the lookout for athletes. What he had no way of knowing was that among this assembly, standing with the young boys, was a kid who'd soon be celebrated as the greatest athlete in the world.

He was eleven years old, not quite five feet tall. His name was Jim Thorpe.

Facing page: Uniformed boys await inspection in their dorm at the Haskell Institute.

**WILD HORSES**

**Jim would never forget that day at Haskell.** He stood at attention as the Carlisle team approached across the snowy field. His eyes were wide, his mouth open in awe, as the players he'd heard about marched up—Frank Hudson, Isaac Seneca, Martin Wheelock, Hawley Pierce— heroes, all of them, to the Indian boys at Haskell.

After a breakfast in honor of the visitors, the Carlisle team headed back to Pennsylvania, and Jim settled back into the school's daily routine. He was actually doing well in classes—until a fall day in 1901, when Jim was thirteen.

"One of my classmates told me that he had seen a letter from my father," Thorpe later recalled. "He had been shot in a hunting accident and, believing that he was dying from the wound in his chest, he had enclosed money for my fare home."

Why hadn't school officials told him? Maybe, Jim figured, they didn't want him leaving school in the middle of a term? But what right did they have to withhold that kind of information—or the money his father had sent?

That night, after lights out, Jim pulled on his overalls and walked away from Haskell. He hiked to the Lawrence rail yard and hopped into a boxcar on an already moving train. Straining to read signposts in the dark, he realized the train was moving east—Oklahoma was south. He leaped off and headed for home. Walking all day, sleeping under the open sky, he covered 270 miles in two weeks.

When he got to his family's cabin, Jim found his father thin and weak, but on the mend. Hiram insisted that Jim turn around and go back to Haskell. Jim absolutely refused.

"One day shortly afterwards," Thorpe remembered, "my dad gave me a licking which I probably deserved but didn't feel like taking. So I lit out."

❖

This time Jim walked nearly 300 miles west, to the Texas Panhandle, where he talked his way into a job on a cattle ranch. He fed animals, fixed fences, and gained a bit of local fame for his uncanny ability to break wild horses.

The first step was to herd a few of the 1,200-pound animals into a round corral. Then the hundred-pound Jim would lasso one of them, tying the other end of the rope to a wooden post in the center of the corral. Approaching slowly, dodging kicks, he'd leap onto the horse's back and hold on for dear life as the furious beast bucked and snorted and twisted its head to try to bite him. Eventually, the horse gave in.

Breaking horses tested Jim's strength and balance, his courage and ability to endure pain. It was his idea of fun.

A cowboy attempting to break an untamed horse on a Texas ranch.

After about a year in Texas, Jim headed home, leading a team of horses he'd saved enough money to buy. He figured his father would have no choice now but to accept him as a man. And this time Hiram really did seem glad to see his son—and was particularly impressed with the horses. "My father took one look at them," Thorpe remembered, "and decided to take me back."

But just a few weeks later, tragedy gashed Jim's life again. His mother, weakened from a difficult childbirth, died at the age of thirty-eight. Charlotte Thorpe was buried in a nearby church cemetery.

Without his mother, life at home would never be the same for Jim. "We didn't sit in front of the house anymore, watching the carefree games," he remembered. He coped as he had after Charlie's death, slipping off into the woods, living alone off the land. But Jim had responsibilities at home now and soon returned to help care for his three younger siblings.

And there was still the matter of his education. Hiram wanted his son back in school, and for once Jim didn't push back too hard—student life sounded pretty soft after a year as a Texas ranch hand. He and Hiram walked to a one-room school just a few miles from their home, a non-boarding public school attended mainly by white children.

Walter White, a teacher at the school, would later describe coming to work that morning and seeing a huge man standing outside the school-house beside a teenage boy. The boy had what White recalled as "a sort of hangdog look."

"Can you teach the boy anything?" Hiram blurted out. He explained Jim's history of running away, how he'd walked out of the nearby Sac and Fox Agency School five or six times.

"Why did you leave the agency school, Jim?" White asked.

Jim was looking at his feet as he said, "I don't like it." None of the Indian boys liked it, he said.

"Will you run away from this school?"

Jim said, "I will not run away."

White got the distinct impression his newest pupil was choosing the lesser of two evils.

On the morning of November 28, 1902, President Theodore Roosevelt ate breakfast in the White House, the newspaper sports page spread open in front of him.

Roosevelt had been elected vice president of the United States in 1900. In September 1901, when President William McKinley was assassinated, Roosevelt, age forty-two, became the youngest president in American history. He had a lot more important issues to ponder than football, but he was still a big fan—and still a vocal defender of the game.

Born to a wealthy family in New York City, Roosevelt had been a small and sickly kid, sidelined with asthma while other boys played in the streets. He took boxing lessons to strengthen his body, and, as a young man, went west to hunt and work on ranches. If he could toughen himself up, Roosevelt concluded, others could, too.

As a student at Harvard, he'd been too nearsighted to play football. But he developed a love of the game, and came to see in it a value far beyond the playing field. For the first time in US history, more Americans were living in cities than on farms. More and more men were working in offices, and Roosevelt worried the country was going soft. The beauty of football, as he saw it, was that it toughened up America's future leaders. "The rough play," he commented, "if confined within manly and honorable limits, is an advantage."

Granted, the sport was not safe. Who said life was supposed to be safe?

At age nineteen, Teddy Roosevelt was fit and proud of it—though poor eyesight kept him off the football field at Harvard.

On this November morning, Roosevelt read descriptions of the previous day's games. Penn had edged Cornell, and, just a few miles from the White House, the Carlisle Indians had shellacked Georgetown University, 21–0. The Carlisle players were scheduled to visit the White House later that day.

And the president was clearly excited, because everyone who went to see him that morning was forced to listen to him talk football. "Portly politicians," wrote the *New York Sun*, "who wouldn't know a center rush from a flying wedge came to say a word for some applicants for office, and went away wondering what making a touchdown meant."

When the attorney general suggested naming a new federal attorney, Roosevelt asked, "Who is the best man?"

"Mr. Beach."

"Beach scores!" Roosevelt shouted. "I'll appoint him."

The president was finishing up a cabinet meeting when the Carlisle players were shown in.

"De-lighted!" Roosevelt bellowed.

Springing up, he thrust his hand out to Jimmie Johnson, the Carlisle quarterback. Then, turning to halfback Ely Parker, he shouted, "De-lighted! Your play was brilliant. You made three touchdowns, didn't you? How in the world did you do it?"

With reporters and government officials looking on, Roosevelt worked his way down the line, shaking hands, reviewing big plays from the Georgetown game.

"I see without asking that you played yesterday," he joked to a player with a bandaged face, "and it didn't improve your beauty."

The students smiled, but didn't chuckle along with the president and the assembled crowd.

Roosevelt asked the next student how Carlisle had fared against his own school, Harvard.

Not so well, the player said, a 23–0 loss.

"That was better than Harvard did with Yale!" Roosevelt said with a laugh.

The whole team stood silently, a bit awkwardly.

Were the Carlisle men sick of being stared at, of being treated like some kind of novelty act? Were they feeling the weight of the moment, the symbolism of standing at the nerve center of a government that had made war on their families just a generation ago?

Or was this just how any group of students in stiff suits would feel in the White House?

They never said. But reporters thought they looked relieved when it was over.

◆❖◆

The White House visit was a memorable finish to what had been a bounce-back year for Carlisle. After that great 1899 season, Pop Warner's team had gone 6-4-1 in 1900, with losses to Penn and Harvard, and a 35–0 thrashing at the hands of Yale. And 1901 had been worse. A beating by Warner's old school, Cornell, set off a seven-game winless streak, and the team finished with a losing record.

Even during these down years, sportswriters continued praising the players for their gentlemanly behavior. Though what writers saw as "gentlemanly" may have been more a case of self-control in the face of bigotry. Before one game in Detroit, as the team checked into a hotel, the desk clerk asked, "Where's your ribbons, and war whoops—and tomahawks?"

The men silently wrote their names in the register.

They'd won eight games in 1902, ending with the Georgetown shutout. Going into 1903, Pop Warner had his best team since his first year at Carlisle. Jimmie Johnson, a Stockbridge Indian from Wisconsin, had matured into a quick-thinking quarterback with a knack for in-game strategy. He was only 140 pounds, and his pants sagged on skinny legs, but Warner was used to this by now. "I never had a team that averaged over 170 pounds," he remembered. "At that, the fury of their attack tore heavier lines to pieces, and their tackling had the force of a catapult."

Carlisle opened the '03 season with four straight shutout wins, then lost to Princeton in a downpour. Warner had seen this before—muddy fields tended to neutralize Carlisle's speed, giving an advantage to bigger teams.

At practice, Warner and the team continued experimenting with new ideas. One day, just to break up the routine, Pop showed the guys a trick play he called "the hidden ball," an outrageous piece of deception he'd dreamed up at Cornell. The players loved it.

Step one was to practice the synchronized steps over and over.

Step two was to have Mose Blumenthal, owner of a clothing store in Carlisle, sew elastic bands into the bottom hem of a few of the players' jerseys.

Step three was to decide exactly when to spring the surprise.

The players looked at the remaining schedule. There were nine more games, but the one on October 31 glowed as if written in red. It was a school to the elite of the elite, the sons of lawyers and bankers and senators. It was President Roosevelt's school. It was a place the Carlisle Indians had never won, a team they longed to beat more than any other.

"Neither the Indian boys nor myself considered the hidden-ball play to be strictly legitimate," Pop Warner would later say. "We did, however, know that the play would work against Harvard and, at least, prove to be a good joke on the haughty Crimson players."

◆▮▸

The Boston press was expecting the Carlisle Indians to play entertaining football, but not much more. "With a team averaging only 165 pounds," commented the *Boston Globe*, "the Indians hardly hope to beat Harvard."

But on the afternoon of October 31, Halloween, Jimmie Johnson kept Harvard's bigger team off balance by faking a handoff to one running back before giving it to another, or faking a punt and running it himself. On defense, Carlisle's "force of a catapult" tackling kept Harvard off the scoreboard. The first half ended with Carlisle clinging to a surprising 5–0 lead.

At some point during the half, Carlisle's Charlie Dillon, a 190-pound lineman, pulled the bottom of his shirt out from his pants and left it untucked. Harvard got used to seeing him this way. No one noticed the elastic hem.

When it was time for the second half to begin, Harvard lined up to kick off. This was it, the perfect moment.

The Carlisle players spread out on their end of the field. Charlie Dillon, his shirt still hanging loose, dropped back beside Jimmie Johnson to receive the kick. Albert Exendine, Carlisle's promising young left tackle, would later describe the mood among the players: excited, nervous, trying not to tip their hand.

The referee signaled for play to begin. Harvard's kick was deep and down the middle of the field—as if made to order. Jimmie Johnson caught it near the goal line. The other Carlisle players bunched into a wedge of blockers. It looked like any other kick return.

And it was, except for one thing—with magician quickness, Jimmie Johnson slid the ball up the back of Charlie Dillon's shirt. The elastic hem held the hump in place.

"Go!" Johnson yelled.

And the Carlisle players scattered, charging toward Harvard's

Just nineteen at the time of Carlisle's immortal "hidden ball" trick play, Albert Exendine would go on to become one of Carlisle's all-time football greats.

onrushing eleven. "Harvard spread out with us," Exendine remembered, "looking for Jimmie with the ball."

Johnson was racing forward, hunched slightly, arms cradled around his stomach. Harvard defenders spotted the returner and dove for him. Johnson went down in a pile.

But Johnson did not have the football.

Several other Carlisle players were also running forward with their arms wrapped around imaginary balls. Harvard defenders knocked them down one by one. Still no ball.

The defenders looked around, confused.

The fans saw it first.

The huge crowd leaped to its feet, roaring and laughing, as Charlie Dillon, with surprising speed for a big man, sprinted down the field, arms pumping freely, a melon-shaped bump on his back. The Harvard men in front of Dillon couldn't see the bump—one even dodged out of his way to avoid being leveled by what he assumed was a blocker.

Dillon flew, untouched, one hundred yards for the score.

The crowd was still going wild as the Carlisle players crowded around Dillon to celebrate. Pop Warner beamed on the sideline. "I don't think any one thing ever gave them greater joy," he recalled.

Harvard's head coach was out on the field, yapping at officials that Carlisle had run an illegal play. But Warner had alerted the refs ahead of time about the hidden ball; there was no rule against it—though one was soon added.

Harvard players channeled their embarrassment into a back-to-basics attack, wearing Carlisle down with a steady diet of short runs. Boring, predictable, and effective. Harvard cut the lead to 11–6, then shoved over the go-ahead score late in the game.

Final: Harvard 12, Carlisle 11.

Pop and the team carried their bags back to the train station. They'd just dropped to 0-7 at Harvard, but Charlie Dillon's touchdown romp removed some of the sting. "For once, there was no mourning after a loss," Warner later said. "On the trip home, the players relived the play over and over again."

**J**im Thorpe's boots clomped along the wood-plank sidewalks of Shawnee, Oklahoma. Beside him walked his older half-brother, Frank. Horse-drawn wagons rolled down the wide, dusty main street, past dry goods stores, banks, and saloons.

The teens pushed through the swinging doors of one of the saloons. Jim took a dollar coin from his pocket and set it on the bar.

When several men looked over, Frank proposed a wager—his brother here could jump up straight into the air, right from where he was standing, and come down on the bar.

The men didn't believe it. They plunked their silver down.

Jim bent his skinny legs and leaped and soared and landed with a crash, two boots on the bar.

Frank scooped up the money. Jim jumped down, and the brothers hurried out the swinging doors.

◆❖◆

This was most definitely not what Hiram Thorpe had in mind when he said his son could live at home.

At the Thorpe farm, Hiram and Jim continued to clash over what Hiram saw as his son's aimless attitude, especially his lack of focus on education. "It was all book work," Thorpe later explained, "and I never did like books."

What he liked was hunting and fishing and riding his horses. As a teenager, Jim didn't think he'd ever be particularly good at organized sports like baseball or football. "I wasn't big enough, for one thing," he later said. "And then we lived way off from everything—made it hard to learn."

Hiram didn't care about sports; he cared about his son's future. And he was sick of arguing about it.

"I have a boy that I wish you would make arrangements to send to school somewhere," Hiram Thorpe wrote in a letter to the government official overseeing the Sac and Fox reservation. "I cannot do anything with him so please at your earliest convenience attend to this for he is getting worse every day—and I want him to go and make something of himself for he cannot do it here."

The Sac and Fox agent arranged for Jim Thorpe to be enrolled in the Carlisle Indian Industrial School.

The night before Jim left home, his father sat him down for what turned out to be the last conversation they would ever have. "Son, you are an Indian," Hiram told Jim. "I want you to show other races what an Indian can do."

◄❚►

On February 6, 1904, Jim Thorpe stepped off the train in Carlisle, Pennsylvania. He was fifteen years old.

It was an unusually warm day and patches of snow were melting in the sun. Jim walked through town, gazing in the windows of jewelry shops and clothing stores. A store called Flickinger's had a window display of Carlisle School merchandise—red-and-gold school pennants and postcards of campus buildings. There were also "before and after" photos of Carlisle students—side-by-side photos, one side showing a student in traditional Indian clothing, the other showing the same boy or girl dressed for the Carlisle School.

Jim found his way to campus and walked across the parade ground to the oldest building, the Revolutionary War–era stone guardhouse. A school official took a look at Jim's entrance papers and told him to report to the infirmary for a physical exam.

Tom Torlino, Navajo, in 1882 (left), and again three years later. Though the changes shown in these "before and after" photos caused great pain to the students, Pratt proudly displayed them as proof of the "progress" he was making at Carlisle.

In the hospital building, he undressed and washed. A doctor examined him and recorded that the new student was in good health, five foot five, narrow shoulders, 115 pounds. Jim was given a haircut and new clothes—black dungarees for the workshops, a uniform for class, nightshirts, and red flannel long johns. He got bedding and towels and a trunk to hold it all.

Jim lugged the trunk to the boys' dorm and up to the room he would share with three other students.

And then came the routine. The early-morning bugle, the marching, the classes and vocational training, the endless lectures about leaving the "old ways" behind. To Jim, it was all familiar.

But there was one unique thing about Carlisle—its famous football team.

Three days a week, as his class walked into the gymnasium to exercise,

Jim walked past a display with photos of Carlisle football players and footballs from the team's big wins. On each ball was painted the score of the game, and above each hung a flag of the vanquished opponent.

It's worth noting that female students used the gym the other days, and a *Washington Post* writer who visited while Carlisle's young women were running races and playing basketball came away convinced that if women had been allowed to play competitive sports they would have filled a wall with trophies of their own.

Young women playing basketball in the Carlisle gym. Even in those heavy shoes and dresses, female students impressed visitors with their athletic skill.

Assigned to the tailor shop, Jim was adjusting well to life at Carlisle. Then, just as had happened at Haskell, a letter arrived from Oklahoma with terrible news. Hiram Thorpe was dead from "blood poisoning," a snake bite, most likely. The funeral was already over by the time the letter arrived.

Jim would never forget the last thing his father had told him. It was a lot to live up to. *Too* much for a lonely, grieving kid.

Withdrawing even more deeply into himself, Jim drifted silently through the dreary routine. The Carlisle staff sensed he was likely to run away. To prevent this, they sent him on an "outing"—Richard Henry Pratt's term for a job on a nearby farm. The Outing Program was a major part of life at Carlisle. The idea was for students to live with a "civilized" family, practice English, and learn how to run a farm. "When you boys and girls go out on jobs," Pratt told students, "you don't go as employees. You go and become part of the family."

These Carlisle students participated in the Outing Program at about the same time as Jim Thorpe. Some had positive experiences living and working with white families—others were treated as nothing more than cheap labor.

That was not Jim's experience. Assigned to a farm near Carlisle, he was put to work mopping floors and doing laundry. He was made to eat alone in the kitchen, and paid half of what a white laborer would typically earn.

Jim did it again. He ran away. But not home this time. He didn't really have a home anymore. He ran back to Carlisle.

For that, they tossed him into the old stone guardhouse. He spent the next few days locked in a windowless cell built to hold prisoners of war.

Then it was back to classes, back to the tailor shop. Jim had zero interest in making clothes, but at least the shop had its own football team. They played against the print shop and blacksmiths and harness makers in a sort of minor league of Carlisle football; players who stood out might eventually move up to the famous varsity squad.

Jim joined the tailors, with dreams of bigger things. And that fall, when he was sixteen, he saw his first Carlisle football game, an early-season matchup with Albright College that was stopped after thirty minutes when Carlisle went up 100–0. That's where Jim wanted to be, out there with the varsity team, running free.

He went to see the team trainer, Wallace Denny, to ask for a practice uniform so he could try out.

"You're too little," Denny said. "Come around later."

Jim definitely planned to come around later.

Before he could, the staff sent him on another outing, this time to a New Jersey farm. Jim spent long days bent over fields of vegetables, hauling heavy sacks. His body grew stronger. But if he dreamed of returning to Carlisle and marching triumphantly onto Indian Field, there was a major problem. It was not at all clear that the sport of football was going to exist for long.

Not at Carlisle—or anywhere else.

**A**fter twenty-five years at Carlisle, Richard Henry Pratt's run as superintendent came to an end. Pratt had clashed frequently with his military bosses, and the War Department finally relieved him of duty at Carlisle in June 1904.

Pratt's departure made Pop Warner nervous about the future of the school, and Warner jumped ship for what felt like a more secure job as head football coach at his old school, Cornell.

Nationwide, meanwhile, football was in serious trouble.

Fans were getting tired of watching the same old mass plays over and over; most of the time they couldn't even see who had the ball. And the game's reputation was only getting worse. Muckrakers—journalists who investigated serious issues like political corruption and dangerous working conditions in factories—went after football as well. One typical article, under the headline BUYING FOOTBALL VICTORIES, reported that top universities were using secret funds to slip payments to favorite athletes, and recruiting kids who were big and strong, though totally unprepared for college academics. When asked what he took at Notre Dame, one football player said, "Baths."

Pop Warner saw this up close at Cornell. "The number of miners, blacksmiths, and plumber's helpers taking art courses was a standing joke," he confessed.

And then there was the violence. Newspapers and magazines printed story after story with descriptions of gruesome injuries, photos of crumpled faces. "The players go on the field expecting to be hurt," said the Columbia team doctor, "and are glad if they come off with nothing worse than a broken bone."

In an article in *McClure's*, a member of the Princeton team admitted to intentionally injuring one of Dartmouth's star players. The targeted player was black—one of the few African American college players at the time—which led to the charge that the attack was racially motivated. Not at all, said the Princeton man; it was just football. "We're *coached* to pick out the most dangerous man on the opposing side and put him out in the first five minutes of the game."

Some writers suggested the solution was to put more referees on the field to watch for dirty play. Harvard president Charles Eliot scoffed. "A game which needs to be so watched is not fit for genuine sportsmen." He sided with a *New York Times* editorial that put it simply: "The sooner the game is discontinued, the better."

Even President Roosevelt was beginning to worry.

"I believe in outdoor games, and I do not mind in the least that they are rough games," Roosevelt declared in a speech at Harvard in the spring of 1905. "I have a hearty contempt for him if he counts a broken arm or collarbone as of serious consequence, when balanced against the chance of showing that he possesses hardihood, physical address, and courage."

But hearty contempt could go only so far. Football needed to change, or schools were going to start banning it. Early in the 1905 season, the president invited coaches from the universities he considered most important—Harvard, Princeton, and Yale—to the White House.

"Football is on trial," Roosevelt told the group over lunch. "Because I believe in the game, I want to do all I can to save it."

There's no detailed record of the discussion that followed, but when it was over the three schools pledged, in writing, to "carry out in letter and in spirit the rules of the game of football relating to roughness, holding, and foul play."

Problem solved? Hardly. At a game soon after, Harvard coach Bill

NEXT!
A president who "does" things.

As this cartoon shows, "Brutality of Football" was one of the many issues Theodore Roosevelt dealt with as president.

Reid watched in horror as one of his players, Bartol Parker, reared back and punched a Penn lineman in the face. Reid knew he'd be hearing from Roosevelt. Sure enough, he was summoned back to the White House.

"Now, Reid," Roosevelt lit into the coach, "what's this I see in the papers about a Harvard man slugging? You and I are both Harvard men, and it puts me in a very awkward position—after our agreement—to have a Harvard man the first one to violate the agreement. What happened anyway?"

"Mr. President, I will tell you exactly what happened without mincing words," Reid said.

The Penn player, he explained, had slugged Parker in the crotch —repeatedly.

"Mr. President," Reid challenged, "what would *you* have done under similar circumstances?"

Roosevelt, through clenched teeth, said, "It wouldn't be good policy for me to state."

In any case, football's real problem was not slugging, or cheap shots to sensitive spots. The real problem was that human heads and necks are not designed to withstand impact with moving walls of massive men. The real problem was the physics of collisions.

On November 25, 1905, in New York City, Union College's William Moore carried the ball into a clump of New York University defenders and was buried under the typical play-ending pile. The refs began pulling people up. Moore lay facedown, motionless. A fan drove his automobile onto the field, and Moore was rushed to a nearby hospital. He died that night from a cerebral hemorrhage.

William Moore was the nineteenth player to die from a football injury—in 1905 alone.

This one got the most attention because it happened in the country's biggest city, in front of reporters from the most widely read papers. THE HOMICIDAL PASTIME, screamed a *New York Times* headline. "In theory boys play football for their health," the *Times* wrote. "The breaking of a youngster's leg, the twisting of his spine, and the fracturing of his skull are of doubtful advantage to his health."

Union College abolished its football program. Columbia and Northwestern dropped football, then so did Duke, California, and Stanford. President Eliot of Harvard badly wanted to do the same. Roosevelt privately called Eliot's anti-football stance a "baby act," but Eliot was not alone. "One human life is too big a price for all the games of the season," said Syracuse University chancellor James Day.

With the crisis reaching a whole new level, and Roosevelt continuing to urge colleges to solve the problem before it was too late, sixty universities hastily arranged the Intercollegiate Athletic Association—soon renamed the National Collegiate Athletic Association, or NCAA. The group completely rewrote the rules of football, making it much more like the game we know today. The yardage needed for a first down was increased from five to ten. Plays would now end when any part of the ballcarrier

# The New Game of FOOTBALL

## Radical changes ••• •• in this year's rules revolutionize the sport

This *New York Times* article explaining football's rule changes was right—it truly was a "New Game," as the Carlisle Indians were about to show the nation.

WITH the period for theorizing passed, college football teams must now face an entirely new condition of affairs on the gridiron. The universal outcry against brutality on the football field and the demand for a more open style of play have been met by a sweeping revision of the rules, the result of many conferences extending over nearly a year and participated in by representatives from colleges and universities all over the country. For months following the long Winter session of the rulemakers coaches have everywhere gone through the rules with the greatest care, racking their brains to analyze them and figure out their possibilities. Many predict the ruination of the game through the drastic reformation, while others profess to see a big improvement. All agree on one point, however, that it will be harder for the unsportsmanlike player to interfere with clean sport, while many of those who see in the coming game greater opportunities for open play believe that the elements of roughness and corresponding injury to players will be method of coaching. This, however, is a consideration for the technical expert and not for the general public.

The old style of starting the game has been retained, but here the old conditions cease, and the new features will at once be apparent. The first and one of the most important changes will be when the opposing teams line up for a scrimmage. Instead of facing each other at close quarters, as in the past, the length of the ball will separate them, and this will affect the entire character of the defensive play. It will put an end to charging, and from a spectator's standpoint will materially improve the game, as it will reduce to a minimum mass plays, which made it next to impossible for the spectators to watch the progress of the ball with any degree of satisfaction. It will prevent one team securing a big advantage on their opponents before the ball is actually in play and favor a defensive rather than an aggressive game.

To eliminate brutality the mode of attack has undergone a sweeping change. Guards and tackles back and tandem plays are things of the past.

other than his hand or foot hit the ground. Stricter rules were added against personal fouls and unnecessary roughness.

And, most important, the forward pass was legalized.

The goal of all these rules was to open up the game, to make football safer—and, the committee hoped, more entertaining—by emphasizing speed and skill rather than mere muscle. Harvard's Bill Reid knew this was football's last chance. "If the game does not stand the test, it will be rooted out completely," he said, "at Harvard and elsewhere."

Reid was right; football would change or die.

The question was, which team had the talent—and the imagination—to invent a new way to play the game?

On a spring afternoon in 1907, Jim Thorpe and a few friends were walking across the Carlisle campus toward the sports fields. Still in overalls and work shirts, they were hoping to get in a few innings of baseball before sunset.

Thorpe was nineteen. Time and farm labor had worked wonders. He'd grown strong and broad-shouldered, nearly six feet tall, a wiry 140 pounds.

As the friends crossed the track, Jim stopped for a moment to watch the track team practice the high jump. One at a time the athletes sprinted forward, leaped, arched their bodies over the bar, and landed on a mat. They raised the bar higher and did it again. When the bar got to five foot nine, no one could clear it. They were about to call it a day.

"Let me try," Thorpe said.

"Move on," someone on the team said.

"He thinks he's a grasshopper," joked another.

It took more than that to discourage Jim. He walked to the start of the runway, and could hear the guys snickering as they reset the bar at five nine. He charged forward, jumped, and sailed over the bar.

He was still laughing as he walked with his friends to the baseball field.

◄❚►

Jim Thorpe at about the time he arrived at Carlisle—before anyone had any idea he was about to become the world's greatest athlete.

The next day, Jim Thorpe met Pop Warner.

Carlisle football had survived without Warner. A series of part-time coaches, including former star Bemus Pierce, had led the team to three winning seasons. And Warner had had three good years at Cornell. But Warner missed Carlisle—he especially missed the freedom to run a football program without unwanted advice from wealthy alumni and fans. When Carlisle's new superintendent invited Pop to return for the 1907 season, he leaped at the chance.

Warner also coached Carlisle's track team, so it wasn't long before he heard about the kid who'd cleared the high jump bar in overalls. He summoned Thorpe to his office.

"You wanted to see me, coach?" Jim said as he walked in.

"Are those the clothes you had on yesterday when you made that high jump?" Warner asked, gesturing to Thorpe's work outfit.

Thorpe nodded.

"Do you know what you have just done?"

"Nothing bad, I hope."

"Bad!" Warner roared. "You've just broken the school record."

Thorpe was relieved; for once, he wasn't in trouble. "That's not very high," he said. "I think I can do better in a track suit."

"Well, you go down to the clubhouse and exchange those overalls for a track outfit." Warner stepped around his desk and put his arm around Thorpe. "You're on the track team now."

◆

"Now Ex, you stick with Thorpe," Warner instructed track and football star Albert Exendine. "He looks like he might be good material."

Exendine—Ex to his teammates—was the son of a Cherokee father and Delaware mother and had grown up on a farm not far from Thorpe's family home in Oklahoma. He'd come to Carlisle at fifteen. He became a standout student and debater, started running track, then discovered football. "I didn't know what a football was until I went to Carlisle, but I was a mean son of a gun," Ex recalled. "I would get the ball and just stand there, pumping my knees, while other fellows pushed me into the line."

Now in his last year at Carlisle, Exendine agreed to mentor Pop's newest recruit. Jim immediately liked Ex, looking up to him like an older brother. They joked together, and wrestled, and worked out on the track. Thorpe was particularly influenced by how intensely Exendine trained. Athletics came so easily to Jim he'd never appreciated the importance of training.

Left to right: Emil Hauser, Jimmie Johnson, Albert Exendine, and Pop Warner.

Best of all, Thorpe was invited to move into the athletic quarters. Renovated with income from football-ticket sales, this building was a palace compared to the student dorms. There were pool tables, a record player, and a comfortable reading room stocked with books and newspapers.

And the special athletes-only kitchen was an almost unimaginable luxury.

Food had never been good or plentiful at Carlisle, and standards had slipped further since Pratt's departure. For years, Jim lived off meager bowls of oatmeal, bean stew, and a mysterious dish called "hash." "It contained different kinds of food mixed together," one student explained, "some were good and some were bad, but the bad outdid the good." Like so many at Carlisle, Jim had often gone to bed hungry. Now, in the athletes' dining hall, he gorged on pancakes and butter, steak and fresh bread.

By late spring, Thorpe was ready to compete in running and jumping events. At a meet against Navy, Warner entered him in the 120-yard high hurdles. Exendine was in the race and favored to win. The starting gun fired, and Ex sped into the lead. But he knew Thorpe was right on his tail, because every time he leaped a hurdle, he heard Jim shouting joyfully from close behind: "Ex!"

As Exendine cleared the last hurdle, he heard, "Ex! I've got you licked!"

Exendine landed and sprinted for the finish line. Thorpe surged ahead and won the race.

"Before Jim hit Carlisle, I was quite the athlete around here," Exendine would later say. "It took Jim just one day to break all my records."

Thorpe spent the summer of 1907 living the good life in the athletic quarters—yet another perk of being one of Pop's chosen was that the school didn't force top athletes to go on farm outings. In late summer, when the football team began to practice, Thorpe went again to see team trainer Wallace Denny. Again, he asked for a practice uniform.

Denny just laughed. "Go away and come back when you have some meat on your bones," he said. "What do you want to do, get yourself killed?"

But Thorpe would not leave the man alone. Denny finally gave in. In a baggy, ragged uniform, Thorpe walked onto Indian Field. The afternoon practice was already under way, and Warner and the team were working hard, preparing for an absolutely brutal slate of games.

"What do you think you're doing out here?" Warner demanded when he saw his track star approaching.

Thorpe said, "I want to play football."

SECOND

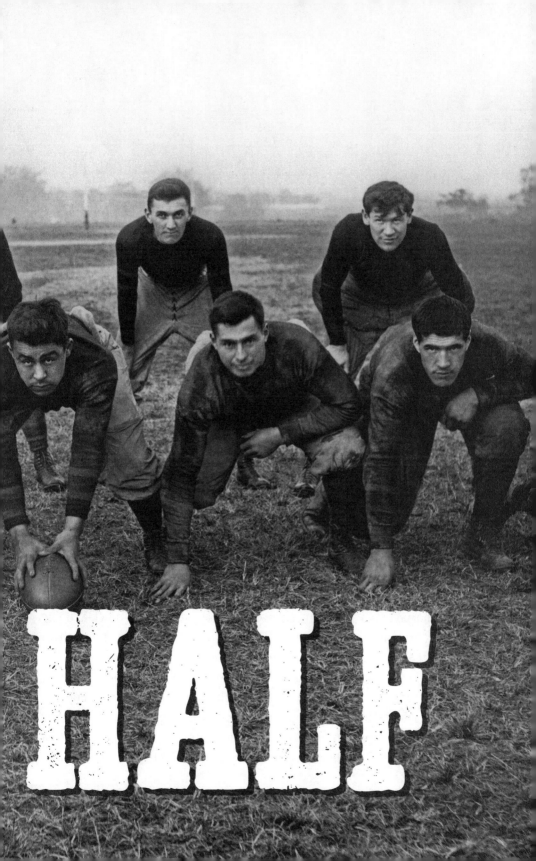

**A**nd that's when Thorpe, dressed like an escaped scarecrow, shocked the coach by running through the entire Carlisle football team, starters and backups. Not once, but twice. That's when Thorpe tossed Warner the ball and said, "Sorry, Pop. Nobody's going to tackle Jim."

Warner was too stunned to respond right away, too steamed at being shown up in front of the team. But beneath the embarrassment, the coach was thinking that he may have just found a very special football player.

"I must admit," Warner would say after a lifetime in the sport, "Jim's performance at practice that afternoon on the Carlisle varsity playing field was an exhibition of athletic talent that I had never before witnessed, nor was I ever to again see anything similar."

With just ten days until the start of the 1907 season, Warner asked Albert Exendine to act as Thorpe's football tutor.

"Thorpe was a good learner," Ex remembered. "He was quick at doing things the way you showed him. He wasn't afraid, and I kept at him about being mean when he had the ball or was blocking or tackling."

Warner liked Thorpe's potential but felt he could wait for the youngster to develop. Carlisle's 1907 team was the most talented bunch Pop had ever coached. They had a stout line, top-tier running backs, and a skinny Tuscarora Indian from western New York named Frank Mount Pleasant who was, arguably, the first great quarterback of football's new era.

Mount Pleasant had come to Carlisle at age thirteen. He'd been sitting in his first class, a history class, when the teacher asked, "Is there a question that anyone would like to have answered?"

Frank raised his hand. "What time does football practice start?"

He was four foot eight. He weighed seventy-one pounds.

He grew to five eight, 135—still small, even for Carlisle. "I nearly missed him as a football player, for he looked too light and frail," Warner later said. "He was always begging, however, and finally, thinking that his speed might be useful, I gave him a chance."

Aside from quickness and intelligence, what Mount Pleasant had going for him was that he was among the first players to see the potential of the forward pass.

"When the pass came out in 1906, nobody knew how to throw it," Albert Exendine recalled. At first, quarterbacks flipped the ball underhand, or held it by one rounded end and shot-putted tumbling, inaccurate throws. Mount Pleasant spent hour after hour experimenting. He spread

Carlisle quarterback Frank Mount Pleasant demonstrates the spiral.

his fingers across the laces and worked out an overhand motion and flick of the wrist that sent the ball spinning off his fingertips in a spiral. By the time practice began in 1907, he could sling it forty yards, and taught teammates to do the same.

Throwing spirals may seem obvious now, but at the time it was revolutionary. "I can still recall the startled looks on our opponents' faces when they first saw the spiral in action," Warner would later say.

Exendine, who'd always been a blocker, started running out to catch passes. While other teams threw very short passes, or none at all, Ex realized he could use his track-star speed to sprint far down the field. Mount Pleasant had the arm strength and accuracy to hit him on the run.

This was all new, *too* new for most coaches—too new even for Pop Warner.

"I opposed the forward pass as entirely foreign to the game," Warner would later admit.

Even the rule makers weren't completely convinced passing was good for the game. In 1907 an incomplete pass resulted in a fifteen-yard penalty. If passing was going to catch on, it would be up to the players themselves.

◂▮▸

Jim Thorpe cheered from the sidelines as Carlisle rolled over its first four opponents by a combined score of 159–5.

In mid-October the team traveled to Buffalo to play Syracuse University. Western New York was—and is—home to a large Native American population; when Carlisle came to town, thousands showed up to cheer on their team. And that's really how they thought of Carlisle, as *their* team. Rather than sitting in stands, Indian fans packed the sidelines to watch shoulder-to-shoulder with Jim Thorpe and the other Carlisle subs.

On the field, in front of his family and friends, Frank Mount Pleasant put on a passing display. Won over by Mount Pleasant's throwing arm, Pop Warner had drawn up another innovation—the quarterback rollout. After taking the snap, Mount Pleasant would sprint ten yards to the left or right, giving his receivers time to get down the field. If someone was open, Mount Pleasant would throw the ball; if not, he'd tuck it under his arm and run.

Bottom: Frank Mount Pleasant (standing) helps younger students with their work. Right: Mount Pleasant in football gear during Carlisle's game-changing 1907 season.

With a comfortable lead late in the game, Warner sent Thorpe in at halfback. Thorpe had to wriggle through fans to get on the field. He'd later admit he hardly knew the signals, but it didn't matter much. He ran the ball for a few short gains, and the clock ran out.

Jim got another shot the next Saturday against Bucknell, a rare home game for Carlisle. On occasion, nearby schools would come to play at Indian Field, and it was a huge treat for the students. "When a touchdown is made the scene beggars description," wrote the *New York World* of the raucous enthusiasm on campus.

In the second half, Warner put Thorpe in to receive a kickoff. The coach wanted to give his new player a chance to run in the open field, see if he could duplicate his tackling-practice show in a game situation.

He could.

The kick was low and deep. Thorpe caught it at his own goal line, exploded forward, and was nearly to the thirty before the first defenders reached him. He barreled through a few tacklers, cut and faked past several more, and was free. The home crowd roared as Thorpe crossed the forty, the thirty, the twenty. He slowed to a cruise inside the ten—a classic rookie mistake. A defender who hadn't quit on the play dove at Thorpe's feet and tripped him. The ball came loose.

Jim Thorpe watched from the ground as teammate Theodore Owl scooped it up and went in for the score.

Carlisle was off to a 6-0 start, and Pop Warner knew he'd been right about this team. It was the best he'd had yet, a "perfect football machine," he'd later say. Not only were they talented, selfless, and smart, they had the poise to handle the unique situation of being pioneers. Forty years later, when Jackie Robinson became the first African American in baseball's major leagues, he'd be provoked by fans and tormented by cheap shots on the base paths.

The Carlisle Indians faced the same challenges. During one game in 1907, Warner watched star fullback Pete Hauser limp off the field. He asked what happened.

"Same old thing," Hauser said. "They kneed me."

"Know who it was?"

"Yep."

Warner was furious. "Well, what did you do? Didn't you say anything?"

"Sure," said Hauser. "I said, 'Who's the savage now?'"

For the first time in his career, Pop Warner had a team that might be good enough to run the table—go undefeated and claim the national championship. With the toughest part of the schedule still to come, Pop pushed the team—and himself—even harder.

Warner's workweek began early Monday morning, at his house, right after breakfast. His two scouts came over, Pop lit one of his pungent Turkish Trophy cigarettes, and the group sat down to dissect Carlisle's next opponent.

"What do they do?" Warner demanded of his scouts, who traveled the country to watch upcoming teams on Carlisle's schedule. "What kind of defense shall we work out?"

Warner chain-smoked as they talked, lighting each new cigarette with the smoldering butt of the last one. "He'd not use another match till about the middle of the afternoon," remembered Pop's secretary, Arthur Martin. "Mrs. Warner would come in with a sandwich or something, and it was time to break it up. The house was full of smoke."

By then they had a game plan, and it was time to practice. Warner worked the players mercilessly, shouting at them, demanding repetition of movements and plays until the timing was perfect.

"You play the way you practice!" Pop preached.

The players kicked and threw and fell on loose balls, but most of the time was spent on Pop's twin keys to the game: "Good blocking and deadly tackling." It was with this in mind that he devised what became known as the tackling dummy—a big bag filled with sawdust and hung from a rope. One by one, the players charged into the dummy, wrapping it up like an opposing runner.

Coach Warner looks on as Jim Thorpe perfects his technique on Pop's tackling dummy.

"There is no system of play that substitutes for knocking an opponent down," Warner lectured. "When you hit, hit hard!"

After two hours of drills, the exhausted players gathered around Pop's blackboard for a strategy session. Warner pointed out mistakes made in the previous week's game and used diagrams to illustrate proper execution. He told them what to expect of their next opponent, specifying the players and plays to watch out for.

When practice was over, and the players were at dinner or studying in the dorm, Warner continued to obsess. Residents of Carlisle would later describe seeing the coach sitting alone in a coffee shop in town, plotting plays in his mind, sliding salt and pepper shakers around his tiny tabletop field.

Books on the history of football often cite a 1913 game between Army and Notre Dame as the moment the forward pass really took off. In that game, the story goes, Notre Dame's long throws brought the passing game to national attention, opening the sports world's eyes to the potential of this exciting new play.

With due respect to Notre Dame's legions of fans, that version of history is nonsense.

The first time the forward pass played a major part in a high-profile game between national powers was October 26, 1907, when the Carlisle Indians went to Philadelphia to take on the University of Pennsylvania. The largest crowd to see any sporting event in Philadelphia that year packed Franklin Field to watch 7-0 Penn host 6-0 Carlisle. Penn had given up just ten points all season; Carlisle had yielded eleven.

Carlisle often held special plays in reserve, saving them for the exact right moment. This time, on just the second play of the game, Frank Mount Pleasant took the snap and handed it to Pete Hauser. Hauser swept to his right, as if looking for a hole to charge through—but he didn't charge. He kept rolling right, rolling right, buying time while William Gardner slipped out from his left end position and started running down the field.

Hauser suddenly stopped, lifted the ball above his shoulder, and heaved.

The spiral sailed high and deep. Astounded fans and reporters bent their necks and looked up at the future of the sport.

Carlisle fullback Pete Hauser ran with the ball, blocked for teammates—and threw what was probably the most significant pass in the history of football.

**W**illiam Gardner ran under the ball and made the catch for a forty-yard gain. Never had such a large crowd seen such a long pass. "It will be talked of often this year," wrote the *Philadelphia North American*. "No such puny little pass as Penn makes, but a lordly throw, a hurl that went further than many a kick."

The stands went quiet. The Penn players looked to the sidelines for guidance.

None was coming. The coaches had never seen this type of offense.

With Penn on its heels, Mount Pleasant orchestrated what sportswriters began calling "whirlwind football," mixing inside power rushes, outside speed runs, and long forward passes. Albert Exendine led a smothering, gang-tackling defense, and about 150 Carlisle students cheered and sang a song they'd written just for the occasion:

*We've come to Philly Billy to Beat old Penn!*

"Well," noted the *Philadelphia Inquirer,* "they beat Old Penn all right."

Carlisle was up 16–0 by halftime. The second half was more of the same.

"I'd see the ball sailing in my direction," Penn's All-American fullback William Hollenback said of the beating he and his teammates took that day. "And at the same time came the thundering of what appeared to be a tribe of Indians racing full tilt in my direction. When this gang hit you, they just simply wiped you out."

From Pop Warner's sideline viewpoint, Penn's utter confusion was a thing of beauty. "Poor Pennsylvania finally reached a point where the players ran around in circles, emitting wild yawps," he later said.

Even Jim Thorpe got in on the fun. Sort of. On his first carry he was hit for a loss.

"I got excited," Thorpe remembered, "and didn't follow my interference."

It was a problem; the young back hadn't learned to wait for his blockers to open holes. It was a problem for another day.

Carlisle won the game 26–6, and it wasn't even *that* close.

The Indians gained 402 yards to Penn's 76; picked up 22 first downs to Penn's 3. The football world was in shock. The Carlisle Indians were no longer delightful "Nomads of the Gridiron," no longer just an amusing traveling show. Playing a brand-new style of football, they had just humiliated one of the country's elite schools on its own field. They had just officially crashed the Big Four party.

The greeting was hostile; in some cases downright racist.

"With racial savagery and ferocity the Carlisle Indian eleven grabbed Penn's football scalp and dragged their victim up and down Franklin Field," wailed the *Philadelphia Press*. "Never has Pennsylvania lost a football game that created greater surprise."

◆❖◆

Six days later, Warner and the team walked into the lobby of a New York City hotel. Newspapermen were waiting, wanting to know if Pop thought his men could clobber its next opponent, Princeton, as it had Penn.

"You know, I never make predictions," Warner said. "But we'll show the crowd that goes to see us play a bully good game."

A swarm of fans formed around Mount Pleasant, Exendine, Hauser, and the other stars. Jim Thorpe was there too, though it's unlikely anyone knew who he was.

"Here, you fellows, off to bed with you," Warner told the team.

Turning back to the reporters, he said, "They have had a hard day's ride, over six hours in cramped cars, and they need their rest."

The Princeton players slept in their own beds that night. The team and coaching staff had spent all week preparing for Carlisle—and they'd gotten plenty of help.

COACHES RUSHING TO PRINCETON'S AID, that Wednesday's *New York Times* had announced, AIM TO CRUSH THE INDIANS. As the story explained, coaches of other teams sent suggestions for beating Carlisle, and former players returned to campus to help at practice. It was even rumored that one of the Penn game refs slipped the Princeton coach a detailed report on Carlisle's playbook.

But none of this helped Princeton nearly as much as a factor beyond anyone's control. Ten hours before game time, it started to pour.

The rain was still falling when the gates of the Polo Grounds opened Saturday afternoon. The field was a swampy mess of slick grass and bare mud, and Carlisle's first play from scrimmage told the story. Pete Hauser took a pitch and swept to the right. The blocking was good and there was a clear path around the edge, but when Hauser planted a foot to cut up-field, he slipped and went down without being touched. This was no day for whirlwind football.

The bigger Princeton team took advantage, settling into a back-and-forth field-position battle, avoiding mistakes, waiting for a break. They got one when Frank Mount Pleasant fell in a puddle as he tried to field a punt. Princeton recovered the loose ball and scored the game's first touchdown.

Princeton students broke out in song:

> *He may have beaten dear old Penn,*
> *But he can't do a thing to the Princeton men.*
> *Poor Mr. Indian!*

TIGERS HUMBLE INDIANS, announced the *New York Times* headline.

PRINCETON DID IT, chimed the *Syracuse Herald*, SOLVED INDIAN PROBLEM.

The sports world celebrated Princeton's 16–0 thumping of Carlisle as if an annoying upstart had been shoved back in its place. As if it was Carlisle against the world.

Pop Warner spent much of the train ride home from New York consoling his downhearted team. He was mighty low himself, having just watched his dream of an undefeated season drown in a sea of mud.

"He was a hard loser," a close friend of Pop's would later say, "a very hard loser."

The only thing to do was move on. The season wasn't over.

In just six days, Carlisle would be back on the train, heading for Boston this time, for their third Big Four matchup in fifteen days. After weeks of exhausting travel, punishing games, emotional highs and lows, they were going back to Harvard, where their record was 0-10.

Warner had once bought into the old stereotype of Indians giving up when the going got tough. Some still believed it. "Their weakness," pronounced the *New York Times* after the Princeton game, "has been the inability to maintain an effective team effort in the face of discouragement."

It was a totally bogus charge; even in their one defeat, Carlisle played to the final whistle, diving for loose balls long after any hope of winning was gone.

But anyway, if the Carlisle Indians had any quit in them, now was the time it would show.

◆❦◆

The skies above Harvard Stadium were clear and blue as Pop Warner and the Carlisle Indian team jogged onto a beautifully firm field of grass.

They looked up at the massive, horseshoe-shaped stands of the biggest football arena in the country, packed, Warner recalled, with thirty thousand Crimson rooters "joyously and continuously" crooning Harvard songs.

"Good thing this isn't a singing contest, hey, Pop?" one of the players joked.

Frank Mount Pleasant was in no mood to laugh. "Remember last Saturday!" he called to his teammates.

Right from the opening kick, Carlisle was back on track. The Harvard defense came out expecting pass plays, and Mount Pleasant caught them off guard by opening with runs. Then, when defenders began bunching closer to the line of scrimmage to stop the run, Mount Pleasant threw passes out of what looked like running formations.

A *Boston Globe* reporter looked on, amazed. "They did not hang out a sign and say, 'Again this time expect a forward pass,'" wrote the *Globe*, "they concealed most skillfully the point of attack." For the past forty years, it had always been easy to tell what an offense was about to do. Carlisle was changing everything.

A twenty-yard pass to Albert Exendine set up Pete Hauser's short plunge over the goal line for a quick 6–0 lead.

"Oh, wait till Harvard wakes up," a Crimson fan was heard bragging, "then you will see the power of the white men assert itself. The Indians will soon give up."

Harvard answered, marching down the field to tie it up. But Carlisle struck right back with another touchdown. Harvard kicked a field goal—now worth four points—right before the half ended. At the break it was Carlisle 12, Harvard 10.

The intensity only increased in the second half. Between plays, Mount Pleasant stalked up and down the Carlisle line shouting, "Remember last Saturday!"

It was the quarterback himself who broke the game's biggest play. Standing at his own twenty-five, he fielded a Harvard punt and side-stepped a charging tackler. The next defender leaped at him, but he ducked low and the Harvard man flipped over his back and thudded to the turf. Then Mount Pleasant took off on what the *Boston Globe* would describe as a "zigzagging sprint"—or, as the *New York Tribune* put it, "He went through the greater portion of the Harvard eleven like a greased pig." Of his eighty-five-yard touchdown run, Mount Pleasant simply said, "I saw only goal-posts in front of me. I made for them."

Jim Thorpe celebrated from the bench. Carlisle was one step closer to the biggest win in school history. But he could only watch.

Harvard struck back, cutting Carlisle's lead to 18–15. There were just a few minutes left. This was the key moment—that pivotal moment in tense games when the underdog gets tight, plays it safe, and blows it.

Not this time.

"We've got to score *again!*" Mount Pleasant roared in the huddle.

The team responded with another long drive. When they got to the Harvard thirty-five, Mount Pleasant faked a handoff and dropped back to pass, looking for Exendine deep down the field. Seeing Ex was covered, Mount Pleasant flipped a short throw to a running back, Bill Winnie, who scampered all the way to the Harvard four. Pete Hauser punched it in, sealing the win.

Final: Carlisle 23, Harvard 15.

When the whistle blew, thousands of fans jumped out of the stands to congratulate the Carlisle players, surrounding them as they limped off the field.

At Carlisle, the celebration lasted into the night. Students sewed and stuffed a human-shaped dummy, dressed it in a crimson sweater with a big H on the front, and set it on a stretcher. Then the school marching band grabbed instruments and led a spontaneous parade through town.

The next issue of Carlisle's student paper said it all: THE 'BIG FOUR' NOW THE 'BIG FIVE.'

If anyone was disappointed with the Carlisle Indians' historic 1907 football season, it was Jim Thorpe. As he later said, "I didn't like it much on the bench."

The lifestyle made it worthwhile. Pop Warner spent freely on private train cars and fancy hotels. Thorpe had run away from every school he'd ever been sent to—being on the football team proved a much cozier means of escape.

Best of all was the camaraderie. For the first time since he was a kid in Oklahoma, Jim was part of a family. And like anyone surrounded by big brothers, he was mercilessly pranked. The older players locked him out of hotel rooms and handed him olive oil when he asked for maple syrup. When he left his shoes in the hotel hallway so the staff could shine them, his shoelaces disappeared. Once, while he was sleeping on a train, the guys stole his clothes, and he had to go searching for them in his boxers.

◆▓◆

Just a few days after beating Harvard, Thorpe and the team hit the road again to play two of the best teams in the Midwest. They beat the University of Minnesota in Minneapolis, then traveled to Chicago to take on the unbeaten University of Chicago—"Champions of the West," newspapers called them.

"Chicago should win today's game," predicted the *Chicago Tribune*,

A sell-out crowd at Chicago's Marshall Field watches Carlisle's showdown with the "Champions of the West."

"and win it through quickness, alertness, and aggressiveness." The Carlisle players got sick of hearing about how much trouble they were going to have with Chicago's All-American quarterback, Wally Steffen, nicknamed "The Wizard of the West."

On Steffen's first carry of the game, Albert Exendine and William Gardner converged on the quarterback and flattened him. Carlisle players never did much trash talking; this time Ex couldn't resist.

"Huh," he grunted at Steffen's crumpled form. "Wizard of the West."

The standing-room-only crowd watched Carlisle dominate both sides of the ball. The only thing keeping the game close was that Chicago's coach, Amos Alonzo Stagg, had prepared for the Carlisle whirlwind by developing football's first pass defense. Stagg assigned two defensive backs to Exendine and two to Gardner. When the receivers ran out for passes, the defenders were all over them. Literally. There were no rules against pass interference.

"They would wait till I almost had the ball, then chop me down," Exendine explained years later. "I don't want to brag, but by comparison, it's a cinch to catch a pass nowadays."

Exendine had an idea. In the huddle he explained it to Pete

Hauser—Hauser was filling in at quarterback for Mount Pleasant, who'd broken his thumb against Minnesota.

"Hold that ball as long as you can," Ex told Hauser, "then throw it to me down by the goal line."

Hauser took the next snap and drifted back. Exendine slanted from his end position toward the Chicago sideline and ran out of bounds. Defenders let him go.

They turned to rush Hauser. The quarterback scrambled, evading tacklers, as Exendine sprinted parallel to the field, *behind* a line of perplexed Chicago backups. Then he swerved back onto the field, and Hauser heaved a fifty-yard bomb. Ex caught it at the Chicago thirty and strolled in for the score.

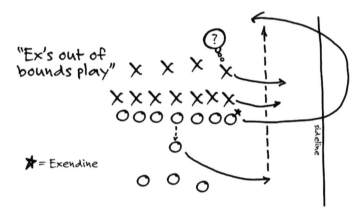

The hometown fans couldn't help it—they burst into cheers.

The Chicago players were furious. Stagg shouted at the officials to call the play back, but the touchdown stood. There was no rule against what Ex had done—though one was added after the season. Carlisle won easily, 18–4.

"They showed themselves masters of modern football," conceded the *Chicago Tribune*, "and gave such an exhibition of its possibilities as will not be forgotten by anyone."

◆◀▮▶◆

"I do not remember a football season more pleasing," wrote Caspar Whitney in his postseason wrap-up. Football under the new rules was faster and higher-scoring, with more action for fans to follow. Serious injuries were down; two college players had died that year, but that was seen as a major improvement.

Harvard coach Bill Reid would later credit Teddy Roosevelt with saving football. But words in a rule book are one thing. Someone had to show the nation a new way to play the game. The Carlisle Indians did that.

"The Indians have had a harder schedule than any team in the country, and they have done marvelously well," praised Yale's football coach, William Knox. "The game of this year owes to them, more than to any other, new developments of the forward pass."

Caspar Whitney agreed. "They used the forward pass successfully, as well as more persistently, than any other team of the year," he wrote. "They seemed to be on a train most of the season, and as travel is very fatiguing, the succession of victories over the strongest elevens in the country was therefore the more notable."

Carlisle finished the season 10-1. Most writers ranked them #3 in the nation, behind only Princeton and Yale.

For Pop Warner, it was an almost impossibly high standard to maintain.

Frank Mount Pleasant, Albert Exendine, and William Gardner graduated from Carlisle in the spring of 1908—the degree was basically equivalent to a high school diploma—and all three enrolled at Dickinson College. Warner was left to rebuild the football team with younger players.

Jim Thorpe seized the opportunity. As the starting left halfback in 1908, Thorpe busted long runs several times a game, immediately becoming a fan favorite. When Warner tried to rest Thorpe during an early-season home game, the Carlisle faithful wouldn't allow it.

"We want Jim!" the students chanted. "We want Jim!"

Pop sent him in. Thorpe took the next handoff up the middle, smashed into one side of a pile of defenders, came out the other, and rumbled for a seventy-yard touchdown, bowling down defenders with raised knees and stiff arms, all the while shouting, "Out of my way! Get out of my way!"

The coach had found his next star.

Out on the field, Thorpe could forget about family tragedies, forget about school and his uncertain future. Even after taking hard hits, one newspaper reported, Jim would leap to his feet, "picking his opponents up off the ground with a belt grip, all the while displaying a grin easily discernible from the stands."

◆❧◆

Suddenly a celebrity in the town of Carlisle, Thorpe took advantage by slipping away from campus to Halbert's Pool Hall or Peanut Joe's saloon. Local bars weren't supposed to serve Carlisle students, but exceptions were made for football players.

The back room of Mose Blumenthal's department store was another favorite hangout. There were photos of Carlisle stars on the wall and a private stash of booze. Warner even set up expense accounts for his players at Blumenthal's, allowing Thorpe and his teammates to charge new suits and hats, all funded by football-ticket sales. "The boys felt they'd earned it," Warner's assistant said of the football fund, "so Pop turned it over to them."

Some of it, anyway. Carlisle football was big business now, one of the top draws in all of American sports. Pulling in the equivalent of four or five million dollars a year in today's money, the football team financed a new hospital on the Carlisle campus, a greenhouse, an art studio—and a brand-new two-story house for Pop and Tibb Warner.

Football paid Pop's hefty $4,000 salary, nearly twice what the superintendent, Moses Friedman, earned. This had once been Pratt's school; now Warner was the most powerful man on campus. If a player got thrown into the guardhouse, a word from Warner to Friedman was enough to spring the athlete in time for the next game.

The one factor Pop Warner couldn't control was his new star.

Jim Thorpe was named third-team All-American at halfback in

## James Thorpe

| Date | Item | Amount | | Date | | Amount |
|---|---|---|---|---|---|---|
| Dec 15 | Gloves | 1 50 | | | By Cash | 75 00 |
| 17 | Bot Hose | 1 00 | Dec 4 | By Cash "Order" | | 50 00 |
| 17 | Handkerchf | 75 | July 13 | | | 10 75 |
| 22 | Midse | 2 00 | | | | |
| Jany 2 | Underwear | 4 00 | | | | |
| 9 | Underwear | 1 50 | | | | |
| 21 | Shirt | 2 50 | | | | |
| 21 | Ties | 75 | | | | |
| 24 | Sox | 50 | | | | |
| | Lock + les | 1 — | | | | |
| 13 | Shirt | 1 50 | | | | |
| 13 | Handkerchf | 1 50 | | | | |
| 7 | Collar Lock | 2 00 | | | | |
| | Midse | 1 00 | | | | |
| | Socks | 50 | | | | |
| 13 | Ties + Sox + Scarf | 2 00 | | | | |
| 26 | Tie Collar | 1 00 | | | | |
| 16 | B V D Under | 1 00 | | | | |
| 2 | Sox | 50 | | | | |
| 17 | Underwear | 1 00 | | | | |
| 17 | Sox | 50 | | | | |
| 30 | Hat | 5 00 | | | | |
| 9 | Underwear | 2 00 | | | | |
| | Shirt | 50 | | | | |
| 10 | Suit | 33 00 | | | | |
| 2 | Suit Pajamas | 3 00 | | | | |
| 2 | pr Hose | 50 | | | | |
| 15 | Coat | 25 00 | | | | |
| | Underwear | 2 00 | | | | |
| | Gloves | 2 00 | | | | |
| | Sox Handk | 75 | | | | |
| 8 | Underwear | 2 00 | | | | |
| | 4 pr Hose | 1 04 | | | | |
| 15 | Suit | 27 00 | | | | |
| 29 | Hat | 4 50 | | | | |
| | Underwear | 1 00 | | | | |
| | Lock | 50 | | | | |
| | | 135 75 | | | | 135 75 |

Mose Blumenthal's department store kept careful records of the purchases Thorpe and his teammates made with the expense accounts Warner set up for them.

1908—third best at his position in the entire country. Warner wanted more. "If he had taken coaching with a better spirit, he would have developed into the best halfback of the season."

This would be a constant sticking point between Warner and Thorpe, a classic case of personality clash. Warner was loud and bossy; Thorpe was quiet and could not be bossed. In practice, Warner berated Thorpe for relying too much on speed—*hit the line*, Warner would plead, *run north-and-south.*

"Oh, hell, Pop," Thorpe would say, grinning, "what's the use of going through 'em when I can run around 'em?"

It was that grin, as much as the obstinacy, that Warner found unsettling.

"It was difficult to know," Pop said, "if Jim was laughing with you or at you."

◆▓▶

Never the most dedicated student, Thorpe's interest in schoolwork—and patience for Carlisle's endless rules—slipped even further after the 1908 football season. He was twenty years old, but between farm outings and all the travel for football and track, he'd missed so much school that he was still years from graduation. He started skipping classes, sometimes disappearing from campus for entire days.

"James was very far from being a desirable student," Superintendent Moses Friedman reported to the Sac and Fox reservation.

When the school year ended, Thorpe watched many of his friends head off on their dreaded farm outings. He had told Friedman he'd stay on campus and take summer classes, but started having second thoughts when several of his track and football teammates told him they were going to spend the summer playing baseball—and getting paid for it. There were more than thirty minor leagues around the country, and hundreds of college athletes found what were essentially summer jobs playing ball.

Thorpe was intrigued. He went to see Superintendent Friedman, told him he'd changed his mind about sticking around Carlisle. Friedman strongly disapproved, but he couldn't get Thorpe to reconsider.

A note was added to Jim's school record: "granted a summer leave to play baseball in the South."

In early June, Thorpe joined fellow football boys Joe Libby and Jesse Young Deer at the train station. Libby and Young Deer were headed for North Carolina, where they'd signed on to play for the Rocky Mount Railroaders. Thorpe went with them.

He would later call it "the greatest mistake in my life."

A few days later **Jim Thorpe stepped up** to the plate for his first at bat in the Eastern Carolina Baseball League. He dug his cleats into the dirt, raised his bat—and struck out.

His second time up, he struck out again.

Well, maybe he can pitch, the Rocky Mount Railroaders manager figured.

"I told him I would give it a whirl," Thorpe recalled. He won his debut, 4–1.

For Jim, who was used to winning track races and outrunning tacklers, baseball didn't come as easily. Thorpe hit a modest .253 for the season, and went 9-10 as a pitcher. The Railroaders finished the summer in last place.

Thorpe had fun anyway. On game days, local kids gathered in the hotel lobby to greet the ballplayers. When Jim came downstairs, his uniform stained tan and green from previous games, he always took the time to joke with the kids.

"He stood about ten feet tall in my eyes," one of the boys would recall. "To me, he was always a gentleman, a very gentle person."

Thorpe earned $25 a week that summer, enough to live on, with a little spending money left over. And between games, he was a free man— or at least freer than he'd ever been at boarding school.

At a time when Jim Crow segregation laws ruled life in the South,

Thorpe and his Carlisle friends occupied an uneasy ground between black and white. While they were not banned from public places like restaurants and hotels, as black Americans were, the Indian athletes never knew how they were going to be treated. Joe Libby later told a story about walking through downtown Rocky Mount with Thorpe and Young Deer. A large white man blocked their way.

"When a white man approaches," he grumbled, "you get off the sidewalk and get into the street."

Thorpe turned to Libby and asked, "Do you like this guy?"

"No, Jim," Libby said, "I don't like him very much."

Thorpe turned to the man and punched him in the face. The three friends walked around his fallen body to the baseball field.

All three, Libby recalled, spent that night in jail.

When the baseball season ended, Thorpe decided not to return to Carlisle. Now a man of twenty-one, he couldn't face giving up the freedom he'd enjoyed over the summer. He moved in with his sister, pitching in on her Oklahoma farm.

Warner thought Thorpe was making a huge mistake—didn't he realize he was on the verge of national fame?

Of course, the coach had his own reasons for wanting his star back on campus. With only average talent in 1909, the football team struggled. More and more colleges were getting serious about the game, and Carlisle's competition intensified as schools like Pittsburgh, Michigan, Penn State, and Army joined the ranks of top teams.

Eager to gain any kind of edge, Warner was constantly telling interviewers how banged up his team was, even inventing injuries to key players in hopes of deceiving upcoming opponents. Before one game with Syracuse, he actually had healthy players limp onto the field with bandages wrapped around limbs and heads. The moment the ball was kicked off, they tore off the bandages.

In late November, Warner and the team traveled to Cincinnati, Ohio, for a game with St. Louis University. Jim Thorpe came and watched from the sidelines as Joe Libby led the Indians to victory.

When the team headed home, Warner traveled back to Oklahoma with Thorpe. They spent a few days hunting together. The coach urged Thorpe to come back to Carlisle, and Thorpe said he would.

Neither left a detailed description of their conversations during these few days, but Warner would later claim that the subject of baseball never came up. He'd claim he had no idea Thorpe had played semipro ball in North Carolina.

◆▧▶

As soon as Pop headed east, Jim had second thoughts about returning to Carlisle.

Sure, there was plenty to miss about the place—the camaraderie, the athletic dorm, football Saturdays. But Thorpe definitely didn't miss the rules, and he wasn't feeling particularly friendly toward Superintendent Friedman. Thorpe had written Friedman, asking the school to send the money he'd earned from his farm outings. Carlisle's policy was to hold on to students' earnings, doling out the cash as administrators saw fit, and Friedman dismissed Thorpe's request, condescendingly noting, "It is customary at this school, when students desert, that all funds to their credit are held until they return."

Thorpe stayed in Oklahoma, helping with the spring planting at his sister's farm.

In the summer, he went back to North Carolina to play baseball. He hit just .236 in 1910, and went 10-10 on the mound. Thorpe had hoped to be picked up by a major-league team, or at least a slightly better minor-league team, but he got no offers. He rode the train back to Oklahoma and tried to settle into life on the farm.

He couldn't, he just couldn't. As he'd done so many times before, he took off.

Thorpe drifted from one town to another, taking odd jobs to get by, completely broke most of the time. He was too restless to stay in one place, but had absolutely nowhere to go.

"I knew I stood at a crossroads," he would later say, "and I was pondering on what I should do."

◄●►

Pop Warner was facing his own crossroads—or maybe, the end of the road.

Carlisle's 1910 football season was its worst in a decade. Even when the team got attention, it was for the wrong reasons—like the erratic antics of Warner's left guard, Asa Sweetcorn. After being tossed from a game yet again, Sweetcorn demanded an explanation.

"Slugging," the ref told him.

"D'yah see me?"

"Out."

"D'yah see blood?"

"Out!"

"When I slugs 'em, you see blood."

Carlisle lost to Syracuse, Princeton, Navy, Brown, and, for the second straight year, Penn. The absolute rock bottom was a 3–0 defeat at the hands of Harvard Law School.

Not the Harvard football team, just a bunch of law students.

Pop Warner knew he could not justify his fat salary much longer. He had some good young players coming up, including a promising quarterback named Gus Welch, but what the coach needed was a difference maker. He needed a player good enough to turn things around in an instant.

◄●►

On a summer day in 1911, the ex-Carlisle star Albert Exendine was strolling the streets of Anadarko, Oklahoma. Now head football coach at Otterbein College in Ohio, Ex was back home on vacation. Far up the street he saw someone he recognized. Not the face—he was still too far away—but something about the man's rolling gait was familiar.

Exendine walked closer and saw he'd been right. It was Jim Thorpe. The kid was more muscular than Ex remembered, thicker through the chest.

Was this really just a chance meeting? Or was Exendine on a mission for his old coach? Ex never said. Either way, the friends were happy to see each other. They shook hands.

"What are you doing?" Ex asked.

"Nothing," said Thorpe.

"What have you been doing?"

"Playing baseball."

"Did you graduate from Carlisle?"

"No."

Thorpe was a man of few words. Exendine didn't need it spelled out; his friend was lost.

"Why don't you go back and finish at Carlisle?"

"They wouldn't want me there now," Thorpe said.

Ex said, "You bet they would."

A scrawny teen in ragged overalls stood on the street in Duluth, Minnesota, staring at a poster that read: CARLISLE INDIANS. The boy's face was thin. His ears stuck out. His eyes were locked on the poster. The famous Indian team was coming to Minnesota. Somehow, he was going to find a way to see them.

This was the fall of 1906. Gus Welch was fifteen years old and not sure he'd make it much longer. His father, an Irish immigrant who'd settled in Wisconsin, had been killed in a logging accident. His mother, a Chippewa Indian, died of tuberculosis, along with three of Gus's brothers and two sisters. Everyone told Gus he had weak lungs; he'd likely be next to succumb to the dreaded disease.

Living with his Chippewa grandmother and younger brother in the woods of northern Wisconsin, Gus spent as much time as possible outside, hoping the cold air would keep his lungs clear. His grandmother taught the boys to paddle a birch bark canoe, to trap animals for their fur, to collect maple syrup and wild rice. Gus earned money for the family by taking furs into Duluth to sell—which is what had brought him to town the day he saw the Carlisle football poster.

After seeing the poster, Welch went home to Wisconsin, trapped a wolf in the woods, sold the pelt, and bought a train ticket to Minneapolis. He found his way to the team's hotel and hung around the lobby.

When the players came downstairs, he marveled at the athletes, amazed by their elegant outfits and sophisticated manners. "I was just a ragamuffin," Gus later said, "wearing odd pieces of cast-off clothing."

The guys liked him. They were heading out for a walk and invited him to stroll with them. At one point, they stopped to look in the window of a clothing store. Gus's eyes locked on a stylish blue suit. The price tag was $15, far more than he could ever afford.

That night the players set up a cot for Welch in their hotel. They took him to the game with Minnesota the next day, and afterward stopped again in front of the clothing store. Gus gazed once more at the blue suit.

It was his, the players told him. They'd taken up a collection, and it was already paid for.

Gus was still crying when he got on the train.

In the twenty-seven years since Richard Henry Pratt founded the Carlisle School, thousands of students had come and gone from the Pennsylvania campus. Several of the football stars, including Bemus Pierce, Albert Exendine, and Frank Mount Pleasant, had found work as college coaches. Some had gone on to college and beyond—former quarterback Jimmie Johnson graduated from dental school at Northwestern University. William Gardner became a lawyer and would later join Eliot Ness's famous "Untouchables," the team of government agents that helped bring down the gangster Al Capone.

As the school newspaper proudly reported, many young women from Carlisle worked as teachers and nurses. Lillian St. Cyr, a Carlisle graduate of Ho-Chuck heritage, became a star of silent movies under the screen name Princess Red Wing.

But these experiences were hardly typical. Most former students simply wanted to go home, which meant returning to impoverished reservations. Beyond a few jobs as clerks or policemen with Indian Services, the government agency overseeing reservations, there was little use for the skills the men and women had learned at Carlisle. Those seeking new lives in cities found that Pratt's dream of assimilation was a fantasy. Many

Carlisle graduate Lillian St. Cyr, known by the screen name Princess Red Wing, performed in more than thirty westerns in the early days of Hollywood movies.

white employers simply wouldn't hire Indians, no matter how qualified they were.

Even more devastating for many students was that the years at Carlisle had cut them off from their traditions; Native American scholars have called this a "soul wound." Students who arrived at Carlisle as young children, for instance, often lost the ability to speak their native language and had the heartbreaking experience of going home and not being able to talk to their own parents or grandparents. This left them caught between worlds. They could not slip seamlessly back into life on the reservation—yet, as those who moved away discovered, they were not welcomed as equals in white society, either.

It's not clear how much Gus Welch knew of Carlisle's mixed reputation, or the bitter disappointment of so many former students. He knew he loved the football team. That was enough.

Nearly two years after meeting the team in Minnesota, Gus boarded a train with his younger brother, Jimmy. They had a jug of spring water and some dried fruit their grandmother had wrapped up for them. Gus and Jimmy had been accepted as students at the Carlisle School and were on their way to Pennsylvania.

The brothers got the usual haircuts and uniforms, and began learning the daily routine. Gus joined the debate team, became a star student, and soon caught Pop Warner's eye as a track sprinter and a quarterback for the blacksmith shop team. At age twenty, Welch got the chance he'd been dreaming about since that unforgettable visit to Minneapolis—Pop Warner picked him to play quarterback for the Carlisle Indians in 1911.

And the wonders kept coming. When Welch moved into the athletic quarters, he met his new roommate, Jim Thorpe.

◆

"It felt good to be back among my own kind," Thorpe would say of his return to Carlisle, "in a football uniform and on the campus of the school I loved."

Warner's decision to room Thorpe and Welch together was inspired. Welch was outgoing, talkative, and the top-ranked student in his class. Under his influence, Thorpe studied more than he had before. And out on the football field, where Thorpe felt most at home, Welch could have no better tutor.

In late September Gus walked nervously onto Indian Field for Carlisle's 1911 season opener, a game with Lebanon Valley College. The quarterback knew he hadn't mastered Pop Warner's complex playbook. In the huddle before the first play, Welch called play Number 48, then turned to his roommate to double-check assignments.

"What do I do if I miss my block?"

"Just keep on running," Thorpe said, "but keep out of my way."

Welch flipped Thorpe the ball and, sure enough, missed his assigned block on a lineman. He tried to hit a linebacker. "But I missed him," Welch remembered. "So I took a shot at the safety, who was coming up fast, and he avoided me. Then I realized that Thorpe was still behind me and we were going for a touchdown."

In the second game, Muhlenberg College safety Walter Reisner made it his personal mission to stop Jim Thorpe. "But I couldn't get both my arms around his legs," Reisner later said. "The best I could do was to hang on to

Gus Welch quickly became a star quarterback at Carlisle—and a best friend to Jim Thorpe.

one leg and slow him down." It proved a better strategy than hitting Thorpe head-on; Reisner tried that, too. "And when I hit the ground, I thought my shoulder was broken," he explained. "It was the first time I was glad to be taken out of a game."

Turned out Reisner's shoulder was fine. It was his collarbone that was broken.

A month into the season, Carlisle was 4-0, outscoring opponents by a combined 148–5. Gus Welch was settling in at quarterback, and Warner knew he finally had the field general he'd been missing since Mount Pleasant graduated. Welch was just five nine, 155, but he was coolheaded, blazing fast, and a natural leader. When a ref's call went against Carlisle, Welch knew how to ease the anger with bitter humor. "What's the use of crying about a few inches," he'd tell teammates in the huddle, "when the white man has taken the whole country?"

Behind Welch in the backfield were fullback Stansil "Possum" Powell and right halfback Alex Arcasa, both emerging young stars. At left halfback was Jim Thorpe, now six feet tall, 190 pounds of solid muscle. It was the best backfield in football—the best Pop Warner had ever seen.

The rest of the country hadn't caught on. In mid-October, when Carlisle began its usual string of brutal road games with a trip to Washington, DC, to play Georgetown, the Indians came in as underdogs.

◄◆►

That was just how Pop Warner liked it.

"I have a better team this year than last," he coyly told reporters in Washington. "While I have not witnessed the Georgetown eleven in action, they will have to go some to best my Indians."

Georgetown head coach Fred Nielsen was a bit bolder. "Georgetown will put a good team on the field against the Indians, and a victory is what I expect."

Nielsen was so determined to beat Carlisle he'd actually skipped his own team's previous game, choosing instead to watch Carlisle play. Then, back in Washington, he'd spent a week trying to get his second-stringers

146

to replicate Carlisle's dreaded whirlwind offense, so his starters could see what they'd be up against. The key, Nielsen lectured, was the first few minutes. The key was to not let the whirlwind start spinning. Easier said than done.

Carlisle came out fast, with Gus Welch's offense humming "like a piece of smooth-running machinery" wrote the *Washington Herald*. Jim Thorpe dragged would-be tacklers all over the field, Possum Powell powered up the middle, and Welch and Alex Arcasa mixed in passes on what looked to the defense like running plays.

"It was smash, smash, smash," said the *Herald*. "Georgetown's line was torn to pieces, her backfield exhausted, and her quick-witted ends bewildered by the hurricane assault."

Carlisle's 28–5 demolition of Georgetown caught the football world's attention. The Indians hadn't been good in a while, now they were good again. But it still wasn't clear *how* good. The next game, at the University of Pittsburgh, would answer that. Pitt was a "big heavy team," Warner recalled, "a lot of bruisers." They had not been beaten, or even scored on, in their last eleven games.

Pitt coach Joseph Thompson drilled his team hard all week. The focus was on finding ways to stop, or at least slow down, Jim Thorpe. It didn't work.

In front of a large crowd at Pittsburgh's Forbes Field, Thorpe rushed for 235 yards, did all the team's kicking, and dominated on defense. "He seemed possessed of superhuman speed," wrote the *Pittsburgh Dispatch*, "for wherever the pigskin alighted, there he was, ready either to grab it or to down the Pitt player who secured it."

The game's most amazing play came on a Jim Thorpe punt, a sky-high sixty-yard spiral. The rule then was that punts were loose balls. Any player on either team could pick up a punt and run with it, and it was common to see the kicking team recover its own punt. What was not common—what no one had *ever* seen—was what Thorpe did that day. Sprinting beneath his own punt as it sailed downfield, Thorpe covered sixty yards fast enough to get there as the ball came down. He leaped above the Pitt player who thought he was about to catch it, grabbed the ball, broke four tackles, and ran twenty more yards for the touchdown. Even the Pitt fans stood and cheered.

But not everyone in the stands was cheering. Reporters noticed a small group of observers who didn't seem to be rooting for either team. As the *Washington Herald* reported, "Scouts for Pennsylvania, Harvard, and other elevens who are to meet the Indians later in the season were here to see the game."

Pennsylvania and Harvard were the ones that counted most. Carlisle's two biggest rivals still lay ahead.

Up until the Georgetown and Pitt games, Jim Thorpe had been known as what sportswriters called an "in-and-outer," the kind of player who can look great one day and be no factor the next. Now it was clear that Thorpe was all in. As one paper put it, "He plays football with the abandon of a man having all competitors outclassed."

If Jim's growing celebrity affected him, no one noticed. Around campus, he was exactly the same—quick smile, easygoing, clowning with friends. And when not in uniform, he dressed the same. "He always went around looking so raggedy," classmate Rose DeNomie remembered. "He had an old long raggedy coat he always wore. But he was always happy."

"He could be very jolly," another female student agreed. "He enjoyed dancing, although he certainly didn't seem to be a ladies' man."

"All the girls had a crush on him," one friend recalled. According to football teammate Henry Roberts, even this didn't go to Jim's head. "He treated all the girls alike," Roberts said.

Actually, there *was* one woman who stood out to Thorpe, an eighteen-year-old student named Iva Miller. Born in Indian Territory, Miller's father was Irish, her mother part Cherokee. Maybe. Iva's parents died when she was five, and her aunt enrolled her in a local Indian school, reporting that Iva was part-Indian on her mother's side. To this day, no one knows if this was true, and it was not unheard-of for white parents to sneak kids into Indian boarding schools, which offered free room and board.

Geronimo was seventy years old when he appeared at the 1904 World's Fair with Iva Miller. The government never allowed him to return home; he died in Oklahoma in 1909.

Whatever her background was, Iva grew up in Indian schools and had her own brush with fame when she was chosen to represent her school at the 1904 World's Fair in St. Louis. At age eleven, she performed in the Indian Territory Building, singing songs and reciting poems for curious crowds. She became friends with the Indian exhibit's main draw, the famous Apache leader Geronimo. Born along what's now the Arizona-New Mexico border, Geronimo had led an armed resistance against settlers on traditional Apache land. He finally surrendered to US forces in 1886, on condition he be allowed to live out his years on the Apache reservation in Arizona. The government broke its promise, holding him instead as a prisoner of war. During the World's Fair, he lived in a teepee outside the Indian Territory Building, where he demonstrated how to make bows and arrows, sold postcards of himself, and sometimes, to the delight of tourists, danced with Iva Miller.

In 1909 Miller transferred to the Carlisle School to study nursing. She was smart and outgoing, active in campus clubs, secretary of the girls' debating society, and, her daughter would later say, "the prettiest girl at Carlisle."

Jim Thorpe thought so. When a teammate introduced Jim to Iva, his first words were, "You're a cute little thing."

She was not impressed.

◆❈◆

Pop Warner was impressed—but didn't show it.

In long afternoon practices, Warner pushed his undefeated team to keep improving. If he didn't like what he saw, he'd take his old place on the line and butt heads with anyone who looked timid.

"You #$%& bonehead!" the red-faced coach roared when players made mistakes.

"I'll knock your @#*& block off!"

Warner's vow to quit cursing long forgotten, he hurled his sharpest barbs at his best player.

"Lazy Indian!" he shrieked at Thorpe. "You don't want to learn! You just want to pout!"

Thorpe flashed that casual grin he knew infuriated his coach and said, "I'm satisfied."

"I tell you what to do, and you start a debate!"

Thorpe was approaching the game more seriously than ever, even getting up early to jog the hilly roads around campus. But out on the field, everything seemed to come easily, and something about that rubbed Pop the wrong way.

"Jim was always a carefree sort of chap and never took things very seriously," Warner would later say. "He was naturally bright," Pop added, but he had "a pretty strong aversion for work."

"But I also had a strong aversion for getting beat," Thorpe fired back, "and I did all right in avoiding that."

◆❈◆

Next up for Carlisle was 5-0 Lafayette College, a strong team that had not allowed a touchdown in two years. The streak ended abruptly when Carlisle came to town.

In another dominating win, Jim Thorpe and the other starters played every down on offense, defense, and special teams. That was normal, but this time it cost them. Late in the game, his team up 19–0, Thorpe rolled his right ankle on a routine run. As he limped to the sideline, he knew from the throbbing pain that the injury was serious.

A doctor took a look at the swollen ankle and diagnosed a severe sprain. He told Thorpe to stay off the foot completely for two weeks.

The next two games were against Pennsylvania and Harvard.

All week Thorpe hobbled around campus on crutches. He watched practice from his least favorite spot—the bench.

On Friday afternoon he boarded the train, along with the team and a large group of students who'd saved up to make the trip to Philadelphia. Iva Miller was among them. She liked Jim, despite that awkward opening line. When the players held a pep rally in the lobby of their hotel the next morning, Iva came as Jim's special guest.

That afternoon, in the locker room of Franklin Field, Thorpe pulled on his uniform. He wanted to give it a go. Gamblers were more realistic— with Thorpe injured, they made Penn the heavy favorite.

Thirty thousand fans watched Thorpe limp onto the field. They watched him loosen up and try to run. Warner watched it too, from much closer up. Every time Thorpe planted his right foot, his face twisted in pain. Warner scratched him from the lineup.

But this was no one-man team. Carlisle overwhelmed Penn with speed and teamwork, and Gus Welch—"the wonderful dodging Welch," as the *Philadelphia Inquirer* put it—never let the defense catch its breath. "We used to call signals so fast the defense didn't have time to get lined up," he remembered. Alex Arcasa and Possum Powell carried the load running the ball, and Welch electrified the crowd by fielding a punt near his own goal line and snaking through the entire Penn team for a ninety-five-yard touchdown.

Final: Carlisle 16, Pennsylvania 0.

"Does it pay to educate the Indian?" an *Inquirer* reporter heard a Penn fan wonder aloud.

"No, no, no," several answered, "not in football."

Carlisle was now 8-0. Pop Warner's thoughts turned immediately to Harvard, a showdown the national press was hyping as "the battle of the year." Warner desperately wanted the win. He knew the players wanted it even more.

Since first coming to Carlisle, the coach had sensed something extra motivating this team, something beyond the typical desire to win football games. "When playing against college teams," Warner would later theorize,

Joel Wheelock crashes through Penn's defensive line in Carlisle's 16–0 drubbing of their longtime rivals. As the photo shows, by 1911 most players chose to wear leather helmets.

trying to explain this X factor, "it was not to them so much the Carlisle School against Pennsylvania or Harvard, as the case might be, but it was the Indian against the white man."

The Carlisle School was supposed to sever these young men from their heritage, to "Kill the Indian in them," as Pratt had famously said. But fans and sportswriters never let the players forget they were Indians—and there's no evidence they *wanted* to forget. They did not call themselves the Carlisle Cardinals or the Carlisle Wildcats. They were the Carlisle Indians.

And their desire to prove themselves, their pride in who they were, was especially strong when facing elite schools. They actually liked and admired Harvard—"Anything very good was always commented on as 'Harvard-style,'" Warner said of his players. But that didn't mean they thought Harvard students were somehow better than they were, more worthy of equality or respect.

"We pointed to this game because it meant more prestige than any other," Possum Powell later said. "On the other hand, Harvard didn't consider us much."

He was right. Harvard had a lifetime record of 11-1 against the Indian school, and Crimson coach Percy Haughton dismissed Carlisle's inventive style as "whiff-whaff," telling reporters, "We'll stick to barnyard football." Haughton even hinted that he might not bother to play his starters, saving them instead for upcoming games with Dartmouth and Yale.

Was Haughton serious, or just gaming Warner? Pop had no idea. He wasn't even sure which of his own players would be on the field. The entire team was feeling the effects of Carlisle's grueling run of road games, and the theme all week on sports pages was that the Indians had simply played too many tough games to compete with "the ruler of the football universe," as papers called bigger, fresher Harvard.

Worst of all, of course, was the injury to Carlisle's biggest star—or, as the *Boston Globe* dubbed him, "Crippled Jimmy Thorpe."

Warner refused to update the press on the state of Thorpe's ankle. He didn't want Percy Haughton to know that Thorpe could barely walk.

Behind closed doors, he and Jim tried everything known to early-twentieth-century medicine, from massages and special ointments to electricity treatments and vibration machines.

On Friday, Thorpe tested the leg on the practice field. Warner's heart sank.

"Jim," he said, "you can't run on that ankle."

"Sure I can," Thorpe insisted.

Warner took a closer look. The ankle was still swollen, Warner pointed out, and Thorpe couldn't put his weight on it without wincing.

Thorpe said, "Wrap it up. I'll play."

O n Saturday afternoon on the Carlisle campus, hundreds of students gathered at Indian Field. On the field was a large blackboard with a diagram of a football field drawn in chalk, and a football symbol stuck to the board. This was 1911's version of ESPN—updates would be telegraphed from Boston to Carlisle and, as each update reached campus, someone would run out to the field and move the ball back and forth on the board so students could follow the action.

In Boston, temporary stands were added to accommodate the turnout of nearly forty thousand at Harvard Stadium. Carlisle vs. Harvard drew a larger crowd than any other American sporting event that year.

In the locker room, Pop Warner wrapped Jim Thorpe's right ankle in a foot-to-shin cast of plaster and tape. Then Warner gathered the team around. He'd never been a big pre-game pep talk kind of coach, but today he told his players to remember Percy Haughton's "whiff-whaff" line. Harvard didn't respect them, was looking past them—here was their chance to take down "the ruler of the football universe."

The huge crowd roared as the Carlisle Indians ran onto the field. Fans spotted Jim Thorpe, limping along behind his teammates.

Henry Roberts was among the players making their first visit to this football cathedral. He looked around, amazed by the skyscraper grandstands, the plush green field—and the enormous Harvard players. "Their line was supposed to be impregnable," he later said. Roberts watched

Thorpe trying to loosen up, trying to figure out how to run and plant and kick with his aching, stiffly bandaged leg. The sight was better than any pep talk.

"Jim didn't say anything," Roberts recalled, "but we all played better because of him."

A scorecard and ticket from the 1911 Carlisle-Harvard game, the most eagerly awaited sporting event of the year. As was so often the case, Carlisle was represented by a stereotyped image instead of a photo of one of the actual players.

Carlisle won the coin toss and elected to receive the opening kickoff.

Harvard sent in the second-string team, holding its starters in reserve. The Crimson backups were still much bigger than Carlisle's players, and Harvard had the advantage of having fifty players in uniform. Carlisle had sixteen.

Pop Warner countered, instructing Gus Welch to open with a relaxed tempo and old-school play selection.

It worked. Harvard came out focused on Jim Thorpe and Carlisle's speed game. Welch used Thorpe as a decoy, giving the ball instead to Possum Powell for power runs up the middle. Carlisle churned all the way to the Harvard five, where the drive stalled.

Welch turned to Thorpe, who did all of Carlisle's kicking. Could his leg handle a short field goal? Thorpe said it could.

Welch knelt in the grass at the thirteen to hold for Thorpe. The old dropkick was going out of style, replaced by the placekick—the technique kickers use today. Gus caught the snap from center and held the ball upright. Thorpe never described the lightning bolt of agony he must have felt as his foot hit the ball. It sailed over defenders' arms and through the uprights. Rule makers had again—and for the last time—changed the value of a field goal, to three points.

At Carlisle, the crowd at Indian Field leaped up, shouting through megaphones, waving red-and-gold flags, as the chalkboard was updated: Carlisle 3, Harvard 0.

At Harvard Stadium, the much smaller Carlisle rooting section—mostly women—made itself heard. "Each girl did her best to encourage our schoolmates with her cheering," a student named Ella Johnson remembered.

Harvard answered Carlisle's score with a dose of barnyard football, tying the game, 3–3. Thorpe hit another field goal to make it 6–3. Then, late in the first half, a Harvard runner broke the game's first big play, trampling Gus Welch on his way to a forty-five-yard touchdown.

At halftime, the scoreboard read Harvard 9, Carlisle 6.

Puffing on cigarettes in the locker room, Pop Warner told his players to stay calm, to trust the game plan. They were the better team, he told them. They were going to open things up in the second half—and Jim Thorpe was going to be more than a decoy.

❖

"It was in the second half that the Indians played their whirlwind football," reported the *Boston Globe*.

Gus Welch handed it to Arcasa running one way, who flipped it to Thorpe going the other. After a gain of twenty, the whole team raced to the line for a quick burst of end runs and reverses. "The Indians played at a speed that was terrific," said the *Globe*. "No one dared sit down in the stands."

Somehow driving the pain from his mind, Thorpe took over. Even with the entire Harvard defense keyed on him, he picked up yards in hard-earned chunks. And after being tackled, he'd come out from under the pile with a smile on his face. "Jim led the Carlisle effort all day," Pop Warner later said, "and showed to everyone in Harvard Stadium that he had the heart of a lion."

At the end of three quarters the score was Carlisle 15, Harvard 9.

That's when the Harvard starters jogged onto the field.

The crowd roared at the sight of the big men in spotless crimson jerseys.

"The Indians were six points ahead, to be sure," wrote the *Boston Globe*, "but all were confident that against the tired team the Harvard varsity men surely would be able to save the game."

Thorpe looked around at his teammates. They were drained, many of them bent over, hands on knees, panting. Their faces showed worry. "Most of the fellows, I guess, believed that we were beaten," Thorpe later said. "Somehow, I never thought so."

❖

Play resumed, and the fourth quarter was an entirely different story from the third. Harvard's fresh defenders stuffed Gus Welch's offense. Carlisle hung tough on defense, tackling in bunches, and the teams punted back and forth while the clock ticked slowly down.

Too slowly for Pop Warner.

Harvard was taking control; it was just a matter of *when* they would break through. And even from the sidelines, Warner could see that Jim Thorpe was suffering.

"Pop wanted to take Jim out because he was about through," Henry Roberts remembered. "But we wouldn't let him. Without Jim, we would have folded up. He was the spark that kept us going."

Carlisle got the ball back, and Thorpe rallied his teammates to make one final push. In the huddle, he told Welch to give him the ball.

"And get out of my way," he told the team. "I mean to do some real running."

Thorpe muscled it across midfield, then inside the Harvard forty. The next run went for no gain. The next was a three-yard loss, setting up a third down and thirteen from the Harvard forty-one.

With only three plays to get a first down, the game came down to this. Quarterbacks, not coaches, made in-game decisions. Gus Welch had a few seconds to decide what to do. The obvious play was to punt. But Welch didn't think his team could stop Harvard's offense again.

They could go for it. But Welch didn't like his exhausted team's chances of gaining thirteen yards in one play against this defense.

They could try a field goal. But to get the ball over the upraised arms of defenders, field goal tries were launched from about seven yards behind the line of scrimmage—in this case, the kick would be from the Harvard forty-eight. That's a long kick even today, and in 1911, with the heavy, lumpy ball, field goals from the middle of the field were simply not part of the game.

And besides, Carlisle's kicker looked like he was about to collapse.

Welch called for the field goal.

Thorpe couldn't believe it. "Who in the hell heard of a placekick from here?" he snapped. "Let's punt the ball."

Other players started to chime in. Welch cut them off with three words: "I'm the quarterback."

They broke the huddle and lined up in field-goal formation. Welch kneeled in the grass seven yards behind the line. Thorpe took a few steps back from there. "As long as I live, I will never forget that moment," he'd later say. "There I stood in the center of the field, the biggest crowd I had ever seen watching us."

The snap came back, the hold was clean, and Thorpe stepped forward and swung his foot into the ball with everything he had left. He knew right away he'd hit it well. He saw the ball barely clear Harvard's charging linemen, then lost sight of it behind the defenders' outstretched hands, and listened for a reaction from the crowd.

It took a few seconds. Fans watched the ball tumbling, low and straight, toward the goalposts. They watched it sail through the uprights and land ten yards behind the goal.

The small group of Carlisle students stood and shouted.

The scorekeeper updated the board: Carlisle 18, Harvard 9.

Jim Thorpe was finished. He laid his arms over his teammates' shoulders and limped off the field.

"His going gave the crowd an opportunity to show appreciation of his playing," wrote the *Boston Herald*. "A long roar of cheering followed him up the sidelines."

◆❖◆

Then Harvard took over, just as Gus Welch had known they would. They scored a quick touchdown, cutting the lead to three.

They got the ball back and were driving again when time ran out.

Final: Carlisle 18, Harvard 15.

Harvard University would not lose another football game until 1915, four years later.

Harvard players, many with tears in their eyes, shook hands with the Carlisle men. Even Coach Percy Haughton offered grudging praise for Jim Thorpe, telling sportswriters, "I realize that here is the theoretical super-player in flesh and blood."

For Jim and for Carlisle, it was the biggest win yet—and the most meaningful.

"Maybe football victories and athletic championships don't mean very much compared to some of the great achievements of famous men," Thorpe would say after his playing days were done, "but I'll bet none of them, in any of their triumphs, ever got a bigger kick out of winning than we Carlisle boys did that day at Boston when we whipped old Harvard."

The headline says it all. But amid the praise for Carlisle, the paper resorts to a typical slur, referring to Thorpe's four field goals as "scalps" (left-hand column, beneath the photo).

The Carlisle Indians were through the toughest part of their schedule. They were a perfect 9-0. They led the nation in scoring. If there had been a week-by-week ranking system at the time, they'd have been the hands-down #1.

Pop took it easy on the team for the next few days. The players were sapped from the endless travel. And like any football team late in a season, they were banged up—more banged up than most, because they had so few subs and their starters hardly ever came out of the game. "Most of the players bear slight bruises," noted a visiting reporter, "and there is quite a number who have from ten to fifteen sore spots on their bodies." Jim Thorpe was still limping. Most troubling was what the papers were calling Gus Welch's "sprained back," sustained in the Harvard game.

But overall, the coach was feeling fine. Next up was a mediocre Syracuse team. "We looked on victory as certain," Warner would later say.

◆❖◆

"Don't ask me how many goals I will kick," Jim Thorpe told reporters Friday night in the team's Syracuse hotel. Thorpe wasn't sure how well he could play on his tender ankle, and never liked talking to sportswriters before games anyway. "I don't have anything to say. You will have to talk to the coach."

They found the coach. As usual, he was more talkative than Thorpe.

"We will probably use the open style of play," Warner mused, "but of course, I can't go into that." He gave his usual line about how he expected a hard match, and let slip one additional worry. "We don't like the rain and snow, but then I guess no one does."

Outside the warm hotel, a storm was rolling south from Lake Ontario. It began dumping heavy rain on Syracuse as the team tried to sleep. The wind picked up overnight, and temperatures fell into the low thirties. By game time Saturday, the football field at Archbold Stadium was a layer cake of mud, slush, and snow.

Five minutes into the first quarter, the players were ankle-deep in the icy mire, and all twenty-two uniforms looked the same—brown. Play was slow and sloppy, and Alex Arcasa, filling in at quarterback for the injured Welch, kept things simple by feeding the ball to a still-limping Thorpe. Thorpe powered in for the game's first touchdown, but his try for the extra point went wide. A Carlisle fumble set up a Syracuse score, and a punt that slipped off the side of Thorpe's shoe led to another. At halftime, it was Syracuse 12, Carlisle 5.

Gus Welch, who'd barely been able to rise from bed that morning, announced he was going in. But the second half was more of the same: turnovers and punts, soggy and shivering players. Thorpe scored another touchdown with two minutes left, and that's how it ended.

Syracuse 12, Carlisle 11.

The team was devastated. Jim Thorpe blamed himself. Playing hurt, he had carried the ball 30 times for 133 yards and both of Carlisle's touchdowns. Still, he insisted he'd "lost the contest for Carlisle" by missing that extra point.

"Coach Glenn Warner's face was glum," reported the *Syracuse Herald*. "He did not say much, but his looks told how hard the defeat has struck him."

When the team boarded a train to head home, Gus Welch almost didn't make it. "He collapsed after the game," the Syracuse school paper explained, "and only the strenuous work of two doctors put him in shape to leave with his team."

164

Carlisle won its last two games to finish the season 11-1. No team had managed to go unbeaten and untied, so football's 1911 national championship was—and still is—open to debate.

*Outing* magazine, in its influential season roundup, gave the title to Princeton. The Tigers had gone 8-0-2, though they'd not exactly dazzled fans with high-flying offense. "Her repertoire of plays was scanty," *Outing* commented, "and the execution was mediocre."

Carlisle outscored Princeton by more than a hundred points, played a much harder schedule, beat twice as many top teams—and did it all on the road.

Media bias in favor of elite schools is the only way to explain the rankings. But Pop Warner dwelt on his own team's letdown at Syracuse. "The Indians, worn out by their series of grueling encounters, played far below their form," he said. Never a word of blame for the man who'd scheduled the grueling encounters—himself, that is.

For Jim Thorpe, named first-team All-American at halfback, it was back to the Carlisle routine.

Between classes, he and Gus Welch shot pool in town and fished in a nearby creek. Sometimes they slipped off to an unused building on campus to drink a can of beer. On Christmas, when nearly three hundred young students gathered for a party in the gym, a man in a long white beard walked in and started handing out presents. One of the boys had the audacity to yank down Santa's beard.

Beneath was the big grin of Jim Thorpe.

The kids cheered and chanted, "All-American! All-American!"

Thorpe spent the winter months training indoors, long jumping and shot-putting in the campus gym. At track meets in the spring, he piled up medals and trophies.

But Pop Warner could see Thorpe's heart wasn't really in it. On the train home after one meet, Thorpe lit up a cigar and walked through the car puffing away. Warner was livid with him for so blatantly flouting team training rules.

"What's the use of bothering with track?" Thorpe shrugged. "There's nothing in it."

No money, in other words. He and Iva Miller had begun talking marriage, and he was worried about his earning potential in the working world. He already knew he didn't want to be a farmer. He wasn't teacher or clerk material, and couldn't see himself as a blacksmith or baker. The best option, he decided, was to find some way to make a living in sports. Today Jim Thorpe could count on being the first pick in the NFL draft—an instant millionaire. But at the time, with no way to support a family playing football, Thorpe figured he'd try to become a college football coach, or maybe a professional baseball player.

Warner didn't want Thorpe thinking that far ahead. He pushed Jim into a seat and launched into a sermon about the famous athlete's duty to his teammates and to Carlisle.

Thorpe was silent for a while. Sighing, he said, "Oh, all right then, but I'd rather play baseball."

Warner offered Thorpe one more reason to stick with track—the 1912 Olympic Games, to be held in Stockholm, Sweden. Pop told Jim he might be good enough to make the American team.

To Thorpe, as restless and competitive as ever, it was a challenge he could not resist.

"I trained as I never trained before—or since," Thorpe later said of his workouts that spring. In the morning he'd go on fifteen-mile runs through the Cumberland Valley. Afternoons he practiced field events, with Pop Warner and Wallace Denny, the football trainer, urging him on. When classes ended at four, Iva Miller would come out to the field—a sight that always gave Thorpe a fresh burst of energy.

Miller graduated that spring and took a summer job at an Oklahoma boarding school. Iva and Jim agreed to stay in touch by mail.

In May, Thorpe traveled to Celtic Park in New York City to compete in an Olympic trial. Some of the country's top athletes stopped what they were doing to stare at the football star.

Iva Miller and Jim Thorpe in a photo taken during the 1911–12 school year.

Jim walked up and said, "When do we start?"

He dominated the trials, even in events for which he'd barely been prepared by his coach. When it was time for the javelin throw, for instance, he just picked the thing up and tossed it. It wasn't until he watched other athletes that he realized you were allowed to take a running start.

"He did everything wrong," a runner named Abel Kiviat later said of Thorpe's technique in the shot put. "His stance, his footwork, his follow-through. It was all backward. Warner never taught him a thing." Thorpe won the event anyway. "That is when I knew he was a marvel,"

Jim Thorpe showed up in top shape for the Olympic Trial event in New York's Celtic Park.

Left to right: Louis Tewanima, Warner, and Thorpe just before leaving for the 1912 Olympics.

Kiviat said. "He was beating all these guys—and *they* were doing it *right*."

◆❖◆

On the morning of June 14, Pop Warner, Jim Thorpe, and a Carlisle track star named Louis Tewanima carried suitcases and duffel bags along a crowded pier in Manhattan. They walked up a ramp and onto the ocean liner *Finland*, the biggest ship Thorpe had ever seen.

Thorpe was on his way to Sweden to represent the United States in the pentathlon and decathlon, all-around events meant to test the world's greatest athletes. He was in an awkward position, though, because the government did not consider Native Americans to be citizens of the United States. He was twenty-three years old, and the best athlete in the country—but, legally, he was a ward of the state. As such, he wasn't even allowed to control his own money. When Thorpe found out he'd made the team, he'd telegraphed the government agent at the Sac and Fox reservation. "Please send me $100 from my account," he wrote. "Will need same this summer in taking trip to Sweden with Olympic team."

The agent refused, suggesting Thorpe quit "gallivanting around the country" and get to work on his land allotment on the reservation. Warner found money in the Carlisle budget to cover travel for Thorpe, Tewanima, and himself.

As the *Finland* pulled slowly into the Hudson River, a crowd of thousands stood on the pier cheering and waving handkerchiefs and American flags. The ship sailed past the Statue of Liberty, through the Narrows between Brooklyn and Staten Island, and out into the Atlantic Ocean.

STOCKHOLM

The next morning, dozens of feet pounded a cork track built onto the deck of the *Finland*.

As athletes circled the eighth-mile loop over and over, weight lifters grunted under barbells and swimmers splashed back and forth in a canvas tank. Tennis players smacked balls against walls and high jumpers leaped over ropes and landed with smacks on piles of wrestling mats. Riflemen—including a young George Patton, later to gain fame as a general in World War II—blasted away at targets launched over the water, and the smell of gunpowder mixed with the cloud of sweat enveloping the ship.

Between training sessions, Jim Thorpe was often seen sitting alone on a deck chair with his eyes closed. Reporters were curious about what they took to be Thorpe's casual attitude.

"What are you doing, Jim?" one of them asked.

Thorpe opened his eyes. "I'm practicing the broad jump," he said. "I've just jumped twenty-three feet, eight inches."

Today we'd call this visualization, a technique of mental rehearsal commonly used by elite athletes. Thorpe was ahead of his time; reporters on the *Finland* didn't get it. Full of typical prejudices about "lazy Indians," they just saw Thorpe relaxing in a chair while other athletes were getting in extra workouts. So that's the story they told.

The other Olympians on the ship knew Jim was training hard, and could see he was serious—"deadly in earnest," remembered Abel Kiviat, who

In spite of rumors to the contrary, photos like this one tell the true story—Thorpe worked out hard aboard the *Finland*.

shared a cabin with Thorpe. "He was pleasant, but he didn't say much," Kiviat recalled. "A perfectly quiet chap who never had a penny to his name."

The other thing Kiviat remembered about the ten-day crossing was that everyone was still talking about the tragedy of the *Titanic*. Just two months earlier, the famous British passenger ship had collided with an iceberg and sunk in the North Atlantic, killing more than 1,500. On the *Finland*, athletes spent spare moments on deck anxiously watching for floating ice.

But the ship sailed safely into Antwerp, Belgium, and the team climbed onto buses for the long drive and ferryboat ride to Stockholm. Thorpe sat alone, watching the scenery roll by outside his window.

"We were pretty nervous by then, but not Thorpe," Kiviat later said. "We all knew he was going to do well. We just didn't know *how* well."

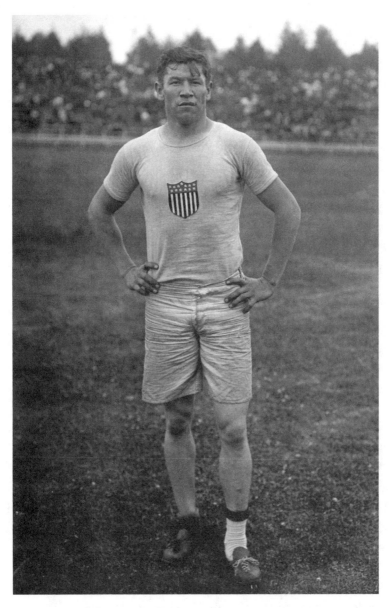

Representing the United States of America: Jim Thorpe.

On a hot afternoon in Stockholm's packed Olympic stadium, Jim Thorpe crouched at the start of the long jump runway, muscles tensed and ready to explode into motion. He wore white shorts and a white shirt with a red, white, and blue American shield on the front.

His eyes were fixed on the sandpit at the end of the runway—specifically, at the twenty-three-foot mark. The moment he'd been visualizing for weeks had finally come.

From the grass field inside the track, Pop Warner watched Thorpe burst forward and tear down the runway. Thorpe leaped, soaring into the air with knees lifted and arms raised high, and fell forward as his feet hit the sand.

Warner clapped the moment Thorpe landed; he knew a quality jump when he saw one. The official measurement was twenty-three feet, two and seven-tenths inches. Good for first place in the running broad jump—the long jump, as it's now known. After the first of the pentathlon's five events, the American was in the lead.

This was definitely not what the experts had predicted.

Conventional wisdom said that Americans were only good at specializing in single events, which Europeans saw as somehow unsporting. European athletes were convinced *they* were the better all-around performers and would prove it on the world stage. Norway's Ferdinand Bie came in as the heavy favorite.

Thorpe took third in the javelin. He won the 200-meter dash, turning at the finish to glance back, with a slight smile, at Ferdinand Bie.

"The Scandinavians couldn't believe their eyes," Abel Kiviat later said. "Thorpe kept getting stronger with each event."

Thorpe started the next day by tossing the discus 116 feet, good for another stunning first-place finish. Going into the last event, the 1,500-meter race, he was leading overall, Bie in second. Bie jumped out to a big lead on the first lap of the 1,500. On laps two and three, Thorpe patiently moved up through the pack, and the crowd stood and screamed as the two leaders entered the fourth and final lap side by side.

With less than three hundred meters to go, Thorpe kicked into a higher gear and pulled away for the gold.

"It is a complete answer to the charge that is often made that Americans specialize in athletics," James Sullivan, commissioner of the American Olympic Committee, told reporters after Thorpe's win. And, aware that snooty Europeans were annoyed that so many US athletes were the children of immigrants, Sullivan again pointed to Thorpe. "It also answers the allegation that most of our runners are of foreign parentage," he said, "for Thorpe is a real American, if there ever was one."

◂▮▸

Next it was Louis Tewanima's turn. Raised in a Hopi village in what's now northern Arizona, Tewanima had grown up running. Running to chase jackrabbits, running to fields that needed tending, running to carry messages to distant villages. As a teenager, Tewanima spoke no English and had zero interest in assimilation into white culture. The government took him anyway, forcibly sending him and a small group of Hopi young men across the country to Carlisle "virtually as prisoners of war," as Pop Warner put it.

For many young men who found themselves at Carlisle, competitive sports offered an escape from the misery of the school. But when the 110-pound Tewanima approached Warner about joining the track team, the coach was skeptical. Then he saw the man run. Tewanima quickly became one of the best distance runners in the country. And in Stockholm he proved to be among the best in the world, winning silver in the grueling 10,000-meter race.

Jim, meanwhile, spent six days recharging. He lounged in a hammock at a house the team was renting and wrote letters to Iva Miller. He told her about the pentathlon, dedicating the victory to her. He went out with teammates a few times, but wasn't able to enjoy the nightlife much.

"He had nothing," Abel Kiviat remembered, "not even a pen to sign an autograph."

Thorpe liked strolling the cobblestone streets of Stockholm—until he realized that everyone was staring at him. Native Americans were a common enough sight on the streets of American cities, but not in Europe. One group of Swedish girls actually stopped Thorpe on the sidewalk and showed him a picture of a man in what they imagined to be typical American Indian clothing. The girls spoke no English, but Thorpe gathered their meaning from gestures to his suit and hat, and the look of doubt on their faces. They didn't believe he was the real thing.

"It seemed they were disappointed," Thorpe recalled, "as I didn't wear war paint or head-feathers."

After that he mostly stayed at the house.

◀◈▶

Finally, it was time for the climactic event of the Olympic Games, the decathlon.

Held over the last three days of the Olympics, this punishing ten-event challenge included all the events in the pentathlon plus the shot put, high jump, 400-meter race, 110-meter hurdles, and pole vault. Twenty-nine of the world's top athletes entered the competition. The favorite was Sweden's Hugo Wieslander, winner of several recent decathlons in Europe.

Right before the first event—the 100-meter sprint—the skies over Stockholm turned gray, and it began to rain. Pop Warner couldn't help but flash back to Carlisle's football struggles on sloppy fields.

He was right to worry. Thorpe ran an uncharacteristically slow 100 on the wet track. In the second event, the long jump, Thorpe's foot slipped over the edge of the takeoff board as he jumped—a fault. He faulted again on his second jump. If it happened a third time, he'd finish last in the event. He'd be out of medal contention.

Warner would later admit to suffering a mild panic attack at this point.

Thorpe, as far as anyone could tell, was as cool as ever. "I had trained well and hard and had confidence in my ability," he'd later say. "I felt that I would win."

He raced down the runway, planted his foot behind the edge of the takeoff board, and leaped twenty-two feet, two and three-tenths inches. Not great by his own standards, but good enough for second place. Thorpe changed into dry clothes and took second in the shot put.

From then on it was sheer domination.

Over the next two days, under sunny skies, Thorpe won the high jump, won the 110-meter hurdles, and finished near the top in everything else.

Thorpe faced the world's best all-around athletes in Stockholm's Olympic Stadium—and beat them all.

When the starter's gun sounded for the closing 1,500-meter race, Thorpe sped into the lead. Fans watched for the moment he'd begin to fade, begin to feel fatigue from the fourteen events that had come before.

It never happened.

Thorpe cruised around the track in long, easy strides, increasing his lead with each lap, and snapping the tape for another gold.

King Gustav V (standing on podium) presents Thorpe (holding his hat) with a wreath, two gold medals, and a bronze bust of, yes, King Gustav V.

At the medal ceremony later that day, Sweden's King Gustav stood on a raised platform, handing out medals. Jim Thorpe's name was called and echoed over loudspeakers.

"There was a great burst of cheers, led by the King," reported the *New York Times*. "The immense crowd cheered itself hoarse."

Thorpe, wearing a blue suit and tie, removed his white straw hat as he stepped to the podium. King Gustav gave Thorpe his gold medals and bent forward to place a laurel wreath on Jim's head.

"Sir," the king proclaimed, "you are the greatest athlete in the world."

Thorpe said, "Thanks, King."

Then came the hard part—the celebrations.

When Jim Thorpe returned to Carlisle, the entire city shut down to greet the conquering hero. Thousands cheered his train as it rolled into the station, waving banners with slogans like "Hail to Chief Thorpe."

Everyone paraded to Dickinson College for a massive outdoor ceremony, where Thorpe and Louis Tewanima were forced to sit on a platform in the blazing sun and endure speeches—long speeches. Carlisle's Superintendent Friedman, after sharing his own thoughts with the crowd, read a congratulatory letter from President William Howard Taft.

"You have set a high standard of physical development which is only attained by right living," the 330-pound Taft wrote to Thorpe, "and your victory will serve as an incentive to all to improve those qualities which characterize the best type of American citizen."

No mention that Thorpe was not actually a citizen—it would be twelve years before Congress would pass a law extending citizenship to all American Indians.

When it was Jim's turn to speak, he stood and said, "You have shown us a splendid time, and we are grateful for it."

Then he sat down.

Louis Tewanima stood and said, "I thank you."

Then he sat down.

Olympic medalists Louis Tewanima and Jim Thorpe share a carriage—and a dislike of being on display—as they parade through downtown Carlisle.

Next it was on to New York City, where a million people lined the streets, cheering and waving flags, as America's Olympic medal winners cruised slowly past in open cars. Thorpe sat in his own car, surrounded by trophies and medals, feeling incredibly awkward. As people shouted his name, Thorpe chomped on chewing gum and pulled the brim of his hat lower over his eyes.

Afterward, reporters crowded around Thorpe and Tewanima, pressing the athletes for stories of their Swedish adventures.

Thorpe made an effort. "The fact that I was able to represent America in such a great thing as an Olympic meet will always be one of the things to which I shall point with pride all my life," he said.

Tewanima looked like he wanted to disappear. Thorpe, bighearted as always, stepped in, telling reporters, "And I believe that in everything I say I voice the sentiments of my teammate, Tewanima, here."

When it was all over, Louis Tewanima gave his track medals to Carlisle students; girls on campus used them as shoe buckles. Then he got permission to head home to the Hopi village he'd never wanted to leave in the first place.

Jim Thorpe returned to the closest thing he had to a home, the Carlisle School.

He gave Gus Welch the hat he'd doffed to King Gustav. The congratulations he cared about most arrived in a letter from Oklahoma. "I'm glad you're back," Iva Miller wrote. "I knew you'd win all the time."

◆❖◆

Football had made Jim Thorpe a star, but now he was *world* famous, acclaimed by sportswriters as "the finest all-around athlete in the world" and "the greatest all-around athlete in the history of sports." Some took it even further. "Goliath and some fabled strong men of history could hardly have competed successfully with Thorpe as an all-around athlete," declared a *New York Times* writer, "as with their great strength they lacked the further combination of speed and agility."

Promoters started showing up at Carlisle, promising Thorpe fat paydays to participate in boxing matches and wrestling tournaments. One offered him $10,000 to join a baseball exhibition tour. That last one was tempting. Jim and Iva wanted to get married, but Jim felt he first needed to earn some money. Gus Welch advised his friend to take the baseball offer.

Pop Warner tugged the other way—he wanted Thorpe back for one more football season. The promoters were just a bunch of "hustlers," he said, "with their own personal version of exploiting Jim's newfound national popularity."

What about Pop's personal version of exploiting Jim?

Didn't exist, the coach claimed; he cared only for Thorpe's best interests.

Thorpe was torn. He'd missed so much school that he was nowhere near graduating, so he wouldn't be returning for the degree. Besides, another year of classes and rules was hard to face. So was another year of being broke. But football was his favorite sport. And he liked and trusted Warner, and felt tremendously loyal to the team.

What helped to tip the scales was the 1912 football schedule. It was deadly, as always, but one late-season game stood out. After the previous year's loss to Carlisle, Harvard had declined to schedule the Indians again. Pop Warner, looking for another big-time opponent, had agreed that on November 9, 1912, Carlisle would visit West Point to play Army.

It was a game bursting with meaning for Thorpe and his teammates. The win over Harvard had been an athletic triumph. With Army, it was personal.

◆❦◆

Dwight Eisenhower was just hoping to get on the field.

Eisenhower would one day lead Allied forces in Europe in World War II and serve as president of the United States. But in the summer of 1912, the twenty-one-year-old had less lofty dreams. He just wanted to make the Army football team.

Dwight Eisenhower as a West Point cadet.

Eisenhower—Ike, as friends called him—had played high school ball in his hometown of Abilene, Kansas, and tried out for the Army team in 1911, his first year as a cadet at the West Point Military Academy. He was too light, coaches told him. His feet were too slow.

For the next twelve months, Ike shoved down extra portions of food. Spare moments between classes and drills were spent in the gym and on the track. Hoping to improve his quickness, he'd crouch like a sprinter about to begin a race and practice exploding forward again and again.

When head football coach Ernest Graves started team workouts in the late summer of 1912, Ike was there, waiting for his chance. Finally, near the end of a scrimmage, Graves sent him in. The kid had put on about twenty pounds of muscle, the coach saw, and had a quicker first step. But what really impressed Graves was Ike's relentless hustle, the way he played through the whistle on every snap. Coaches talk about wanting players who have a "motor"—Ike was not a gifted athlete, but he had a serious motor.

After practice, as everyone else headed for the showers, Ike tossed down his leather helmet and started jogging laps around the football field. He heard someone yell, "Eisenhower!"

He stopped and turned. Coach Graves was standing about twenty yards away. Ike ran to the coach and saluted, saying "Yessir!"

Graves asked, "Where did you get those pants?"

They were two sizes too big, and Ike had to keep yanking them up. They were what the equipment manager had given him; he didn't rate any better.

"Look at those shoes," Graves said, pointing to Ike's mangy cleats. "Can't you get anything better than that?"

"I'm wearing what I was issued."

The manager was standing nearby. Graves told him, "Get this man completely outfitted with new and properly fitting equipment."

That's when Eisenhower knew he'd made the team. Army was on a collision course with the Carlisle Indians, and Ike would be there for the impact.

"**Keep your eye on him this year,**" Pop Warner told reporters one day at practice, gesturing to his star player. "He's going to captain the team again, and I have a vague suspicion that he's going to be worth the price of admission."

That's what you call an understatement. In 1912 Jim Thorpe would treat football fans to a display of brilliance the sport had never seen.

In an early game with Dickinson College, Thorpe was back to punt, twelve yards behind the line of scrimmage. He called for the snap, and it came—and sailed over his head and skipped toward Carlisle's end zone. Thorpe turned to chase the still-rolling ball as Dickinson defenders broke through the line.

Pop Warner screamed for Thorpe to fall on the loose ball. This would give Dickinson great field position, but would at least prevent the added disaster of a Dickinson player picking up the fumble and running for a score.

Thorpe ignored his coach. He snatched the ball cleanly off the grass. Turning to see six defenders closing in, Thorpe sprinted toward the sidelines, hopping over outstretched arms, then turned upfield and faked out some tacklers, stiff-armed a few more to the turf, and went all the way for the score.

The headline of Dickinson's school paper read: WORLD'S GREATEST ATHLETE—PLUS TEN OTHER PARTS OF A POWERFUL MACHINE—DEFEAT US.

Football had come a long way from the shoving matches Pop Warner learned at Cornell. And, as the Carlisle team had shown the nation, a faster, more open game was somewhat safer—and a lot more entertaining. With this in mind, football's rule makers introduced another slew of changes for the 1912 season. The playing field was shortened to one hundred yards, and teams would have four downs to get a first down. Penalties for incomplete passes were scrapped, and ten-yard end zones were added to each end of the field to allow for touchdown passes, which previously had not been permitted. The value of a touchdown was increased to six points; seven with an extra-point kick.

The goal was to increase scoring. The Carlisle Indians were built to score.

Opposing defenses got used to chasing Carlisle players all over the field.

The greatest backfield in football. From left to right: Alex Arcasa, Stancil "Possum" Powell, Gus Welch, and Jim Thorpe.

Carlisle averaged an eye-popping forty-nine points a game through the first month of the season, and once again Pop Warner was having championship dreams. His entire 1911 backfield was back: Thorpe, the speedy Alex Arcasa, the power back Possum Powell, and, at quarterback, class president Gus Welch. He added promising youngsters like Joe Guyon, a nineteen-year-old Chippewa from Minnesota, who helped solidify the line, and Pete Calac, a Mission Indian from California, also nineteen. For these newcomers, it was both thrilling and intimidating to suddenly be playing alongside Jim Thorpe.

"He was my idol!" Pete Calac remembered. "Actually, he was the idol of every Indian boy." Thorpe didn't play the idol, though. "Jim never acted like he was better than any of us, in spite of his great fame," said Calac. "He always tried to be just one of the guys."

And Thorpe *was* just one of the guys. He also happened to be the best athlete on the planet.

Everywhere Thorpe went that season, crowds followed. In Harrisburg, before a Wednesday afternoon game with Villanova, the start was briefly postponed when a singer named Belle Story ran onto the field to offer Thorpe her treasured rabbit's foot.

"It brought me lots of good luck," she said, "and I know it will bring you luck, too."

Thorpe smiled. He took the paw. The game began. By halftime Carlisle was up 58–0.

Story told a reporter, "See, that's the rabbit's paw."

After the game, hundreds of children raced from the stands and surrounded Thorpe. As always, he took the time to shake hands and sign autographs.

◆

Just three days after Villanova, a scrappy Washington & Jefferson College team gave Carlisle a major scare. Right from the opening kickoff, Warner's team was a step slow, a beat out of sync.

This was Carlisle's third football game in just eight days—a schedule Warner, looking to maximize profits, had constructed. But he preferred to blame Gus Welch, saying, "The team's play-calling of fancy end runs and daring passes sapped them of their energy in the hot weather."

Carlisle moved the ball all day but fumbled it away several times, including once on the Washington & Jefferson one-yard line. Jim Thorpe missed three field goals. His long punts and four interceptions kept the opponents off the scoreboard, and the game ended in an ugly 0–0 tie.

Warner fumed over what he saw as a dangerous letdown in intensity. He knew all too well what a single loss could do to a team's chances of finishing #1. A tie wasn't disastrous; they'd dodged a bullet. But the whole team headed home in a foul mood.

In Pittsburgh, with a few hours to kill between trains, several of the players walked to a bar near the station. Thorpe and Welch sat together with glasses of beer. Welch soon left to join the team for dinner, but Thorpe stayed and drank, brooding over his missed kicks.

He was still at the bar a couple hours later. Warner found him there and told him the train was about to leave. Thorpe wouldn't budge. He and Warner exchanged angry words. Thorpe finally got up and wobbled out the door, but he and the coach continued shouting at each other in the street. A crowd gathered to watch. Several players jumped in and pulled Thorpe into the lobby of a nearby hotel. They guided him out the back door and onto the train.

It was a minor incident. Jim Thorpe's fame made it major.

THORPE AND WARNER IN FIGHT AFTER GAME, read one newspaper headline the next morning.

According to the press's embellished version, Thorpe and Warner had gotten into a furious fistfight, and Warner had decked his drunken halfback. Thorpe, wrote the *New York World*, was now "nursing a few bruises he didn't get in Saturday's game."

Exaggeration or not, it was a huge embarrassment for everyone involved.

"Thorpe, you've got to behave yourself," Pop said, showing Jim the articles. "You owe it to the public as well as your school. The Olympic Games made you into a public figure, and you've got to shoulder the responsibility."

The next day, at practice, Thorpe asked the team to gather around. He apologized and promised to stay focused the rest of the year.

At West Point, Dwight Eisenhower was not making any headlines. But he was at least getting some playing time.

Coach Graves put Eisenhower at left halfback on offense and linebacker on defense, the same positions as Jim Thorpe. Ike was slated as a second-stringer, but he moved up when the starter hurt his knee. And he quickly won over coaches and fans with his bruising, no-nonsense runs. He couldn't speed around defenders, but often dragged them several yards before going down himself, and after Army's 19–0 victory over

Though not the most gifted athlete, Dwight Eisenhower impressed coaches with his hard work and determination to improve.

Rutgers, a *New York Times* article called Ike "one of the most promising backs in Eastern football."

"Ike was the first cadet on the field for football practice and the very last to leave," remembered the equipment manager who'd given Eisenhower his first uniform. After practice, he'd stay out on the field and work on his punting. The manager wasn't thrilled about that part. "I used to curse him because he would practice so late that I would be collecting footballs he had kicked away in the darkness."

On October 12, the day Army beat Rutgers, Carlisle played in Syracuse. Pop Warner paced the sidelines of Archbold Stadium, watching his recurring nightmare.

It was another rainy day. Another muddy field. Another slow and sloppy game. Play was stopped often so players could rinse grime from their eyes with wet sponges. At the half, there was no score.

This Syracuse team had ruined Carlisle's perfect season the year before, and Warner had been hoping to pay them back. He berated the team in the locker room, ripping into Gus Welch for calling too many finesse plays. Then he turned his wrath on Jim Thorpe.

"Where's your sense, Jim?" Warner screamed. "Don't you see that speed isn't getting you anything on this slippery ground? For heaven's sake, use your weight!"

The whole team came out of the locker room angry. Syracuse paid the price. Battering the defense with power runs up the middle, Carlisle scored three touchdowns in the first seven minutes of the third quarter. The final score was 33–0. Only Thorpe was disappointed. "Had the field not been soft and soggy, I surely believe we would have run up a higher score," he told reporters after the game.

Next week it was Carlisle's opponent, Pittsburgh, looking for payback. Still stinging from the lashing Carlisle had given them the year before, one Pitt official vowed to turn the tables. "Thorpe will never run through us," he announced. "We've got him figured."

That's what coaches call "bulletin board material"—worthy of hanging in the locker room to fire up the team. Thorpe saw it. The whole team saw it. "We did everything we could to help him break loose and get out in the open," Pete Calac later said.

They didn't need to do much. Early in the game, Thorpe caught a short

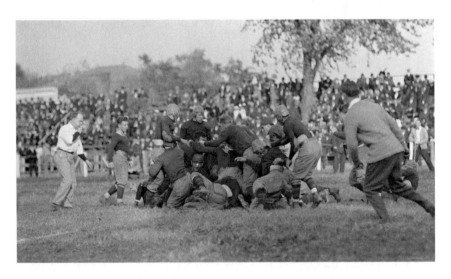

An old-fashioned pile-up at the Carlisle-Georgetown game.

Carlisle's whirlwind offense seems to have left these Georgetown fans in a state of shock.

pass and bowled over the entire defense on his way to a long touchdown. On other plays, he simply outran everyone. Thorpe rushed for 266 yards and scored 32 points on the way to Carlisle's 45–8 win.

So much for Pittsburgh's revenge.

A week later, so many football fans drove to Georgetown that the city of Washington, DC, experienced a problem new to cities—there was absolutely nowhere to park. Policemen stood in the street vainly trying to break the gridlock. "It was worth one's life to attempt to get through the line of automobiles," reported the *Washington Post*.

The Georgetown team had spent the past two weeks prepping for Carlisle's offense. They came in expecting to win.

"Break up that interference!" fans shouted.

"Get Thorpe!"

"Hold 'em, Georgetown!"

They couldn't hold 'em.

Thorpe broke free for long gains, Alex Arcasa powered it over the middle, and cheers turned to groans, and then silence, as Carlisle jumped to a 34–0 lead. The Georgetown players "had not been called upon to face such a whirlwind attack this season," noted the *Washington Herald*; "they were bewildered, shocked, and stunned."

Instead of heading home from DC, the Carlisle Indians got on yet another train and hurried to Canada for a Monday matchup with the University of Toronto rugby club. This was an unabashed money-grab by Warner, who knew his team could sell tickets anywhere—even in a country that didn't play football.

And the crowd in Toronto was huge, if slightly confused. In the first half, played under American football rules, Thorpe scored at will, opening up a 44–0 lead. As fans chanted his name, he walked to the sidelines, bowed stiffly, and smiled.

The second half was played with rugby rules, allowing Toronto to cut into the deficit. Kind of. The game ended 49–1.

Yet again, an undefeated season was coming into view.

A s the games got bigger, Pop Warner ramped up the intensity on the practice field—and the security around it.

Knowing that upcoming opponents would try anything to get a glimpse at Carlisle's latest innovations, that any innocent-looking visitor could really be an undercover scout, the coach hired guards to patrol the edges of Indian Field. As the guards watched for spies, Warner continued to tinker with a new formation he'd been sketching in his mind.

Teams started every play the same way, with the quarterback standing behind the center, and three backs lined up behind the quarterback. Warner's game-changing twist, the "single wing," was to spread things out by shifting one of the backs over to the edge of the offensive line. The ball was snapped shotgun-style to any of the other backs—often right to Jim Thorpe—and from that point he could run, hand off, or pass, based on what he saw the defense doing. The variations were endless, but the idea was simple: give Carlisle's playmakers more ways to make plays.

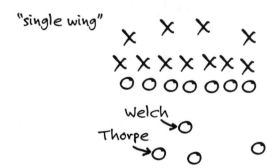

It was a system that required precision and timing and hours of practice. The team finally began to master the single-wing partway through the season, but hadn't yet used it in a game. Given how closely they were watched by scouts, Pop and the team knew they could truly shock only one opponent with the formation. The question was: when to spring the surprise?

Their next game was against a very good Lehigh team that was coming off an impressive win over Navy. Two weeks after that they'd be in Philadelphia to play their oldest rival, Penn. But in between those two was the game the team had been pointing to all year, the one players wanted to win more than any they'd ever played.

"Which team do you boys want to use this new formation on first?" Warner asked the players.

Several shouted at once, "The soldiers!"

The soldiers were getting ready, too.

Earlier that year, at the West Point officers club, someone had asked Coach Ernest "Pot" Graves why he stuck to his old-school, smash-mouth style of football—power running and physical defense. Graves pointed out the window at a steamroller in the street below.

"There is my idea of football," he said.

"Pot was a supreme proponent of designed butchery," one Army lineman remembered. "And he was right. Football is not a game. You can't get anywhere in it by going out and exuding an aroma of good fellowship." Players bought in, or they didn't play.

"I want to see blood!" Graves would yell to his linemen at practice.

Midway through the season, Army had the best defense in the country, led by its first-team All-American lineman, the six-four, 225-pound Leland Devore. "They are a wall of bone and muscle, and they have grit enough for a regiment," wrote the *Washington Herald*. "The charging of the West Point line is a spectacle in itself."

Next up for Army was Holy Cross—until current events intervened. A few days before the game, US Vice President James Sherman died suddenly. Out of respect for Sherman, West Point officials canceled the November 2 game. President Taft, incidentally, may have wished he could cancel the 1912 presidential election, set for November 5. With no time to pick a new running mate, Taft was in the awkward position of running on a ticket with a dead man. He lost to Woodrow Wilson.

Coach Graves made the most of the week off. While players healed from previous games, Graves prepped his team for the Carlisle whirlwind.

"Our coaches told us that these people are tricky," Dwight Eisenhower remembered. "They are very tricky players. And you people got to be on your mettle or you're going to be surprised."

⚬

Carlisle's November 2 game against Lehigh went ahead as scheduled. Early on, it was too close for comfort.

As Pop Warner paced the sidelines, Lehigh's All-American quarterback, Vince Pazzetti, led his team all the way to the Carlisle three. On the next play, Pazzetti took the snap and scrambled, looking for an open man. Spotting a receiver, he fired the ball. Jim Thorpe knifed in front and picked it off five yards deep in the crowded end zone.

The safe play was to take a knee—the touchback would give Carlisle the ball at its own twenty. Thorpe did not play it safe.

"He started weaving his way out of that mass of players," remembered one stunned Lehigh fan. "It seemed impossible that he could get through, but the next thing anybody knew, Jim was on the twenty-yard line headed for a touchdown." When Pazzetti, Lehigh's fastest man, gave chase, Thorpe waved with the back of his hand and accelerated so quickly it looked to fans like Pazzetti was nailed to the ground.

With a comfortable lead by halftime, the Carlisle team spent the break out on the field, goofing around and laughing. Teams take on the personality of their leaders, and Jim Thorpe was, at heart, a big kid. On campus, he'd wrestle other students just for the joy of messing up their uniform. In the dining hall, when everyone stood with their hands behind their backs, he'd sneak up behind an unsuspecting victim's open palm and drop in a squishy prune or a scorching potato. The press always depicted Thorpe as serious and shy, but friends saw a different side of him. "Introverted is not the way I knew him," Albert Exendine once told an interviewer. "In comparison with whites, he might have been. But whites like to talk a lot."

In the second half, the team's fun-loving approach spilled over into the game. Gus Welch stood at the line before one play and shouted, loud enough for the defense to hear, "What about going around right end this time?"

And Carlisle ran the ball around the right end.

They lined up again, and Thorpe called out, "How about through left tackle this time?"

And they ran behind the left tackle.

Lehigh caught on, but still couldn't stop the drive. By the time Carlisle neared the Lehigh goal line, both teams were cracking up. As Carlisle bashed in for another score, lineman William Garlow entertained the defense with his running commentary. "Gentlemen, this hurts me as much as it does you, but I'm afraid the ball is over. We regret it, I am sure you regret it, and I hope nothing happening here will spoil what for us has been a very pleasant afternoon."

Fans in the stands, who couldn't hear Garlow, had no idea why players who'd just surrendered a touchdown were doubled over with laughter.

❖

Then the joking stopped. It was time to prepare for Army.

For years the government had avoided pitting these two schools against each other. "When Indian outbreaks in the West were frequent," explained the *New York Times*, "government officials thought it unwise to have the aborigines and future officers combat in athletics."

Now soldiers were no longer fighting Native Americans in the West. Did the Carlisle players think that by beating Army they could reverse the results of those bloody wars? Of course not. Did they think a few touchdowns could right the wrongs of history? Not a chance.

But to Jim Thorpe, Gus Welch, and the entire team, the Army game mattered. It mattered a lot.

Pop Warner thought he knew why. "It was not that they felt any definite bitterness against the conquering white, or against the government for years of unfair treatment," Warner later said. "But rather they believed the armed contests between the red man and the white man had never been waged on equal terms." That's what made the Army game so much *more* than a game. "On the athletic field," Warner said, "where the struggle was man-to-man, they felt that the Indian had his first even break."

It's hard to know if Pop had this exactly right. Is it humanly possible for the players to have felt *no* bitterness? Isn't it conceivable that Thorpe and the team were looking for a bit of symbolic revenge?

The players never spoke about it, at least not on the record. But they knew how much pride Native Americans all over the country took in their success. They knew copies of the Carlisle school paper, with accounts of their games, were passed from hand to hand on reservations. All this created enormous pressure to make the most of the opportunity against Army.

And even if the players *had* wanted to treat the game like any other late-season showdown, the press wouldn't have let them. As game day approached, newspapers described the coming contest as if the previous century's wars were about to reignite, and all the old prejudices and stereotypes came flowing out.

A *New York Times* headline declared: INDIANS TO BATTLE WITH SOLDIERS.

The *Philadelphia Inquirer*: INDIAN ATTACK FEARED.

The *Brooklyn Eagle*: INDIANS OUT TO SCALP THE CADETS.

◆◆◆

All week Warner woke the team early to exercise on the track before class. At afternoon practice, they ran new plays over and over until after dark, Warner barking all the while, demanding perfection.

The Carlisle-Army game was so heavily anticipated that even these workout sessions made the news. "Coach Warner fully appreciates the hard task that will fall to the Indians' lot on Saturday," reported the *Washington*

*Post*. "He has prepared several spectacular football evolutions." A *Scranton Republican* reporter informed readers that Gus Welch and Possum Powell both had "leg sprains" from previous games, but were ready to go. "Captain Thorpe," added the paper, "barely feels his bruises."

The big news at West Point was that team leader Leland Devore's knee had fully recovered from an early-season injury. The whole team was healthy and confident. "The soldiers expect to make an even battle against the Indians," wrote one reporter after visiting West Point. "The Army feels that once Thorpe is stopped, there is a chance for victory."

That was the question: *could* Thorpe be stopped?

Some writers thought so. "Carlisle may have a good team, equipped with all the tricks known to a crafty coach," pronounced the *Washington Times*, "but the Army relies on hard tackling, speedy running, and that never-say-die spirit characteristic of all Army elevens. Who will pick the Indians?"

On Friday afternoon the Carlisle players met on Indian Field for one last full-speed run-through of their game plan. Reporters tried to elicit predictions from the team, with no luck. "Neither Warner nor Captain Thorpe cared to express an opinion as to the possible outcome of the game," wrote the *New York Times*.

Actually, Captain Thorpe did have an opinion, just not one he wished to make public.

"We were confident that we were a high-rolling team," he'd later say, "and would give the cadets a very bad afternoon indeed."

Built as a fort during the American Revolution, West Point sits on high ground above a bend in the Hudson River, about fifty miles north of New York City. This was such a strategically vital spot in the war with Britain that George Washington called it "the key to America." It was at West Point that Benedict Arnold betrayed his country in 1779, trying to turn the fort over to the British. After the fort became a military academy in the early 1800s, it was here that Ulysses S. Grant, William Tecumseh Sherman, Robert E. Lee, George Armstrong Custer—all the famed generals of the Civil War and Indian Wars—learned to be soldiers.

On November 9, 1912, the sky above West Point was low and stone gray. The air was cold and wet, with temperatures in the mid-thirties, and a steady breeze blowing off the Hudson. The season's last brown leaves clung to mostly bare branches on the forested hills above campus.

As the three o'clock kickoff approached, fans streamed off trains at the nearby station and poured from boats at the waterfront. Sportswriters from major papers all over the East, pencils and notebooks ready, took their places in the filling grandstands of Army Field. Hundreds of cadets paraded into the stadium, their long capes blowing in the wind.

In the Army locker room, slogans on the blackboard reminded players of Coach Graves's keys to victory:

"Carry the fight to the opponent and keep it there all afternoon."

"The team that makes the fewer mistakes wins."

The 1912 Army team, including Dwight Eisenhower (third from left) and Omar Bradley (far right). These two men would later help lead American forces in World War II.

In the visitors' locker room, the Carlisle players sat on long wooden benches, pulling on their dark red game jerseys, lacing up black cleats. Pop Warner lit a cigarette and asked the team to gather around. The players stood. Some stepped onto benches for a better view. Pacing between players, Warner launched into an uncharacteristically emotional appeal.

"I shouldn't have to prepare you for this game," he began. "Just go read your history books."

These men knew their history, and not from books. Their families had lived it. If there ever was a game that required no pep talk, this was it. But Pop was on a roll.

"Remember," he continued, "that it was the fathers and grandfathers of these Army players who fought your fathers and grandfathers in the Indian Wars. Remember it was their fathers and grandfathers who killed your fathers and grandfathers." And in a voice rising to a roar: "Remember all of this on every play! Let's go!"

The Carlisle players charged onto the field and began warming up. Moments later Army ran out in their uniforms of black and gold.

As had so often been the case since Carlisle's first games in the 1890s, the size difference was immediately striking. Army players were, on average, a few inches taller than the Indians, about twenty-five pounds heavier. Leland Devore thought the visitors looked intimidated.

Some were. "I didn't think we had a chance against Army," Pete Calac later admitted. "They were very big, much bigger than we were."

Thorpe's face revealed nothing. He was silent and focused, kicking field goals and throwing long spirals to teammates. Warner knew he'd be relying on his star today, even more than usual. "He was primed for that battle," the coach recalled. "He and I had planned it ever since our trip to Stockholm."

A cannon fired, and fans cheered as Thorpe and Devore met at midfield. The captains shook hands. Thorpe won the coin toss and elected to receive. Strapping on his leather helmet, he lined up near the Carlisle end zone.

The kickoff sailed right to Thorpe, and the adrenaline may have been pumping harder than he was letting on—he bobbled the ball and it fell to the grass. He snatched it up and took it to the Carlisle twenty-eight.

Gus Welch lined the team up in the standard formation. Then, before taking the snap, he barked another signal, and Thorpe motioned out to the left edge of the offensive line. They were going to hit Army with the new formation right away.

Welch caught the snap from center. The defense keyed on Thorpe, but Gus pitched it to Alex Arcasa, who sped around the right end for a gain of fifteen.

The second play started out with another pitch to Arcasa heading left. This time the defense followed Arcasa, who flipped it to Thorpe heading right for another gain of fifteen.

Pop looked on like a proud father. "The cadets had never seen such a formation—or anything similar to it," he remembered. Yet again, Carlisle was changing everything.

The confusion on the faces of defenders was visible from the stands.

"The shifting, puzzling, and dazzling attack of the Carlisle Indians had the cadets bordering on panic," wrote the *New York Tribune*. "None of the Army men seemed to know just where the ball was going or who had it."

Dwight Eisenhower and the other Army defenders tried to stay focused on what they'd talked about all week—the idea was to hit Thorpe, early and often. When Thorpe broke free for another long run, Eisenhower and fellow linebacker Charles Benedict slammed into him at the Army fifteen. The ball came loose as all three men crashed to the ground. An Army player covered the fumble. The crowd roared—"it was a crowd made up almost entirely of West Point sympathizers," noted the *New York Times*.

Ike and Benedict popped up. Thorpe stayed on the turf. He reached for his right shoulder.

Warner sprinted onto the field. Kneeling, he ran his hand over Jim's collarbone, and was relieved to feel no fracture.

The ref told Warner he needed to get the injured man off the field so play could resume.

Leland Devore, who'd come over to have a look, said, "Hell's bells, Mr. Referee. We don't stand on technicalities at West Point. Give him all the time he wants."

Devore may have meant this as a courtesy, but to Thorpe's ears it sounded like pity—or worse, gloating. Thorpe pushed himself up. He stayed in the game.

The defense held Army, forcing a punt. Carlisle then drove to the Army one-yard line, but lost the ball on a fourth-down pass that fell incomplete. Carlisle forced another punt and again got down inside the Army five. Again, Welch chose to go for the touchdown on fourth down.

Again, Army's vaunted line stuffed Carlisle inches short of the end zone.

The first quarter ended with no score. Carlisle was dominating, with nothing to show for it.

Army got rolling in the second quarter, helped along by a major penalty. Possum Powell, who'd been taking shots from Army's Charles Herrick, finally responded by punching Herrick. The ref tossed Powell for slugging.

Warner charged onto the field, protesting the call. To no avail; Carlisle's starting fullback was done, and the penalty moved the ball all the way to the Carlisle thirty-two.

It was exactly the break the opportunistic Army team needed. Eisenhower, Leland Hobbs, and Geoffrey Keyes took turns powering it down to the Carlisle goal line. On third down, Ike threw a key block, and Hobbs went in for the score. Cannons blasted in celebration behind the south end zone.

The extra-point try went wide. The scoreboard read Army 6, Carlisle 0.

In what everyone expected to be a low-scoring game, those points looked huge.

Carlisle needed to answer, but on their next drive they were stopped deep in their own end. Thorpe dropped back to punt. This was a dangerous moment for Carlisle. Army had the momentum, and with good field position could seize control of the game. Thorpe caught the snap from center, stepped forward, and boomed a high spiral that flew seventy yards. The ball sailed over the punt returner's head and bounced even deeper into Army territory.

Just like that, the momentum flipped again. Carlisle's fired-up defense quickly forced Army to punt.

"Then Mr. Thorpe got into action," wrote the *New York Sun*. If Thorpe's right shoulder was still hurting, no one could tell. "He twisted this way and that, shook off Army tacklers and promenaded down the field." From the Army six, Gus Welch slipped the ball to the stout Joe Bergie, who the defense assumed was in the game as a blocker. Bergie muscled it up the middle for the touchdown. Thorpe added the point after. The crowd went quiet.

Carlisle 7, Army 6.

On the Army bench, backup center Omar Bradley heard teammates saying, "Thorpe runs too fast. We can't keep up with him."

The Carlisle defense pinned Army deep again and forced another fourth and long. Now it was Carlisle that could grab control with a score. Army's punter kicked it high, giving his coverage team time to surround the most dangerous open-field runner in the sport. The ball came down in Thorpe's arms near midfield.

"His catch and his start were but one motion," wrote an amazed *New York Times* reporter. "In and out, zigzagging first to one side and then to the other, while flying cadets went hurling through space, Thorpe wormed his way through the entire Army team. Every cadet in the game had his chance, and every one of them failed."

By the time Thorpe crossed the goal line, the West Point crowd was on its feet, cheering him on. Thorpe's teammates ran up to celebrate with him—then noticed a referee waving his arms. He'd thrown his penalty flag way back where Thorpe had caught the punt.

Holding, on the receiving team. The spectacular return was called back.

The first half ended with Carlisle up by one, 7–6.

Gus Welch would forever refer to the Army game as "the rattling of the bones." Both teams walked to their locker rooms feeling the pain.

Dwight Eisenhower would never forget the experience. "I was thoroughly enjoying the challenge that Jim was presenting," he later said. "On the football field, there was no one like him in the world." But as much as Ike admired Thorpe, the point was to win the game. Army's strategy was to gradually wear down the smaller Carlisle team. That might still work. It wouldn't matter, though, if they couldn't stop Thorpe.

And by halftime, it was pretty obvious they couldn't stop Thorpe. In the locker room, Eisenhower and Leland Hobbs made plans to hit the Carlisle star high and low at the same time from different directions. The objective now was to knock Jim Thorpe out of the game.

The day's cold gray light was already beginning to fade when Carlisle kicked off to start the second half.

Army got the ball first but was quickly forced to punt.

On Carlisle's first offensive play, Welch pitched it to Thorpe, and the Army defense gave chase, determined not to let Thorpe beat them. Thorpe let the defenders get close, then threw it downfield for a long gain. Welch then mixed runs and passes, keeping the defense on its heels. Eisenhower and Hobbs shadowed Thorpe but couldn't get a solid hit on him.

Even more frustrating was that Carlisle's smaller linemen were consistently gouging holes in Army's massive line. "The West Pointers were smeared in every scrimmage," wrote the *New York Sun*, "and the ball advanced from five to fifteen yards at a clip."

For all Carlisle's athleticism, their most powerful weapon was teamwork. "We played as one perfect, moving unit," Thorpe later said. He set the tone by selflessly playing the decoy on some plays, blocking for teammates on others. He didn't care who got the credit, or who took it over the goal line. Early in the third quarter, Thorpe and Joe Guyon plowed into big Leland Devore, sealing the edge of the Army line, allowing Alex Arcasa to run untouched into the end zone.

Thorpe added the kick. Carlisle 14, Army 6.

Devore was fuming at this point. On the ensuing kickoff, he blindsided Guyon away from the ball, knocking him nearly unconscious. The crowd hissed Devore. The ref threw him out. With the game still in the balance, Army's best player trudged to the bench.

The ball was punted back and forth. Late in the quarter, Carlisle took over at its own twenty-five.

"We knew Thorpe would take it on the next play," Eisenhower remembered of this pivotal moment, "and we knew he'd come through the line because the line had never stopped him before." Ike's team was not built to play from behind; Army didn't have the offensive firepower to erase big deficits. They could not allow any more points.

As Thorpe broke through the line, Ike launched himself like a missile at Jim's chest. At the exact same moment, Leland Hobbs drove his lowered shoulder into Jim's knees. The crack of the collision was audible in the stands. Then silence.

Eisenhower and Hobbs got up. "We were sure we'd laid him out for good," Ike recalled.

He was stunned to see Thorpe push himself up and join his teammates in the huddle.

"Even then we weren't worried," Ike said, "because we were sure we'd ruined him for the rest of the day."

Gus Welch could see exactly what was going on. He gave it to Thorpe again.

Again Ike and Hobbs charged at the runner from different angles and left their feet for maximum impact. This time, Thorpe went from sprint to stop in a single step—and the defenders collided midair. Thorpe continued downfield for a big gain.

"When we got up, we staggered a little," Eisenhower recalled.

He limped to the sidelines and dropped onto the bench beside Omar Bradley. Three decades later, these two men would help lead the Allies to victory in World War II.

But on this day, there was nothing more to be done.

In the fourth quarter, Thorpe bulled over exhausted defenders one play, swerved around them the next. "More than once," wrote the *New York Tribune*, "it took a half a dozen men to drag him to earth." Thorpe carried it twenty-four times on the day for nearly two hundred yards. "He simply ran wild," was how the *Times* described Jim's domination. "It was like trying to clutch a shadow."

Alex Arcasa scored again with just eleven minutes to play, giving Carlisle an insurmountable lead.

The game's last highlight provided a welcome bit of comic relief. Under a darkening sky in the unlit stadium, Army was forced to punt from its own end zone. The Army punter accidentally booted the ball into his own goalpost, which was planted at the goal line—the posts weren't moved to the back of the end zone until 1974. The ball bounced off the post, spun out to the ten, and was covered there by Carlisle. Arcasa scored his third touchdown a few plays later.

Final: Carlisle 27, Army 6.

"The cadets had been shown up as no other West Point team has been in many years," wrote the *New York Times*.

It was a crushing loss for Army, but the players were good sports about it. They surrounded Jim Thorpe, each taking a turn to shake his hand. Thorpe and Eisenhower walked together to the locker rooms. Ike remembered Jim as "very quiet and kind."

In the Army locker room, reporters approached Leland Devore. The Army star appeared shocked, dejected, and, when asked about Jim Thorpe, somewhat in awe. "That Indian is the greatest player I have ever stacked up against," Devore said. "He is superhuman, that's all. There is no stopping him."

# LAST GAMES

**T**he movie ends right there.

The Hollywood version of the Carlisle story—if there was one—would end in the fading light at West Point, with Jim Thorpe and Dwight Eisenhower walking off the field side by side.

Then credits roll as the victorious Carlisle players walk out of the locker room, showered, hair combed, in their blue school uniforms. They get on the train and there, finally away from reporters and crowds, the celebration erupts. Thorpe and Welch and the rest of the players gather in the aisles, shouting and laughing and reenacting plays from their historic victory.

And as the credits end, there's one last little scene. Walter Camp, the sportswriter and former Yale coach, walks through the train car. Camp stops to congratulate the Carlisle team, but his football philosophy is old-school, conservative, and he can't help but nitpick. For instance, why did Carlisle keep going for it on fourth down inside the Army five? Why not kick short field goals and put points on the board?

"At Yale we don't play that kind of ball," Camp lectures. "Your quarterback should have used Thorpe's kicking ability."

"Mr. Camp," one of the players says, "we wanted *touchdowns*."

Camp has another criticism of Gus Welch. "Your quarterback calls plays too fast. He doesn't study the defense."

Jim Thorpe jumps in. "Mr. Camp, how can Gus study the defense when there isn't any defense?"

The entire car explodes into laughter. Even Camp cracks a smile.

We see the exterior of the train as it clatters and rolls through the night.

Fade out.

◄█►

All of the above is true—but this is not a Hollywood movie. The story isn't over.

Back on campus, Pop Warner gave the players one day to savor their victory over Army and all it meant to their fellow Carlisle students, and to Native Americans everywhere. One day to revel in headlines like the *New York Times*'s THORPE'S INDIANS CRUSH WEST POINT.

On Monday it was back to work.

Warner drilled the players hard all week. He lectured them at the blackboard after dark. Everyone was emotionally drained from the Army win, physically sapped from eleven football games, thousands of miles of travel, and nearly thirty nights on the road. But the coach kept them focused on their last major challenge of the season—the first Big Four team they'd ever played, the first they'd ever beaten, the University of Pennsylvania.

The *Philadelphia Inquirer* set the scene at Franklin Field that Saturday: "It was 2:25 pm when the Indians, looking the part of the best football team in America, with the world's greatest athlete, their captain, Jim Thorpe, at their head, came running on the field."

The crowd hailed Thorpe and the visiting team. Fans had seen so many classic showdowns between Carlisle and Penn. They were hoping for one more.

Just three plays into the game, with Carlisle facing a third and long, the snap sailed over Alex Arcasa's head and bounced into the end zone. Arcasa ran back and lunged for the ball, but a Penn lineman knocked it free, and another fell on it for a touchdown.

The sloppy mistakes kept coming. Two more Carlisle fumbles led to two more Penn touchdowns. With a minute left in the half, Penn was up 20–6. Jim Thorpe tightened things up with an eighty-yard run through the entire defense. The score at halftime was Penn 20, Carlisle 13.

Warner threw an absolute tantrum in the locker room. It seemed to help. Carlisle dominated the third quarter, with Thorpe in on almost every play on both sides of the ball. At the end of three quarters, it was Carlisle 26, Penn 20.

But the furious comeback—and everything that had come before—took its toll. With one twelve-minute quarter standing between Carlisle and its dream season, Jim Thorpe could see that his teammates were simply out of gas. Thorpe put the team on his back and tried to carry his friends home. "He was fatigued to a degree that in most men would mean submission," one writer described, "yet he would gather all of himself together each time and hurl it at that rival phalanx."

Penn ground out gains with power runs, then tried a long pass. Thorpe backpedaled into pass coverage, shadowing the receiver down the field. He saw the quarterback heave it high and far and could tell the ball was overthrown. He slowed up, and the receiver sped past—and under the ball to make the catch. Thorpe spun and leaped on the Penn player's back. They staggered together into the end zone.

With six minutes to go, the score was Penn 27, Carlisle 26.

When Carlisle got the ball back, the Penn defenders knew exactly what was coming.

"Penn played and waited for Thorpe," reported the *Philadelphia Inquirer.* "The great Indian was invariably smothered by Quaker tacklers in the closing minutes." After catching a short pass near the sideline, Thorpe was hit hard and the ball came loose. Penn fell on it. The fans went wild, leaping onto their seats and watching the rest of the game from there.

The crowd rushed the field as time expired. Penn players and fans sought out Thorpe, but for the first time in his life, Jim shoved away outstretched hands. For the first time, he couldn't wait to get off the field.

The locker room was a different kind of torture. Warner was in there, venting.

Thorpe collapsed onto a bench. The coach prowled over and ripped into Thorpe for allowing the long touchdown pass to go over his head.

"I never thought the receiver had any chance to reach the ball," Thorpe said glumly.

Warner exploded with fury, blaming Jim for being careless, blaming the team for wearing down, blaming everyone—but himself—for throwing away everything they'd worked for.

Thorpe sat in front of his locker, staring at nothing that anyone else could see.

⁂

Ten days later the Carlisle Indians were in Worcester, Massachusetts, preparing for their final game of the season, a Thanksgiving Day matchup with Brown in nearby Providence, Rhode Island. When word spread that Jim Thorpe and company were tossing the ball around in a town park, a crowd quickly gathered. Kids, adults, even a few local reporters lined the edge of the field.

Among those watching was Charles Clancy, a former baseball manager in the Eastern Carolina League. He was standing next to Roy Johnson of the *Worcester Telegram* when Jim Thorpe ran past.

"Why, I know that guy," Clancy said. "He played for me a couple of years ago."

Clancy told Johnson that he'd managed the Fayetteville team while Thorpe was at Rocky Mount and that late in the 1910 season, Fayetteville had traded for Thorpe.

Johnson didn't seem surprised. Hundreds of students played summer ball; most used phony names, since college students weren't technically allowed to earn money playing sports. But this wasn't just any student-athlete. This was Jim Thorpe. That made it a story, Johnson knew. A very big story. He decided to do some digging before publishing the explosive scoop.

Jim Thorpe had no idea the course of his life had just changed.

⁂

On Thanksgiving Day heavy snow fell on Brown's Andrews Field as the Carlisle Indians, draped in red capes, marched from the locker room and onto a field of white.

Jim Thorpe felt a chill in his heart that had nothing to do with the weather. "I was losing something I would never be able to regain," he would say, looking back on those moments before his final game in a Carlisle uniform. "I felt as though I wanted to fling my arms about the field, the goalposts, and hold them tight."

For Brown, as for so many schools, Carlisle's visit was the event of the season. "The team realizes," wrote the *Boston Journal*, "that upon the outcome of the Carlisle game depends to a considerable extent whether the season has been a success or a failure."

They would soon wish they'd chosen a different yardstick.

Carlisle's dream of an undefeated season was gone, but this team was nothing if not resilient. And they made sure Jim Thorpe went out in style.

On a slippery field, with snowflakes swirling in icy wind, Thorpe gained 275 yards, ran for three touchdowns, threw for a fourth, kicked two field goals, and was in on nearly every defensive play. Sportswriters were running out of ways to describe what they were seeing. "He eluded the outstretched arms of the tacklers with ridiculous ease," said the *Providence Journal*. The *Boston Journal* wrote: "He plunged, dodged, ducked, side-stepped, wriggled, squirmed, swerved, and sped up and down the white stretches with consummate skill, certainty, speed and grace."

Five and a half years earlier, Thorpe had earned his way onto the Carlisle team by running through an entire team of tacklers. He ended his Carlisle career the exact same way—"in a blaze of glory," as many papers put it. Late in the game, Thorpe took a direct snap from the center and proceeded to knock over, swerve around, or sprint past every defender on his way to the end zone.

Carlisle finished the season 12-1-1. Jim Thorpe was again a first-team All-American, scoring twenty-seven touchdowns and rushing for nearly two thousand yards—and since no stats survive from two Carlisle games, the real totals were certainly higher.

Opinions were split on the national champion; some writers picked Harvard, others said Penn State. But it was the Carlisle Indians who had once again changed the game. Rule makers wanted more offense, and Carlisle reached new heights with 504 points. No other team scored even 400. Penn State scored 282. Harvard scored 176.

Jim Thorpe scored 224.

In Thorpe's four seasons with Pop Warner, practically living on the road, playing a schedule no other school would dare to attempt, Carlisle compiled an almost impossible forty-three wins, against only five losses and two ties. Along the way, they managed to pull football, kicking and screaming, out of the Stone Age and into the modern era, putting it on the road to becoming the country's favorite sport. In the decades ahead, schools like Notre Dame, Alabama, and Oklahoma would replace the Big Four as perennial elites, and today many fans have no idea that one of football's all-time greatest teams was the Carlisle Indians.

"Whenever I see one of these All-America teams," Pop Warner would say years later, "I cannot help but think what an eleven could have been selected from those *real* Americans who blazed such a trail of glory across the football fields of the country."

Over the Christmas break, Thorpe traveled to Oklahoma for some well-deserved rest. Strolling streets he'd known as a kid, he called out to old friends as if nothing had changed. Only now, when Jim Thorpe walked by, everyone stopped.

"The Indians are very proud of the record made by their now illustrious kinsman," reported a local paper. "With the folks here he is more than a hero."

In January Thorpe returned to Carlisle to finish up the school year. He entered a waltz contest in the school gym and took first prize, a chocolate cake.

Two days later, on January 22, 1913, the story broke in the *Worcester Telegram*:

THORPE WITH PROFESSIONAL BASEBALL TEAM SAYS CLANCY.

The article quoted Charles Clancy as saying that the world-famous Jim Thorpe had been paid to play minor-league ball in North Carolina in 1909 and 1910. Pretty much everything else in the article was false; much of it sounded like some sort of racist cartoon. According to the story, "Big Chief" Thorpe had made a habit of staggering down main streets throughout the South, emitting "war whoops" and swigging whiskey from a gallon jug.

An apparently remorseful Charles Clancy denied having told any such tales, but it was too late. By January 23, the story was in newspapers all over the country. What made this front-page news was Thorpe's gold-medal performance at the 1912 Olympics. Olympic athletes were supposed to be amateurs. Headlines asked:

IS THORPE A PRO?

Absolutely not, commissioner of the American Olympic Committee James Sullivan told newspapers. Warner backed Sullivan, pointing out to reporters that Clancy had retracted his claims. The next day's papers declared:

JIM THORPE VINDICATED.

Thorpe watched in agony. Sullivan and Warner seemed to be hoping the whole thing would blow over, but how could it? Thorpe had played under his own name in North Carolina, and thousands of people had seen him. There were photos, signed checks, box scores. Sure enough, reporters quickly found "evidence" that Thorpe had played ball for Rocky Mount. On January 26 headlines announced:

CASE AGAINST JIM THORPE SEEMS TO BE FULLY PROVED.

"I don't understand, Pop," Thorpe said to Warner, his trusted adviser. "What's that two months of baseball got to do with all the jumping and running and fieldwork I did in Stockholm? I never got paid for any of *that*, did I?"

It was a fair point. The rules of amateurism were vague, and different in different countries, and in any case Thorpe had never tried to hide his participation in baseball. He'd told Superintendent Friedman before leaving campus in 1909, and had talked about it ever since coming back. "I never made any secret about it," Thorpe later said. "I often told the boys, with the coaches listening, about things that happened while I was at Rocky Mount." There's simply no way Pop Warner didn't know about Thorpe's summer baseball.

After all they'd accomplished together, all they'd been through, *this* was the moment Thorpe needed Warner the most. This was Warner's chance to stand by Thorpe's side.

He didn't do it.

"All I know about the charges against Thorpe have been gleaned from the newspaper reports," Warner told the *New York Times*. He called Thorpe's summer baseball "news to everyone connected with Carlisle because it was supposed that he had been at his home in Oklahoma from the time he left the school in 1909 until he returned in 1911."

Friedman echoed the lie, declaring: "The faculty and athletic director, Mr. Glenn Warner, were without any knowledge of this fact until today. It is a most unpleasant affair and has brought gloom on the entire institution."

Scrambling to save their own hides, Warner and Friedman drafted a "confession" that put all the blame on Jim Thorpe.

"I played baseball at Rocky Mount and at Fayetteville, N.C., in the summer of 1909 and 1910," they wrote. "I was not wise in the ways of the world and did not realize this was wrong, and that it would make me a professional in track sports, although I learned from the other players that it would be better for me not to let anyone know that I was playing and for that reason I never told anyone at the school about it until today."

The document ended with an apology to Sullivan and the Olympic committee. "I hope I will be partly excused by the fact that I was simply an Indian schoolboy and I did not know all about such things."

Thorpe wasn't sure where else to turn for help. Though he'd later call it "hard and cruel," he wrote out the statement in his own hand and signed it.

The papers declared:

### THORPE CONFESSES TO HIS ERRORS.

### OLYMPIC HERO, CARLISLE FOOTBALL MARVEL, IS BRANDED A PROFESSIONAL.

### ALL INDIAN'S OLYMPIAD PRIZES WILL HAVE TO BE RETURNED.

## "JIM" THORPE PROFESSIONAL, PLEADS GUILTY TO CHARGE

### Admits That He Played Baseball for Money—Means Great Indian Athlete Must Give Up Olympic Medals and All Other Trophies Won by Him Since 1909.

New York, Jan. 27.—James Thorpe, the Indian athlete and Olympic champion, to-day admitted that charges of professionalism brought against him were true, and formally retired from amateur athletics. Thorpe's confession was contained in a letter to the registration committee of the Amateur Athletic Union, which met to-day to investigate his case.

The letter admitted that Thorpe had played baseball for a salary on a professional team three years ago while a student of the Carlisle Indian School, but that on the same team there were several northern college men who were regarded as amateurs, and Thorpe did not realize his participation was wrong. Thorpe added that he did not play for the money he earned, but for the love of the game.

### Greatest Modern Athlete.

Thorpe's winning of the penthalon and decathlon events at the Olympic games in Stockholm, and later his wonderful performances which won for him the all-round championship of the A. A. U. at Celtic park last September, had stamped him the most marvelous all-round athlete of modern times. In addition, his prowess as a football player had earned for him last season, by unanimous choice of leading sporting writers, the position of half-back on the annual all-American football team.

the A. A. U., after I had answered the questions and signed it, and I received my card allowing me to compete in the winter meets and other track sports. I never realized until now what a big mistake I made by keeping it a secret about my ball playing and I am sorry I did so. I hope I will be partly excused by the fact that I was simply an Indian school boy and did not know all about such things. In fact, I did not know that I was doing wrong, because I was doing what I knew several other college men had done, except that they did not use their own names.

### Money No Attraction.

"I have always liked sport and only played or run races for the fun of the thing and never to earn money. I have received offers amounting to thousands of dollars since my victories last summer, but I have turned them all down because I did not care to make money from my athletic skill. I am very sorry, Mr. Sullivan, to have it all spoiled in this way and I hope the Amateur Athletic Union and the people will not be too hard in judging me. Yours truly "JAMES THORPE."

Mr. Friedman in his letter says that neither the faculty of the Carlisle Indian School nor Athletic Director Warner had knowledge of Thorpe's professionalism, and declares the confession has brought

... and the honors which ... entire institution.

# WORLD'S GREATEST ATHLETE IS DISCREDITED

## JIM THORPE ADMITS PROFESSIONALISM

### Confession Is a Matter of International Significance

### All Indian's Olympiad Prizes Will Have to Be Returned

**Touch of Pathos in His Letter To A. A. U. Secretary; Did Not Realize Wrong He Was Doing**

NEW YORK, Jan. 27.—James Thorpe, the Indian athlete and Olympiad champion, today admitted that the charges of professionalism brought against him were true and formally retired from amateur athletics.

*[remainder of column body text illegible]*

#### LOS ANGELES MAN MOVES UP

#### UNITED STATES STILL HOLDS LEAD

#### PLAYED FOR LOVE OF GAME

#### DID NOT REALIZE OFFENSE

#### OTHER COLLEGE MEN DID IT

#### "THREW THORPE"

#### INEXPERIENCE SOME EXCUSE

**Two Polo Matches Today On Crossways**

**Washington Park Soccer Champions**

**Connie Mack's Son Takes Job Like Dad's**

---

### JAMES THORPE,
### Discredited Athlete

---

## DON'T LET THE HAMMER THROW BE DISCARDED FROM ATHLETIC GAMES

### Develop Javelin and Discus, but Keep Hammer and Make It Safer

By WILLIAM UNMACK

#### EASY THROWS VALUABLE

#### CROWDS ENDANGERS SELVES

---

## Bill Would Put the Lid on Athletic Clubs

### Another Angeleno Hatches Weird Measure

### Senator Gates Hitches Cart Before Horse

CALL BUREAU, SACRAMENTO HOTEL,
SACRAMENTO, January 27.

---

## POLY LOSES TO LICK BY POOR TEAM WORK

All Sorts of Basket Ball Contests Between School Fives

---

## MAJOR ROSS NOSES OUT CHICAGO GOLF PLAYER

Close Match Features First Round at the Coronado Tournament

SAN DIEGO, Jan. 27.

#### Dundee Puts It All Over "Special Delivery"

NEW YORK, Jan. 27.—Johnny Dundee...

#### South End Rowing Club To Hold Banquet

---

## PUPPIES SHOW CLASS IN OPENING TRIALS AT BAKERSFIELD MEET

### Opening Day Is Marked by Ideal Conditions and Lots of Birds

(Special Dispatch to The Call)
BAKERSFIELD, Jan. 27.

#### Maude Lowell Shines on Stanford Courts

(Special Dispatch to The Call)
STANFORD UNIVERSITY, Jan. 27.

---

---

As these articles from the *Washington Post* (left) and *San Francisco Call* (above) show, Thorpe's story was major news across the entire country.

Pop Warner called the entire affair "a brutal business," but he continued to deny any responsibility. To Jim's teammates, this was nothing less than a knife to the back.

"Mr. Warner is a good football coach," said a disgusted Gus Welch, "but a man with no principle."

James Sullivan demanded that Thorpe name the college students he'd played baseball with. Thorpe refused. That only tipped public opinion—which had been with Thorpe all along—further in his favor.

First off, sportswriters didn't buy Warner's cries of ignorance. "Glenn Warner must have known—it was his business to know, as one in charge of the government's Indian wards—that Thorpe played professional baseball," wrote *The Sporting News*.

More important, papers pointed out, was the blatant hypocrisy behind the whole overblown controversy. It was an open secret that college athletes took money to play ball, and that so-called "amateur" track stars accepted payments disguised as "travel expenses" to appear at meets. "There are any number of professionals masquerading as amateurs," pointed out the *Washington Times*. Why single out Thorpe? Why the talk of stripping medals for what amounted to a minor infraction that had nothing to do with competition on the track?

The articles never came out and said it, but it was there between the lines. This would not have been happening to a student from Harvard. This would not have been happening to a white American.

"There is no reason for the hysteria exhibited in America," the *London Daily Citizen* cautioned. A Swedish paper pointed out that, regardless of the details of Thorpe's summer baseball, objections to his amateur status were being raised too late. The International Olympic Committee's own rules were clear: "Objections to qualifications of a competitor must be made in writing to the Swedish Olympic Committee before the lapse of thirty days from the distribution of prizes."

James Sullivan moved ahead anyway. Just six months earlier, Sullivan had stood before reporters and pointed to Thorpe as a shining example of American greatness. Now he deleted Thorpe's records from the books and ordered the return of Thorpe's trophies and medals.

When Sweden's Hugo Wieslander, who had won silver in the decathlon, was told he'd now be getting the gold, he joined the chorus backing Thorpe. "I don't know what your rules are in regard to amateurism," Wieslander wrote to Sullivan's committee, "and apparently Thorpe didn't either, but I do know that we met in honest competition and he beat me fairly and decisively. I didn't win the Olympic decathlon. Jim Thorpe did."

Thorpe never found out exactly when it happened, or who did it, but someone went into his room at Carlisle and took his trophies and gold medals. They were put on a ship and sent back to Sweden.

Early on the afternoon of **February 1, 1913,** Jim Thorpe walked along New York City's Fifth Avenue in a blue suit and dark purple fedora. Beside him was Pop Warner.

They entered a building together and stepped into the offices of the New York Giants baseball team. Thorpe was news everywhere he went, and the Giants' offices were packed with reporters and photographers. Giants manager John McGraw greeted Thorpe and showed him to a desk. On the desk was a contract to play ball for the Giants in 1913. Photographers lifted their cameras as Jim sat down and picked up a pen.

There had been plenty of other options. Boxing promoters wanted Thorpe in the ring. Motion picture producers offered movie contracts. A theatrical agent promised him $1,000 a week to perform feats of strength on stage. The women of America wouldn't leave him alone—"He has received on the average of 30 proposals of marriage a day," one paper reported.

The ladies never had a chance. Jim was still committed to Iva Miller, and she wrote him often throughout the bad times, assuring him their engagement was still on. It was about this time that Iva began referring to Jim by a nickname no one else would have dared to use: "Snooks."

As for the other offers, none of them sounded right to Thorpe. He was an athlete; he wanted to earn a living in sports. The decision would have been easy if professional football had existed, but baseball was the big game, and even as the Olympic controversy raged, offers from big-league teams had flowed in to the Carlisle campus. Thorpe seems to have still trusted Pop Warner, or at least felt he needed his coach's advice. Pop helped negotiate a one-year deal with the New York Giants for $6,000, a huge payday for a rookie ballplayer.

Now, in the crowded Giants office, flashbulbs popped as Jim Thorpe signed the contract.

"I haven't any doubt that he will develop into a first class ball player," Pop Warner told the newspapermen. "He has the ability, mental and physical."

Warner went on and on, but reporters really wanted to hear from Thorpe.

"I am pleased to get a chance to play for the Giants," Jim said. "Whether I will make good I cannot say. I am going to try my best."

New team, new city, new sport—Thorpe with the New York Giants in 1913.

Then came questions about the scandal. One reporter even pointed out that Thorpe's medals were, at that very moment, on their way back to Europe.

Thorpe was quiet for a long moment.

"No one knows how sorry I feel about that," he finally said. "That is all over now, and there is nothing more to say about it."

◆❖◆

Two weeks after signing with the Giants, Thorpe packed up his stuff, said goodbye to Gus Welch and his friends at the Carlisle School, and headed for Texas to report for spring training. In Carlisle, citizens began taking up a collection to purchase replacement trophies and medals for Thorpe. People dropped coins in jars at stores all over town.

When Thorpe heard of the effort, he asked that the money be given to charity.

For the rest of his life, Jim Thorpe would talk about his life in terms of two distinct eras: pre- and post-Olympic scandal. This was the start of part two, and he was eager to do what he had always done—what the Carlisle football team had always done after a bitter defeat—to quietly, stubbornly, forge a new path.

Fifteen years earlier, after the 1897 football season, the Carlisle players gathered for a post-season dinner. The Carlisle Indians had lost three games to the Big Four that year. Their overall record against those top schools was 0-9. But when star halfback Frank Cayou rose to speak, he insisted that, in spirit, the team was still undefeated. "Our greatest glory consists not in never falling," he told teammates, "but in rising every time we fall. Let that be our motto!"

It certainly was for Jim Thorpe.

"They tell me I have gained my share of fame in athletics and in football," he told reporters at spring training. "If I have, I did not do it by moping, but by hustling."

When the team workouts began, Thorpe grabbed a glove and ran onto the field.

222

EPILOGUE: BACK ON TOP

Jim Thorpe got just thirty-five at-bats for the New York Giants in 1913. He watched from the bench as the team cruised to the World Series, where they lost to a Philadelphia Athletics club led by former Carlisle student—and future Hall of Fame pitcher—Charles Albert "Chief" Bender.

As for his Olympic trophies and medals, Thorpe mentioned them only once. It was late one night, at the team's hotel, and the Giants' star catcher, John "Chief" Meyers, a Cahuilla Indian from California, was getting ready for bed (yes, the media really did nickname every Native American player "Chief"). Jim Thorpe came in, tears rolling down his cheeks.

"You know, Chief, the King of Sweden gave me those trophies," Thorpe said. "He gave them to me. But they took them away from me. They are mine, Chief! I won them fair and square."

In October, with the frustrating season finally behind him, Thorpe returned to Carlisle for a happier occasion—his wedding to Iva Miller. Jim and his best man, Gus Welch, stood in a church decorated with autumn leaves and packed with friends from school. Iva walked down the aisle in a white gown and veil, a wreath of flowers around her head.

That night, in the school gym, everyone danced to Jim and Iva's song, "You Tell Me Your Dream and I'll Tell You Mine."

Jim and Iva at their wedding in Carlisle. Jim's best man, Gus Welch, stands to his right.

Carlisle football went on without Thorpe. The team was still loaded with talent, but many of the best players, including the new captain, Gus Welch, simply didn't trust Pop Warner anymore. The Carlisle Indians had changed football forever. Everything today's fans love about the game—creative strategies, up-tempo offense, deep passes, highlight-reel plays—Carlisle did it all.

But the glory years were over. Carlisle would never again beat one of the Big Four.

In 1914 Congress began investigating allegations of misconduct by Pop Warner and Superintendent Friedman. Students came forward to testify about skimpy meals for non-athletes and cruel treatment, including beatings, by teachers. Welch focused his fury on Warner, telling investigators of Pop's verbal abuse of players and his habit of selling tickets in hotel lobbies and pocketing the profits.

Warner denied breaking any rules, but his career at Carlisle ended under a cloud. He knew how to win football games, though—then, as now, that buys you another chance.

As head coach at the University of Pittsburgh, Warner won his first thirty games, including national championships in 1915 and 1916. He also had successful coaching stints at Stanford and Temple, and he is still among the winningest coaches in football history. In 1934, while he was at Temple, the coaches of a Philadelphia youth football league named their league for Pop. Today more than three hundred thousand kids play in Pop Warner football leagues around the country. Warner retired from coaching in 1938 and settled in Palo Alto, California, where he died in 1954, at the age of eighty-three.

Like so much of this story, Pop's legacy at Carlisle is tough to summarize in a sentence. Did he genuinely love the Carlisle players like sons? Did he love them only so long as he could exploit them for all they were worth? Different players had different opinions—and they knew him a lot better than we possibly can.

Warner certainly benefited from his years at Carlisle, so it's not surprising that his own recollections were nothing but warm. "After thirty-six years of coaching," he wrote late in life, "the experiences that stand out most vividly in my memory are those connected with the Indian lads."

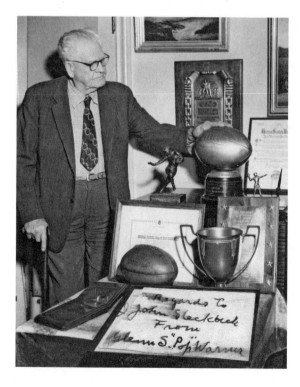

From the moment he first walked onto the field at Cornell to his retirement in California, football was the center of Pop Warner's life.

Gus Welch graduated from Carlisle in 1914 and enrolled in law school at Dickinson College. When the US entered World War I in 1917, he enlisted in the army and was accepted into an officer-training program. Welch had suffered a serious head injury in his last football game and worried the lingering headaches would hurt his chances of completing the competitive training program. He somehow powered through. "I have done my best," he wrote to a friend, "keeping always in mind that I was a Carlisle man."

When Welch heard that many white officers were refusing to lead an all-black troop of combat engineers, he volunteered. He served with them in combat in France, came home, married, and settled in Virginia, where he coached football and lacrosse, and ran a popular outdoor camp for boys.

In 1939 the Department of the Interior announced plans to extend a highway through Welch's property in the Blue Ridge Mountains. The government offered to buy the land from Welch—for far less than he'd paid for it. Gus went to court, lost, and was forced to sell.

"It's the same old story," he told reporters. "The white man has been taking land from the Indian so long that it has become a habit with him."

Welch continued coaching and teaching, and he was invited often to give speeches about the early days of football and the legendary Carlisle teams he'd quarterbacked. Every chance he got, he campaigned for the return of Jim Thorpe's gold medals.

With US forces fighting in World War I, the War Department needed hospital and rehabilitation space for soldiers returning from Europe. On September 1, 1918, Richard Henry Pratt, aged seventy-seven, returned to Carlisle to watch a Pueblo student named J. F. Duran lower the flag for the final time. The school became an Army hospital and, years later, the US Army War College, which it still is.

For visitors today, one of the few reminders that the Carlisle Indian Industrial School ever existed is the cemetery, lined with small white stones above the graves of 192 boys and girls who died very far from home.

From 1879 to 1918, about 8,500 students attended Carlisle. Only 741 graduated—twice as many students ran away from Carlisle as got degrees there. Many of the football players remembered Carlisle fondly, but they got to skip classes and travel the country, treated as celebrities both on and off campus. Reading accounts of non-athlete students from Carlisle and other government-run Indian boarding schools, it becomes clear that these schools inflicted enormous and lasting pain on entire generations of young people.

What does this say about Richard Henry Pratt and his life's work? Was he a man who cared about the future of Native Americans at a time few other white leaders did? Was he a man who put down his rifle only to use his school as a weapon against the very people he was claiming to save? Can there be truth in both of the above?

One thing that can be said for sure is that Pratt failed at his goal of permanently severing Native Americans from their culture and identity. According to the 1920 US census, the Native American population of the United States had fallen below 250,000, an all-time low. In 2010 more than five million Americans identified themselves as "American Indian alone" or "American Indian in combination with one or more other races."

The last word on the Carlisle School belongs to Ota Kte—renamed Luther Standing Bear at Carlisle—who was among Pratt's original students in 1879. Standing Bear valued the knowledge he'd gained at Carlisle, but he had no interest in turning his back on Lakota traditions. "I kept the language, tribal manners and usages, sang the songs and danced the dances," he explained. "I still listened to and respected the advice of the old people of the tribe."

Standing Bear went on to be a successful writer and actor, and spoke eloquently about the massive mistake at the heart of Pratt's school. The mistake was beginning with the small-minded idea that one side was "savage" and the other "civilized."

"While the white people had much to teach us, we had much to teach them," Standing Bear wrote fifty-four years after first arriving at Carlisle, "and what a school could have been established upon that idea!"

Luther Standing Bear in a Carlisle Indian School portrait.

Luther Standing Bear in 1904.

In a life scarred by tragedy, the cruelest blow fell on Jim Thorpe in the fall of 1918. Jim and Iva's first child, a son they named James Junior, fell sick with what doctors diagnosed as inflammatory rheumatism. The four-year-old boy died in Jim's arms.

Thorpe and his son had been inseparable, just like Jim had once been with his twin brother, Charlie. When Iva took Junior to Giants games, she had to grip the child tight to keep him from running onto the field to be with his father.

"Jim was never the same," one Giants teammate said after Junior's death.

"He was brokenhearted," Iva remembered. He started staying out later, drinking more, and she felt them drifting apart. Jim and Iva would have three healthy daughters together, Gail, Charlotte, and Grace, but eventually agreed to split up.

Jim Thorpe holding Junior, his newborn son.

Jim Thorpe never did become a great baseball player, though he improved steadily, hitting .329 in part-time action in 1919, his last year in the majors. He also found a way to earn some cash playing the sport he was built for, football.

These were the very early days of professional football, and the owner of a struggling club called the Canton Bulldogs recruited Thorpe to join the team in 1915. Attendance at Bulldogs games jumped from 1,200 to 8,000, and Thorpe led Canton to the championship of its Ohio-based league in 1916, 1917, and 1919. He was nearly thirty when he started playing pro football—ancient by running back standards—but the old magic was still there. "Thorpe," wrote the *Canton Daily News*, "by sheer strength, shook off rivals like the wind blows leaves to the ground."

In 1920 the Bulldogs owner invited the owners of competing teams from Ohio and beyond to meet at his auto dealership in Canton. The objective was to discuss the formation of a more organized professional league. Sitting on the running boards of cars in the auto showroom, the men banged out a deal to form what they named the American Professional Football Conference. For the league's first president, they chose the country's most famous and popular player, Jim Thorpe. Two years later, when the league had grown to eighteen teams, owners changed its name to the National Football League.

Thorpe, meanwhile, was still playing. In 1922 he teamed up with the owner of Oorang Dog Kennels (Oorang is a type of terrier) to found a team called the Oorang Indians. It was the NFL's one and only all-American Indian team, featuring former Carlisle stars Joe Guyon, Pete Calac, Possum Powell, and Carlisle's original enforcer, Bemus Pierce, now forty-seven.

This could be a movie all to itself—Jim and his aging friends on the road again, trying to recapture the glory days of their youth, and all the while battling stereotypes that just wouldn't die. "White people thought we were all wild men," Oorang quarterback Leon Boutwell remembered, "even though almost all of us had been to college and were generally more civilized than they were." The Oorang Indians were disbanded in 1923, after just two seasons.

Now, in the twenty-first century, should any team, at any level or in any sport, continue to call itself the Indians? Or some stereotypical variation, like Braves or Redskins?

Daniel Snyder, owner of the NFL's Washington Redskins, vows never to change his team's name. "It represents honor," he insists, "represents respect, represents pride."

Ray Halbritter, of the Oneida Indian Nation, sees it differently. "*Redskins* is defined in the dictionary as an offensive label for Native Americans—that was used against them when they were forcibly removed from their lands at gunpoint," Halbritter says. "It's hard to believe that Washington's NFL team continues to use this name, even though it's the sort of slur that would never be used in polite conversation."

A protester outside a recent Washington football game held a sign that put it even more directly: "I'm not your mascot."

◆❚▶

Jim Thorpe went on juggling jobs in minor-league baseball and pro football until 1929, when he was forty-one. Over the years, he and Pop Warner made a few public appearances together. Thorpe never said a word against Warner, not even in private.

"I never heard anything bad about Pop Warner from Dad," Grace Thorpe, Jim and Iva's daughter, later said. "I did hear Momma say that Pop Warner knew all the time that Dad had played baseball."

But Jack Thorpe, Jim's son from a second marriage, believed his dad's silence didn't mean he wasn't hurting. "The people that he trusted turned on him, for their own personal gain," Jack said. Thorpe carried the pain of that betrayal with him for the rest of his life.

With his career in sports over, Thorpe struggled to earn a living. He appeared in a few Hollywood movies, gave lectures around the country, and in lean times worked as a bouncer in a Los Angeles bar. One night, over drinks with his daughter Charlotte, Thorpe reflected on the name his mother had given him, Bright Path. "I can't decide whether I was well-named or not," Thorpe said. "Many a time the path has gleamed bright for me—but just as often it has been dark and bitter."

In 1950 nearly four hundred sportswriters were asked to list the best college football players of the first half of the twentieth century. Many of the writers had been around long enough to have seen all the big stars of the past five decades. The vote was not even close—the winner was Jim Thorpe.

Writers were also asked to pick the single greatest American athlete of the century so far. Thorpe topped that poll, too. Coming in a very distant second was Babe Ruth.

Soon after the vote, the residents of Carlisle invited Jim Thorpe back to town for a ceremony in his honor. The school was long gone, but the old football field was still there. Thousands cheered as Thorpe walked, one last time, onto what had been Indian Field.

This was the field Bemus Pierce and his teammates had flattened and planted with grass. It was here that Frank Hudson perfected the drop-kick, and Frank Mount Pleasant figured out how to throw a spiral. It was here that Jim Thorpe, looking like a teenage scarecrow, had run through the entire Carlisle team on his way to football immortality.

Now sixty-one, his hair still thick and black, his face fleshy, his body rounder than in playing days, Thorpe spoke of the old times. He told the crowd of the high jump he'd made in overalls, and relived his favorite football memories.

Jim Thorpe was never one to seek attention, but the warm reception felt good. After walking off the field, he told a reporter, "It was great to see the folks haven't forgotten old Jim."

In 1951 Warner Brothers released a movie based on Jim Thorpe's life called *Jim Thorpe—All-American*. Burt Lancaster, a white, thirty-seven-year-old movie star, played the college-aged Jim. Thorpe, at least, was paid $15,000 to be an adviser on the set.

Just two years later, on March 28, 1953, Jim Thorpe died of a heart attack. He was sixty-four.

Gus Welch, who had remained close with Jim over the years, wanted people to remember his friend as a champion, both on and off the field.

Thorpe flashes his famous smile at the premiere of the movie *Jim Thorpe—All-American*.

"One of the most wonderful, good-hearted men I've ever known," Gus said.

Until his own death in 1970, Welch continued campaigning to get Thorpe's gold medals returned. Leading this effort was Charlotte Thorpe, who spent thirty years writing letters, making phone calls, and arranging meetings with anyone who might be able to help persuade the US Olympic Committee to reverse the 1913 ruling that had disqualified Jim Thorpe.

"I will not quit," she told a friend, sounding exactly like her father. "I will never give up."

Finally, seventy years after the Stockholm Olympics, the committee conceded that Thorpe had been wrongly disqualified. That cleared the way for the International Olympic Committee to offer Thorpe's family two replica gold medals—the real ones had been given to second-place finishers, and the IOC didn't think it would be fair to ask for them back.

On January 18, 1983, in a ceremony at a Los Angeles hotel, the IOC presented two gold medals to Thorpe's children. "My dad's life was like a Greek tragedy," Grace Thorpe told reporters that happy day. "He went from the bottom to the heights and back down to the bottom again."

But now Jim Thorpe was—and always will be—back on top.

Reporters asked Grace how her father would have responded to the return of his medals.

She thought he would simply have said, "It's about time."

# SOURCE NOTES

## Tryout

2 Jim Thorpe later described this memorable tryout in Thorpe, "This Is My Story," *Sports World*, September 1949, 68; and in his personal scrapbook, which is excerpted in Wheeler, *Jim Thorpe*, 54–55.

2 Pop Warner's recollections of the tryout are found in his collection of autobiographical writings published as, Bynum, *Pop Warner*, 121–122; additional details in Jenkins, *The Real All Americans*, 230.

## The Star

6 "No college player I ever saw": Crawford, *All American*, 144.

7 "Don't be afraid of the water": Buford, *Native American Son*, 15.

9 "a superior race": Andrew Jackson's fifth annual message to Congress, excerpted in Ward, *The West*, 83.

9 Jim describes his parents and the origin of the name Bright Path in Thorpe, "This Is My Story," *Sports World*, September 1949, 44; more family background in Steiger and Thorpe, *Thorpe's Gold*, 15–19; Newcombe, *The Best of the Athletic Boys*, 27–29; Buford, *Native American Son*, 12–13.

9 General Allotment Act and land rush described: Buford, *Native American Son*, 19–21.

10 Keokuk Falls details can be found in Thorpe, "The Jim Thorpe Family, Part II," *The Chronicles of Oklahoma,* Summer 1981, 186–187; Steiger and Thorpe, *Thorpe's Gold*, 44.

11 "Our lives were lived out in the open": Crawford, *All American*, 14.

12 Thorpe recalls details of his childhood in Thorpe, "This Is My Story," *Sports World*, September 1949, 44–45; additional details in Buford, *Native American Son*, 15–17. One of Thorpe's teachers recalls the twins in Gilstrap, "Memoirs of a Pioneer Teacher," *The Chronicles of Oklahoma*, Spring 1960, 22.

## The Coach

13 Pop Warner recalls childhood scenes, including the nickname "Butter," in his autobiographical writings, collected in Bynum, *Pop Warner*, 37–38.

13 "This battle showed me a new way": Bynum, *Pop Warner*, 37.

14 "We used anything that we could": Bynum, *Pop Warner*, 38.

15 "I soon became depressed": Bynum, *Pop Warner*, 41.

15 "At the time, I considered this": Bynum, *Pop Warner*, 42.

15 Warner describes his first day at Cornell and being recruited by Carl Johanson: Warner, "Battles of Brawn," *Colliers*, November 7, 1931, 10.

## The Game

17 Descriptions and recollections of the historic Rutgers-Princeton football game can be found in Weyand, *Saga of American Football*, 2–4; Danzig, *Oh, How They Played the Game*, 3–8.

18 "Early-day football": Warner, "Battles of Brawn," *Colliers*, November 7, 1931, 10; additional details on early football are from Anderson, *Carlisle vs. Army*, 59–60; Weyand, *The Saga of American Football*, 29–35; Revsine, *The Opening Kickoff*, 26–29.

20 "The stronger team": Bynum, *Pop Warner*, 115.

20 "In fact, one who wore homemade pads": Danzig, *Oh, How They Played the Game*, 70.

20 "This sometimes had its disadvantages": Warner, "Battles of Brawn," *Colliers*, November 7, 1931, 10.

20 "Good work, Pop!": Anderson, *Carlisle vs. Army*, 27; Warner discusses origin of "Pop" in Bynum, *Pop Warner*, 53.

20 "If a player was too good-natured": Warner, "Battles of Brawn," *Colliers*, November 7, 1931, 10.

22 Warner describes the origin and execution of play Number 39: Bynum, *Pop Warner*, 54–55.

23 "My first play as an interim coach": Bynum, *Pop Warner*, 55.

## The School

24 Carlisle's first game and the Stacy Matlock injury are described in Steckbeck, *Fabulous Redmen*, 12; Hall, *Go, Indians!*, 7–8; Pratt, *Battlefield and Classroom*, 317.

24 "It's Stacy, sir!": Hall, *Go, Indians!*, 7; Pratt describes Matlock injury and his dislike of football in Pratt, *Battlefield and Classroom*, 317.

26 Pratt's career before Carlisle is described in Robert Utley's introduction to Pratt, *Battlefield and Classroom*, xvii–xxi.

27 "I had concluded": Crawford, *All American*, 53.

28 Pratt's background and ideas behind Carlisle are described in Fear-Segal, *White Man's Club*, 159–163; Pratt describes the origin of the Carlisle School in Pratt, *Battlefield and Classroom*, 213–219.

29 "I believe in immersing": Newcombe, *The Best of the Athletic Boys*, 68.

29 "Left in the surroundings of savagery": Pratt's "Kill the Indian" speech is reprinted in Prucha, *Americanizing the American Indians*, 260–271.

30 Pratt describes his trip to Rosebud in Pratt, *Battlefield and Classroom*, 220–221.

30 Ota Kte's recollections of the day Pratt came to Rosebud are in his memoir: Standing Bear, *My People the Sioux*, 123–124.

30 "The white people": Pratt, *Battlefield and Classroom*, 222.

31 History behind Rosebud and the Battle of Little Bighorn: Brown, *Bury My Heart at Wounded Knee*, 276–313; Ward, *The West*, 292–304.

31 "Do you want to go, son" and Ota Kte's initial feelings about the school: Standing Bear, *My People the Sioux*, 125.

31 "But I could not get to sleep"; Standing Bear, *My People the Sioux*, 128.

## Alien World

32 Ota Kte describes the harrowing trip east in Standing Bear, *My People the Sioux*, 127–132; Pratt's recollections of the trip: Pratt, *Battlefield and Classroom*, 228–229.

32 "Many of the little": Standing Bear, *My People the Sioux*, 130.

32 "I was thrust into an alien world": Cooper, *Indian School*, 10.

35 "Do you see all these marks": Standing Bear, *My People the Sioux*, 137; he describes haircut details in the same book, 141; additional details of the first days at Carlisle can be found in Witmer, *The Indian Industrial School*, 19–22.

35 "I've always hated that name": Ball, *Indeh, An Apache Odyssey*, 144.

36 Early years at the Carlisle School are described in Pratt, *Battlefield and Classroom*, 230–244; Standing Bear, *My People the Sioux*, 144–150; Fear-Segal, *White Man's Club*, 184–187; Witmer, *The Indian Industrial School*, 23–29.

36 "We keep them moving": Crawford, *All American*, 56.

38 Maggie Stands Looking story is from Pratt, *Battlefield and Classroom*, 275; the fire is described in an untitled front-page roundup of campus news in the *Red Man*, February 1898; White Thunder details from Fear-Segal, *White Man's Club*, 245.

38 "Boys and girls actually suffered": Cooper, *Indian School*, 46.

40 "You've got to stick to it": Bell, *Telling Stories Out of School*, 63.

40 "I was not especially pleased": Pratt, *Battlefield and Classroom*, 317.

40 "Carlisle teams will no longer": Hall, *Go, Indians!*, 8.

## The Team

41 "Sir, we understand your reasons": Pratt describes his meeting with these pro-football students in Pratt, *Battlefield and Classroom*, 317–318; see also Hall, *Go, Indians!*, 13–15.

41 "We are not afraid of injuries" and subsequent quotes from this discussion: Pratt, *Battlefield and Classroom*, 317–318.

42 The utter domination of the Big Four in the late 1800s is described in detail in Weyand, *The Saga of American Football*, 36–54.

43 Vance McCormick's first visit to Carlisle is described in Pratt, *Battlefield and Classroom*, 318; details of early training are also in Steckbeck, *Fabulous Redmen*, 13; Jenkins, *The Real All Americans*, 124.

45 Steckbeck gives well-researched accounts of Carlisle's early games, including complete year-by-year schedules and results. For 1893 and 1894 seasons: Steckbeck, *Fabulous Redmen*, 12–15.

45 "obvious delight" and additional game details: "Indians Failed to Score," *Washington*

*Times*, November 25, 1894; "Lo, the Poor Indians: C.A.C. Defeat Carlisle Indian School 18 to 0," *Washington Post*, November 25, 1894.

## Restless Disposition

46 "I was always of a restless disposition": Buford, *Native American Son*, 17.

46 "We made our own balls": Crawford, *All American*, 49.

46 "Any kid who failed to follow": Thorpe describes his childhood version of follow-the-leader in Thorpe, "This Is My Story," *Sports World*, September 1949, 44–45.

46 Hiram and Charlotte's commitment to education, and details of Sac and Fox Agency School: Buford, *Native American Son*, 24; Thorpe, "This Is My Story," *Sports World*, September 1949, 45.

47 "Our lives were just one bell": Newcombe, *The Best of the Athletic Boys*, 40.

48 "calm, even-tempered": Thorpe boys' report cards and school behavior are quoted in Steiger and Thorpe, *Thorpe's Gold*, 41; Newcombe, *The Best of the Athletic Boys*, 44; Buford, *Native American Son*, 26.

48 Warner describes his brief legal career and coaching job at Iowa State in Bynum, *Pop Warner*, 58–59.

49 "bare and hard as an iron griddle" and other Butte game details: Bynum, *Pop Warner*, 61–62; Warner, "Battles of Brawn," *Colliers*, November 7, 1931, 46; "Butte Wins from Iowa," *Carrol Sentinel* (Carrol, IA), September 16, 1895.

49 "made the law seem pretty tame": Warner, "Red Menaces," *Colliers*, October 31, 1931, 16.

49 Bemus Pierce background: Bemus Pierce Student File, National Archives and Records Administration; for his love of football and participation on early teams: Benjey, *Doctors, Lawyers, Indian Chiefs*, 85.

50 1895 game results: Steckbeck, *Fabulous Redmen*, 15–17.

50 Historical background is found in Deloria, *Indians in Unexpected Places*, 23–24; Brown, *Bury My Heart at Wounded Knee*, 440–442; historical studies of scalpings are cited in Dunbar-Ortiz, *An Indiginous People's History*, 64–65, 137; Bigelow and Peterson, *Rethinking Columbus*, 58–59.

52 "There was an uprising": "Indians Play Good Football," *New York Times*, November 29, 1895; biased treatment of Carlisle in press described in Adams, "More Than a Game," *The Western Historical Quarterly*, Spring 2001, 31–34.

52 1896 schedule and early-season results: Steckbeck, *Fabulous Redmen*, 17–18.

## Carlisle vs. the Big Four

53 Descriptions of the 1896 Carlisle-Princeton game: "Princeton 22; Carlisle 6," *Washington Post*, October 15, 1896; "Princeton Scored On," *Philadelphia Inquirer*, October 15, 1896; "Princeton 22; Indians 6," *Daily Princetonian*, October 15, 1896.

53 "Then, the unlooked for": "Princeton Scored On," *Philadelphia Inquirer*, October 15, 1896.

54 "You must remember": Jenkins, *The Real All Americans*, 142.

56 "the crowd at once began": "Yale's Narrow Escape: Carlisle Indians Play Practically a Draw with the Blue," *New York Sun*, October 25, 1896.

56 Descriptions of the 1896 Carlisle-Yale game: "Yale's Narrow Escape: Carlisle Indians Play Practically a Draw with the Blue," *New York Sun*, October 25, 1896; "A Stolen Triumph for the Pale Children of Civilization," *New York Sun*, October 25, 1896; "Lively Football Row on Manhattan Field," *New York Journal*, October 25, 1896; "Carlisle Indians Score Against Yale," *Brooklyn Daily Eagle*, October 25, 1896; "Yale's Narrow Escape," *New York Tribune*, October 25, 1896; "Indians Surprise the People," *New York World*, October 25, 1896.

56 "After the game": "Yale's Narrow Escape: Carlisle Indians Play Practically a Draw with the Blue," *New York Sun*, October 25, 1896.

56 *Hello! Hellee! Who are we?*": Ryan, *The Carlisle Indian Industrial School*, 142.

57 "That's one!" Anderson, *Carlisle vs. Army*, 60.

57 "The Yale men looked at each other": "Indians Surprise the People," *New York World*, October 25, 1896.

57 "They've scored once": Hall, *Go Indians!*, 22.

57 "We will score again" and teammates' responses: Hall, *Go, Indians!*, 23.

57 "The official didn't see it": "Yale's Narrow Escape: Carlisle Indians Play Practically a Draw with the Blue," *New York Sun*, October 25, 1896.

58 "Never did New York see": "Indians Surprise the People," *New York World*, October 25, 1896.

59 "Now, if we have a right": *Rochester Advertiser*, excerpted in Carlisle's student newspaper, *Red Man*, November 1896.

59 Descriptions of the 1896 Carlisle-Harvard game: *Red Man*, November 1896. "Indians Scalped," *Boston Post*, November 1, 1896; "A Victory for Harvard," *New York Times*, November 1, 1896.

59 "Mr. Donald, you have been hitting me" and "I remember charging": Edwards, *Football Days*, 421.

59 Descriptions of the 1896 Carlisle-Penn game: "The Game with Pennsylvania University," *Philadelphia Press*, November 8, 1896; "Carlisle Indians Beaten," *New York Times*, November 8, 1896; "On Goal Line," *Boston Globe*, November 8, 1896; "No Team More Praised," *Kansas City Star*, excerpted in the *Red Man*, November 1896.

## Charlie

60 "I took care of them": Thorpe's teacher recalls the epidemic and Charlie's death in Gilstrap, "Memoirs of a Pioneer Teacher," *The Chronicles of Oklahoma*, Spring 1960, 22.

61 "I asked my father where he got all his strength": *Jim Thorpe: The World's Greatest Athlete*, a Moira Productions film, 2009.

61 "But I took a shortcut": Thorpe, "This Is My Story," *Sports World*, September 1949, 45. Hiram's "Now I'm going to send you" quote is from the same article.

## The Carlisle Rut

62 "Ever scrub before": Gansworth describes his first week at Carlisle, including Pratt's lecture in the chapel: Gansworth, "My First Days at the Carlisle Indian School," *Pennsylvania History*, October 1, 2004, 479–493.

64 The history textbook used at Carlisle is described in Adams, *Education for Extinction*, 146–147.

64 "I could not eat": Adams, *Education for Extinction*, 141.

64 "Somebody would have a coughing": Interview with John Alonzo, Dickinson Archive.

64 "When we were in school": Adams, *Education for Extinction*, 223.

65 Descriptions of the 1896 Carlisle-Wisconsin game: "Indians Get the Scalps," *Chicago Tribune*, December 20, 1896; "Greatest Game of the West," *Chicago Sentinel*, December 20, 1896.

65 "Too much praise cannot be given": Whitney, "Amateur Sport," *Harper's Weekly*, November 14, 1896.

65 Von Gammon story: Moore, "Football's Ugly Decades, 1893–1913," *Smithsonian Journal of History*, Fall 1967, 49–68; Miller, *The Big Scrum*, 156.

66 "Football Must Go; Stop the Deadly Game," *Rome Tribune*, November 1, 1897.

66 "Grant me the right": Revsine, *The Opening Kickoff*, 95.

67 "Death on the Football Field," *New York Herald*, November 13, 1897.

68 "I emphatically disbelieve": Miller, *The Big Scrum*, 214.

68 "Their chief shortcoming": "Facts About the Indians," *Boston Globe*, October 31, 1896.

68 "We only need a little more time": "Past, Present and Future of the Carlisle Indian School Team," *Red Man*, January 1898.

## Football Imagination

69 Information on Haskell Institute and Thorpe's first impressions can be found in Steiger and Thorpe, *Thorpe's Gold*, 51–52; Buford, *Native American Son*, 27–29.

70 "An Indian on the Haskell squad": Thorpe, "This Is My Story," *Sports World*, September 1949, 45.

70 "We played in our hickory-cloth": Interview with Henry Roberts, October 2, 1972, "American Indian Oral Histories," Oklahoma Historical Society.

70 Thorpe describes meeting Archiquette in Thorpe, "This Is My Story," *Sports World*, September 1949, 45; additional details in Wheeler, *Jim Thorpe*, 17.

71 Warner describes Cornell's crushing loss to Princeton in Bynum, *Pop Warner*, 77.

71 "There is winning, and there is misery": Benson, *Winning Words*, 112.

71 Descriptions of the Carlisle-Cornell game: "Cornell 23, Carlisle 6," *Boston Globe*,

October 9, 1898; "The Red Men Vanquished," *Cornell Daily Sun*, October 10, 1898;
Warner describes his impressions of the Carlisle team in Bynum, *Pop Warner*, 82.

71 "The twelfth member of the Cornell team": Crawford, *All American*, 35.

71 "We outscored 'em": Anderson, *Carlisle vs. Army*, 37.

72 Warner recalls his decision to leave Cornell for Carlisle, including the quote "The
Indian boys appealed to my football imagination," in Bynum, *Pop Warner*, 81–82.

## New Team

73 Warner's job interview with Pratt: Bynum, *Pop Warner*, 83; Anderson, *Carlisle vs.
Army*, 65.

74 "Having been coached": Warner, "Heap Big Run-Most-Fast," *Colliers*, October 24, 1931,
19.

74 Warner's favorite curses described: Crawford, *All American*, 77.

74 "You haven't been to practice" and response from players: Wheeler, *Jim Thorpe*, 47.

75 "I had all the prejudices": Warner, "Heap Big Run-Most-Fast," *Colliers*, October 24,
1931, 18.

76 "Speed had little place": Bynum, *Pop Warner*, 114.

76 Frank Hudson background: Benjey, *Doctors, Lawyers, Indian Chiefs*, 54–56; Anderson,
*Carlisle vs. Army*, 71; see also the American Indian Athletic Hall of Fame website for
biographical info on many of the Carlisle greats, including Hudson.

76 "Okay, son": Hall, *Go, Indians!*, 30.

77 "This is a new kind of team": Hall, *Go, Indians!*, 30.

77 "The Indians took to it": Warner, "The Indian Massacres," *Colliers*, November 17,
1931, 61.

77 "Now get down here": this scene is described in Benjey, *Doctors, Lawyers, Indian
Chiefs*, 67.

77 "When you're on defense" and following quotes from this practice: Anderson, *Carlisle
vs. Army*, 69.

78 The team's preparation for the Penn game is described in "Indians Leave Carlisle,"
*Philadelphia Times*, October 14, 1899.

## Carlisle vs. Pennsylvania

79 "a varying mass of color": "Penn Defeated by Fine Play of the Indians," *Philadelphia
Times*, October 15, 1899.

79 Descriptions of the 1899 Carlisle-Penn game: "Indians 16; Pennsylvania 5," *New York
Times*, October 15, 1899; "Penn Defeated by Fine Play of the Indians," *Philadelphia Times*,
October 15, 1899; "Pennsy's Big Fall: Outplayed by the Indians in Every Way," *Sunday
Gazette* (York, PA), October 15, 1899; "The Football Season," *Red Man*, December 1899.

81 "The Indians were tearing through": "Penn Defeated by Fine Play of the Indians,"
*Philadelphia Times*, October 15, 1899.

81 "This is the time": Hall, *Go, Indians!*, 33.

82 For Carlisle's 1899 football schedule, with scores and game descriptions, see Steckbeck, *Fabulous Redmen*, 29–31.

82 "one of the most interesting football battles": "Columbia and Indians Battle Here This Afternoon," *New York Sun*, November 30, 1899.

82 Descriptions of the 1899 Carlisle-Columbia game: "Indians in Great Form: They Crush Columbia's Varsity," *New York Sun*, December 1, 1899; "Indians' Big Triumph," *New York Tribune*, December 1, 1899.

82 "played the fastest game seen": "Indians' Big Triumph," *New York Tribune*, December 1, 1899.

83 Carlisle's rising stature in the football world discussed: "Earned Its Place," *New York Telegram*, December 1, 1899; "Honor for the Red Man," *New York Herald*, December 1, 1899.

83 "At one point along the road": "Famous Indian Football Men Have Arrived from the East," *San Francisco Call*, December 22, 1899; Warner describes the trip to California in Bynum, *Pop Warner*, 86–87.

83 Descriptions of the 1899 Carlisle-Cal game: "Masters of the Gridiron Against Local Champions," *San Francisco Call*, December 23, 1899; "Carlisle Barely Defeats California," *San Francisco Call*, December 26, 1899; "California Virtually Ties Carlisle," *San Francisco Chronicle*, December 26, 1899.

84 Carlisle ranked Number 4: Weyand, *The Saga of American Football*, 65.

85 Carlisle's visit to Haskell: Steiger and Thorpe, *Thorpe's Gold*, 63; Anderson, *Carlisle vs. Army*, 94.

## Wild Horses

86 Thorpe's Haskell experience described: Buford, *Native American Son*, 28–29.

86 "One of my classmates told me": Thorpe, "This Is My Story," *Sports World*, September 1949, 45.

87 "One day shortly afterwards": Thorpe, "This Is My Story," *Sports World*, September 1949, 45.

87 Jim's time in Texas: Wheeler, *Jim Thorpe*, 18; *Jim Thorpe: The World's Greatest Athlete*, a Moira Productions film, 2009.

88 "My father took one look": Thorpe, "This Is My Story," *Sports World*, September 1949, 45.

88 "We didn't sit": Buford, *Native American Son*, 30.

88 "a sort of hangdog look": Walter White's recollections of meeting Hiram and Jim Thorpe are excerpted in Crawford, *All American*, 43–44.

## Haughty Crimson

89 Roosevelt's longtime love of football discussed: Abbott, "Score One for Roosevelt," *Smithsonian.com*, September 20, 2011; Miller, *The Big Scrum*, 169–173; "T.R.'s Son Inspired Him to Help Rescue Football," *New York Times*, August 1, 2014.

89 "The rough play": Miller, *The Big Scrum*, 149.

90 "Portly politicians" and "Who is the best man?": "President Talks Football: Receives Members of the Carlisle Indian Team," *New York Sun*, November 29, 1902.

91 "De-lighted! Your play was brilliant" and "I see without asking": "President Talks Football: Receives Members of the Carlisle Indian Team," *New York Sun*, November 29, 1902.

91 "That was better than Harvard": "Indians at White House," *Washington Post*, November 29, 1902.

91 For game-by-game results of 1900–1902 seasons: Steckbeck, *Fabulous Redmen*, 32–41.

92 "Where's your ribbons": Adams, "More Than a Game," *The Western Historical Quarterly*, Spring 2001, 37.

92 Jimmie Johnson background: Carlisle's student files are held by the National Archives and Records Administration; many, including that of James Johnson, are available online at the Carlisle Indian School Digital Resource Center: carlisleindian.dickinson .edu; more on Johnson in Benjey, *Doctors, Lawyers, Indian Chiefs*, 95–96.

92 "I never had a team that averaged": Warner, "The Indian Massacres," *Colliers*, November 17, 1931, 7.

92 For game-by-game results of 1903 season: Steckbeck, *Fabulous Redmen*, 42–47.

92 "Neither the Indian boys nor myself": Warner describes the origin of the "hidden ball" play in Bynum, *Pop Warner*, 104–105.

93 "With a team averaging": "Lot of Tricks: What Harvard Expects from Indians," *Boston Globe*, October 31, 1903.

93 Descriptions of the 1903 Carlisle-Harvard game, including "hidden ball" play: "Indians Tricked Harvard," *Washington Post*, November 1, 1903; "Harvard 12, Indians 11," *New York Times*, November 1, 1903; "Coach Glenn Warner Explains the Tricks," *Boston Globe*, November 1, 1903; "Harvard 12, Carlisle 11: Spectacular Game," *Harvard Crimson*, November 2, 1903.

94–95 "Harvard spread out with us": for Albert Exendine's recollections of the "hidden ball" play: Newcombe, *The Best of the Athletic Boys*, 88; Warner describes the play, including quote, "I don't think any one thing," in Bynum, *Pop Warner*, 106–107, and Warner, "The Indian Massacres," *Colliers*, November 17, 1931, 7–8.

95 "For once, there was": Warner, "The Indian Massacres," *Colliers*, November 17, 1931, 8.

## Before and After

96 Jack Thorpe tells the story of young Jim jumping onto the bar: interview with Jack Thorpe, conducted by Joseph Bruchac for *Jim Thorpe: The World's Greatest Athlete*, a Moira Productions film, 2009.

96 "It was all book work": Thorpe, "This Is My Story," *Sports World*, September 1949, 68.

97 "I wasn't big enough": Crawford, *All American*, 49.

97 "I have a boy": Newcombe, *The Best of the Athletic Boys*, 60.

97 "Son, you are an Indian": Wheeler, *Jim Thorpe*, 20.

97 Thorpe's arrival in Carlisle: Crawford, *All American,* 53–55.

98 Carlisle's gym described, including praise of female athletes: "Carlisle Indians Taught by One of Their Own Race," *Washington Post*, April 8, 1906.

100 Hiram's death described: Buford, *Native American Son*, 35.

100 "When you boys and girls": Newcombe, *The Best of the Athletic Boys*, 71.

101 Thorpe describes his outing experience: Thorpe, "This Is My Story," *Sports World*, September 1949, 68.

101 "You're too little": Jenkins, *The Real All Americans*, 213.

## Football on Trial

102 The end of Pratt's Carlisle career is summarized in Robert Utley's introduction to Pratt, *Battlefield and Classroom*, xxiv–xxv.

102 The growing controversy over football described: Miller, *The Big Scrum*, 173–190; Revsine, *The Opening Kickoff*, 93–104; Moore, "Football's Ugly Decades, 1893–1913," *Smithsonian Journal of History*, Fall 1967, 49–68; Brooks, *Forward Pass*, 13–16.

102 Corruption in football described in Jordan, "Buying Football Victories," *Colliers*, November 25, 1905, 21–24; "baths" quote is from Revsine, *The Opening Kickoff*, 54.

102 "The number of miners": Warner, "What's the Matter with Football?," *Colliers*, November 14, 1931, 26.

103 "The players go on the field": Moore, "Football's Ugly Decades, 1893–1913," *Smithsonian Journal of History*, Fall 1967, 59.

103 "We're *coached* to pick out": Needham, "The College Athlete," *McClure's*, July 1905, 271.

103 "A game which needs": Moore, "Football's Ugly Decades, 1893–1913," *Smithsonian Journal of History*, Fall 1967, 51.

103 "The sooner the game is discontinued": "Facilis Descensus," *New York Times*, November 28, 1904.

103 "I believe in outdoor games": Miller, *The Big Scrum*, 177.

103 "Football is on trial": Miller, *The Big Scrum*, 187; Harvard coach Bill Reid briefly describes this meeting and the agreement made in Reid, *Big-Time Football at Harvard, 1905*, 194–195.

104 "Now, Reid, what's this I see": Miller, *The Big Scrum*, 192.

105 William Moore's death described: "Football Player Killed," *New York Times*, November 26, 1905; Miller, *The Big Scrum*, 193.

105 "In theory boys play football": "The Homicidal Pastime," *New York Times*, November 29, 1905.

105 "One human life": Weyand, *The Saga of American Football*, 82.

105 Formation of the NCAA and new rules: Weyand, *The Saga of American Football*,

83–84; Brooks, *Forward Pass*, 25–26; Morrison, "The Early History of Football's Forward Pass," *Smithsonian.com*, December 28, 2010.

106 "If the game does not stand": Miller, *The Big Scrum*, 211.

## High Jump

107 Thorpe describes the high jump and meeting Pop Warner in Thorpe, "This Is My Story," *Sports World*, September 1949, 68; Warner's version is in Bynum, *Pop Warner*, 119–120; both quoted in "Jim Thorpe Leaps to Fame on Carlisle Athletic Field," *Washington Post*, December 15, 1912.

109 "Now Ex, you stick with Thorpe": from recording of Exendine oral history used in *Jim Thorpe: The World's Greatest Athlete*, a Moira Productions film, 2009.

109 "I didn't know what a football was": "Mr. Ex Walking, Talking History," *Great Bend (KS) Tribune*, August 25, 1967; Exendine describes his friendship with Thorpe: interview with Albert Exendine, September 30, 1972, "American Indian Oral Histories," Oklahoma Historical Society.

110 "It contained different kinds": Adams, *Education for Extinction*, 115.

110 "Ex! I've got you licked!": Buford, *Native American Son*, 43.

110 "Before Jim hit Carlisle": "Jim and Exie Meet Once More," *Muskogee (OK) Daily Phoenix*, May 12, 1929.

110 "Go away and come back": Wheeler, *Jim Thorpe*, 54.

## The Forward Pass

114 "I must admit": Crawford, *All American*, 8.

114 "Thorpe was a good learner": Benjey, *Oklahoma's Carlisle Indian School Immortals*, 87.

115 "Is there a question": "Interesting Yarns of the Gridiron," *Altoona Tribune*, November 16, 1911; additional Mount Pleasant background: Benjey, *Doctors, Lawyers, Indian Chiefs*, 111; American Indian Athletic Hall of Fame website.

115 "I nearly missed him": Warner, "Red Menaces," *Colliers*, October 31, 1931, 16.

115 "When the pass came out": "Mr. Ex Walking, Talking History," *Great Bend (KS) Tribune*, August 25, 1967.

115 Warner discusses the evolution of the forward pass and spiral, including photos of Mount Pleasant demonstrating proper technique, in Warner, *A Course in Football for Players and Coaches*, 35–37.

116 "I can still recall": Benjey, *Doctors, Lawyers, Indian Chiefs*, 114.

116 "I opposed the forward pass": Warner, "Battles of Brawn," *Colliers*, November 7, 1931, 47.

116 Descriptions of the 1907 Carlisle-Syracuse game: "Beaten After Game Fight," *Syracuse Herald*, October 13, 1907; coverage of Buffalo newspapers excerpted in the *Arrow*, October 18, 1907.

117 "When a touchdown is made": "Indians Crush the U.P.," *New York World*, excerpted in *Arrow*, November 2, 1906.

117 Thorpe's early action: Crawford, *All American*, 78–79; "Bucknell Fails to Score," *Arrow*, October 25, 1907.

118 "perfect football machine": Buford, *Native American Son*, 57.

118 "Same old thing": Warner, "Heap Big Run-Most-Fast," *Colliers*, October 24, 1931, 19.

118 "What do they do?": Newcombe, *The Best of the Athletic Boys*, 155.

119 "He'd not use another match": Crawford, *All American*, 139.

119 "You play the way you practice": Buford, *Native American Son*, 46.

119 "Good blocking and deadly tackling": Warner, "Heap Big Run-Most-Fast," *Colliers*, October 24, 1931, 18.

120 "There is no system of play": Jenkins, *The Real All Americans*, 251.

120 Dickinson quarterback Hyman Goldstein recalls seeing Warner at café with salt and pepper shakers in Wheeler, *Jim Thorpe*, 44.

120 Descriptions of the historic 1907 Carlisle-Penn game: "Indians Beat Penn by Score of 26 to 6," *Philadelphia Inquirer*, October 27, 1907; "Red and Blue Team Defeated by Carlisle," *Philadelphia Inquirer*, October 27, 1907; "Penn Gives Poor Football Exhibition; Loses to Indians," *Washington Post*, October 27, 1907; "Indians Humble Pennsy's Eleven," *New York Times*, October 28, 1907; "Indians Win Exciting Game from Varsity by 26 to 6," *Pennsylvanian*, October 28, 1907; "Victory over Pennsy," *Arrow*, November 1, 1907.

## Carlisle against the World

122 "It will be talked of often": Newcombe quotes the *Philadelphia North American* in his book *The Best of the Athletic Boys*, 118.

122 "We've come to Philly Billy": "Indians Beat Penn by Score of 26 to 6," *Philadelphia Inquirer*, October 27, 1907.

122 "I'd see the ball sailing": Bynum, *Pop Warner*, 118.

123 "Poor Pennsylvania": Warner, "The Indian Massacres," *Colliers*, November 17, 1931, 62.

123 "I got excited": Buford, *Native American Son*, 58.

123 "With racial savagery": Anderson quotes the *Philadelphia Press* in his book *Carlisle vs. Army*, 157.

123 "You know, I never make predictions" and subsequent Warner quotes in hotel lobby: "Indians Primed for Tigers' Game," *New York Times*, November 2, 1907.

124 Princeton receives help from coaches and former players: "Coaches Rushing to Princeton's Aid," *New York Times*, October 30, 1907.

124 Descriptions of the 1907 Carlisle-Princeton game: "Tigers Humble Indians and Win by 16 to 0," *New York Times*, November 3, 1907; "Indians No Match for Tiger Eleven," *New York Tribune*, November 3, 1907; "Princeton Did It: Solved Indian Problem by Straight Football on Wet Field," *Syracuse Herald*, November 3, 1907; "Indian Tricks Prove Unavailing Against Tigers' Weight," *Washington Times*, November 3, 1907; "Tigers Masters of the

Redskins," *New York Sun*, November 3, 1907; "Princeton Wins," *Daily Princetonian*, November 4, 1907; additional coverage and excerpts in the *Arrow*, November 8, 1907.

124 "He may have beaten dear old Penn": "Tigers Humble Indians and Win by 16 to 0," *New York Times*, November 3, 1907.

124 "Tigers Humble Indians," *New York Times*, November 3, 1907; "Princeton Did It: Solved Indian Problem by Straight Football on Wet Field," *Syracuse Herald*, November 3, 1907.

125 "He was a hard loser": "Dr. Waite Remembers Pop's Daring, Love of Horses, and His Snoring" clipping from Concord, New York, Historical Society archives, September 11, 1954.

125 "Their weakness has been": "Indians' Stiff Schedule: No College Team Would Dare Undertake Carlisle's Hard Program," *New York Times*, November 3, 1907.

125 "joyously and continuously" and "Good thing this isn't": Warner, "Heap Big Run-Most-Fast," *Colliers*, October 24, 1931, 19.

125 "Remember last Saturday!" Hall, *Go, Indians!*, 47.

126 Descriptions of the 1907 Carlisle-Harvard game: "Indians Do Up Harvard Team," *New York Sun*, November 10, 1907; "Indians Beat Crimson," *New York Tribune*, November 10, 1907; "Indians Better in Every Way," *Boston Globe*, November 10, 1907; "Speedy Indians Crush Harvard," *New York Times*, November 10, 1907; "Carlisle Indians Triumph Over Harvard 23 to 15," *Boston Post*, November 10, 1907; "Mt. Pleasant, as Usual, Thrilled the Stadium," *Boston Post*, November 10, 1907; "The Scene in the Stadium," *Boston Post*, November 10, 1907; "Indians Scalp Harvard," *Arrow*, November 15, 1907.

126 "They did not hang out a sign": "Indians Better in Every Way," *Boston Globe*, November 10, 1907.

126 "Oh, wait till Harvard": "The Scene in the Stadium," *Boston Post*, November 10, 1907.

126 "zigzagging sprint": "Indians Better in Every Way," *Boston Globe*, November 10, 1907.

126 "He went through": "Indians Beat Crimson," *New York Tribune*, November 10, 1907; "I saw only goalposts": "Mt. Pleasant's Laconic Comment upon Victory," *Boston Herald*, November 10, 1907.

127 "We've got to score *again*": Anderson, *Carlisle vs. Army*, 159.

127 "The 'Big Four' Now the 'Big Five'": *Arrow*, November 15, 1907.

## Modern Football

128 "I didn't like it much": Crawford, *All American*, 83.

128 Warner recalls some of the team's pranks: Warner, "Heap Big Run-Most-Fast," *Colliers*, October 24, 1931, 19; more on pranks in Newcombe, *The Best of the Athletic Boys*, 119; Steiger and Thorpe, *Thorpe's Gold*, 93.

128 "Chicago should win": "Maroons and Indians Ready: Game of Thrills Expected Today," *Chicago Daily Tribune*, November 23, 1907.

129 Descriptions of the 1907 Carlisle-Chicago game: "Aborigines Win over Palefaces,"

*Chicago Daily Tribune*, November 24, 1907; "Indians' Fast Play Routs Chicago," *New York Times*, November 24, 1907; "Carlisle Gets Another Scalp: Chicago Beaten 18 to 4 on Own Ground," *Boston Globe*, November 24, 1907; "Maroons Beaten by Better Team," *Chicago Daily Tribune*, November 24, 1907; "Carlisle Too Fast: Chicago Falls Before Superior Play of Indians," *Washington Post*, November 24, 1907; additional articles excerpted in the *Arrow*, November 29, 1907.

129 "Huh, Wizard of the West": Johnson, "Albert Andrew Exendine: Carlisle Football Coach," *The Chronicles of Oklahoma*, Autumn 1965, 321.

129 "They would wait till I almost": "Mr. Ex Walking, Talking History," UPI article, August 17, 1967.

130 "Hold that ball": Benjey, *Oklahoma's Carlisle Indian School Immortals*, 87.

130 "They showed themselves": "Aborigines Win over Palefaces," *Chicago Daily Tribune*, November 24, 1907.

131 "I do not remember" and "They used the forward pass": Whitney, "The View-Point," *Outing*, January 1908, 497.

131 "The Indians have had a harder": Knox, "The New Football," *Harper's Weekly*, December 7, 1907, 1766.

131–132 "We want Jim" and "Out of my way": Wheeler, *Jim Thorpe*, 66.

132 "picking his opponents up": Buford, *Native American Son*, 75.

132 Thorpe's activities in town: Buford, *Native American Son*, 64.

132 "The boys felt they'd earned it": from an oral history interview with Arthur Martin held at the Cumberland County Historical Society; this historical society even has (and I was able to see) the actual handwritten ledgers in which the players' expense accounts were kept.

132 Warner living the good life: Crawford, *All American*, 88.

134 "If he had taken coaching": Warner, "Review of the Football Season of 1908," *Outing*, January 1909, 516.

134 "Oh, hell, Pop": Warner, "Here Come the Giants," *Colliers*, November 21, 1931, 20.

134 "It was difficult to know": Buford, *Native American Son*, 72.

134 "James was very far": Buford, *Native American Son*, 90.

134 Thorpe's decision to play summer baseball: Crawford, *All American*, 118–119; Steiger and Thorpe, *Thorpe's Gold*, 129.

135 "granted a summer leave": Crawford, *All American*, 119.

135 "the greatest mistake in my life": Thorpe, "This Is My Story," *Sports World*, September 1949, 69.

## Crossroads

136 "I told him I would give it a whirl": Steiger and Thorpe, *Thorpe's Gold*, 129.

136 Thorpe's stats from 1909 summer season: Steiger and Thorpe, *Thorpe's Gold*, 130; more on his minor-league experience in Buford, *Native American Son*, 85–89.

136 "He stood about ten feet": Newcombe, *The Best of the Athletic Boys*, 142.

137 "When a white man approaches": Mike Koehler, Jim Thorpe's grandson, relates this story in an interview conducted by Joseph Bruchac for *Jim Thorpe: The World's Greatest Athlete*, a Moira Productions film, 2009.

137 Warner's struggles without Thorpe: Steckbeck, *Fabulous Redmen*, 78–85.

138 Thorpe returns home, tries farming: Buford, *Native American Son*, 89–91.

138 "It is customary at this school": Newcombe, *The Best of the Athletic Boys*, 143.

138 Thorpe's 1910 baseball season: Buford, *Native American Son*, 91–93.

139 "I knew I stood": Buford, *Native American Son*, 93.

139 Sweetcorn's slugging: Steckbeck, *Fabulous Redmen*, 104; this source also includes game-by-game results for the 1910 season.

139 Exendine describes meeting Thorpe in Anadarko in an oral history interview conducted on September 30, 1972, held by the Oklahoma Historical Society.

## The Quarterback

141 Welch's childhood, including seeing poster for Carlisle game in Duluth and meeting the team in Minneapolis: "Athletic Career of Gus Welch," *Richmond Times Dispatch*, February 12, 1928; "Last Stand of the Indians," *Bedford (VA) Bulletin*, October 9, 1952; more on background in Benjey, *Doctors, Lawyers, Indian Chiefs*, 189–190.

142 "I was just a ragamuffin": "Last Stand of the Indians," *Bedford (VA) Bulletin*, October 9, 1952.

142 Careers of Carlisle graduates discussed in: Deloria, *Indians in Unexpected Places*, 94; Benjey, *Doctors, Lawyers, Indian Chiefs*, 100, 131.

143 "soul wound": Buford, *Native American Son*, 41.

144 Welch moves in with Thorpe: Newcombe, *The Best of the Athletic Boys*, 153.

144 "It felt good to be back": Buford, *Native American Son*, 98.

144 "What do I do if I miss": Newcombe, *The Best of the Athletic Boys*, 154.

144 "But I couldn't get": Newcombe, *The Best of the Athletic Boys*, 150.

146 "What's the use of crying": Jenkins, *The Real All Americans*, 275.

146 For Carlisle's 1911 team lineup and game-by-game results: Steckbeck, *Fabulous Redmen*, 85–92.

146 "I have a better team" and "Georgetown will put": "Georgetown Meets the Indians Today," *Washington Herald*, October 14, 1911.

147 Descriptions of the 1911 Carlisle-Georgetown game: "Large Crowd of Enthusiasts Throng Hilltop to See Georgetown-Indian Game," *Washington Times*, October 14, 1911; "Carlisle Eleven Wins from G. U. by 28 to 5," *Washington Post*, October 15, 1911; "Carlisle Indians Humble Georgetown," *Washington Herald*, October 15, 1911.

147 "like a piece of smooth-running": "Carlisle Indians Humble Georgetown," *Washington Herald*, October 15, 1911.

147 "big heavy team": Buford, *Native American Son*, 100.

147 Descriptions of the 1911 Carlisle-Pitt game: "Carlisle Indians Trim Pittsburgh," *Washington Herald*, October 22, 1911; "Carlisle Indians Beat Pitt in Football, 17 to 0,"

*Pittsburgh Post-Gazette*, October 22, 1911; "Indians Win Easily: Play Great Game in Defeating Pittsburgh, 17 to 0," *Washington Post*, October 22, 1911; "About Carlisle Athletics," *Arrow*, October 27, 1911.

147 "He seemed possessed": *Pittsburgh Dispatch*, excerpted in Wheeler, *Jim Thorpe*, 87.

148 "Scouts for Pennsylvania": "Carlisle Indians Trim Pittsburgh," *Washington Herald*, October 22, 1911.

## All In

149 "He plays football with the abandon": "Carlisle Indians Beat Pitt in Football, 17 to 0," *Pittsburgh Post-Gazette*, October 22, 1911.

149 "He always went around": oral history interview with Rose DeNomie Roberts, held by the Oklahoma Historical Society.

149 "He could be very jolly": Newcombe, *The Best of the Athletic Boys*, 170.

149 "All the girls had a crush" and "He treated all the girls": Buford, *Native American Son*, 109.

149 Iva Miller background: Buford, *Native American Son*, 109–111; Steiger and Thorpe, *Thorpe's Gold*, 159.

150 Geronimo background and World's Fair experience: King, "Geronimo's Appeal to Theodore Roosevelt," *Smithsonian.com*, November 9, 2012.

151 "the prettiest girl at Carlisle": Crawford, *All American*, 162.

151 "You're a cute little thing": Steiger and Thorpe, *Thorpe's Gold*, 159.

151 Warner's continued cursing: Newcombe, *The Best of the Athletic Boys*, 156; Steiger and Thorpe, *Thorpe's Gold*, 144.

151 "Lazy Indian": Rice, *The Tumult and the Shouting*, 233.

151 "I'm satisfied" and Pop's response: Pope, *Football's Greatest Coaches*, 297.

151 "Jim was always a carefree": Thorpe gives Warner's quote and his own response in Thorpe, "This Is My Story," *Sports World*, September 1949, 70.

152 The Lafayette game and Thorpe's injury: Steckbeck, *Fabulous Redmen*, 88; Newcombe, *The Best of the Athletic Boys*, 158; "Carlisle Wins from Lafayette," *Arrow*, November 3, 1911.

152 Iva's trip to Philadelphia: Anderson, *Carlisle vs. Army*, 214.

152 Descriptions of the 1911 Carlisle-Penn game: "Indians Outplay Red and Blue and Are Cheered by Fair Maids," *Philadelphia Inquirer*, November 5, 1911; "How Game Was Won and Lost at Franklin Field," *Philadelphia Inquirer*, November 5, 1911; "Indians Scalp Quakers, *New York Tribune*, November 5, 1911.

152 "the wonderful dodging Welch": "Indians Got Jump on Penn in First Period," *Philadelphia Inquirer*, November 5, 1911.

152 "We used to call signals": Crawford, *All American*, 139.

153 "Does it pay to educate": "Indians Outplay Red and Blue and Are Cheered by Fair Maids," *Philadelphia Inquirer*, November 5, 1911.

153 "When playing against college teams": Cooper, *Indian School*, 75.

154 "Anything very good": Crawford, *All American*, 140.

154 "We pointed to this game": Buford, *Native American Son*, 101.

154 "whiff-whaff": Crawford, *All American*, 140.

154 "We'll stick to barnyard football": Whelan, "Football Coaches—Drivers and Diplomats," *Outing*, October 1913, 193.

154 "the ruler of the football universe": "Jim Thorpe Acclaimed as America's Greatest Gridder in Mid-Century Poll," *Syracuse Post-Standard*, January 25, 1950.

154 "Crippled Jimmy Thorpe": *Boston Globe*, quoted in Buford, *Native American Son*, 101; more pregame hype: "Indians to Face All Substitutes," *Boston Globe*, November 11, 1911; "Harvard to Use Subs," *New York Tribune*, November 11, 1911.

155 "Jim, you can't run": Hall, *Go, Indians!*, 69.

## Carlisle vs. Harvard

156 The system of the blackboard updates on Indian Field is described in "Victory over Pennsy," *Arrow*, 1907.

156 "Their line was supposed to be": Crawford, *All American*, 140.

157 "Jim didn't say anything": Newcombe, *The Best of the Athletic Boys*, 166.

158 "Each girl did her best": "My Trip to Boston," *Arrow*, April 19, 1912.

158 Descriptions of the 1911 Carlisle-Harvard game: "Indians Win in Stadium: Thorpe's Good Toe Gives Them 18–15 Victory," *Boston Globe*, November 12, 1911; "Indians Not One-Man Team," *Boston Herald*, November 7, 1911; "Weak Harvard Team Is Beaten by the Indians," *Boston Herald*, November 12, 1911; "Remove Crimson Scalp," *New York Tribune*, November 12, 1911; "Thorpe's Four Field Goals Beat Harvard," *New York Times*, November 12, 1911; additional excerpts in the *Arrow*, November 24, 1911.

159 "It was in the second half" and "The Indians played at a speed": "Indians Win in Stadium," *Boston Globe*, November 12, 1911.

159 "Jim led the Carlisle effort": Bynum, *Pop Warner*, 128.

159 "The Indians were six points": "Indians Win in Stadium," *Boston Globe*, November 12, 1911.

159 "Most of the fellows": Thorpe recalls the Harvard game in an extended interview in Paddock, "Chief Bright Path," *Colliers*, October 12, 1929, 80–81.

160 "Pop wanted to take Jim": Crawford, *All American*, 142.

160 "And get out of my way": Paddock, "Chief Bright Path," *Colliers*, October 12, 1929, 81.

160 "Who in the hell heard": this discussion in the huddle in from Gus Welch's description, quoted in Jenkins, *The Real All Americans*, 266.

161 "As long as I live": "Chief Bright Path," *Colliers*, October 12, 1929, 81.

161 "His going gave the crowd": "Weak Harvard Team Is Beaten by the Indians," *Boston Herald*, November 12, 1911.

161 "I realize that here": Steiger and Thorpe, *Thorpe's Gold*, 157.

162 "Maybe football victories": "Chief Bright Path," *Colliers*, October 12, 1929, 81.

## All-American

163 "Most of the players bear": "Indians Have Day of Rest," *New York Times*, November 14, 1911.

163 "We looked on victory": Warner, "The Indian Massacres," *Colliers*, November 17, 1931, 63.

163 "Don't ask me how many": "Carlisle Indians and Orange Eleven Clash Before Thousands Today," *Syracuse Daily Orange*, November 18, 1911; Warner's pregame quotes are also from this article.

164 Descriptions of the 1911 Carlisle-Syracuse game, including weather conditions: "Orange Triumphs over the Indians in Grand Battle," *Syracuse Herald*, November 19, 1911; "Carlisle Indians Set Back," *New York Times*, November 19, 1911; "Carlisle Indians Lose in Fiercely Fought Game," *Brooklyn Daily Eagle*, November 19, 1911; "Syracuse Defeats Carlisle," *Syracuse Daily Orange*, November 20, 1911; additional excerpts in the *Arrow*, November 24, 1911.

164 "lost the contest for Carlisle": Thorpe, "This Is My Story," *Sports World*, September, 1949, 69.

164 "Coach Glenn Warner's face": "Orange Triumphs over the Indians in Grand Battle," *Syracuse Herald*, November 19, 1911.

164 "He collapsed after the game": "Alumni Present Coach with a Gold Watch," *Syracuse Daily Orange*, November 20, 1911.

165 For 1911 football results: "The Football Schedule, 1911," *Arrow*, December 8, 1911.

165 Season wrap-up and "Her repertoire of plays": "Football in 1911," *Outing*, January 1912, 507.

165 "The Indians, worn out": Warner, "The Indian Massacres," *Colliers*, November 17, 1931, 63.

165 Christmas at Carlisle and Thorpe's appearance: "Christmas Festivities at Carlisle," *Arrow*, January 12, 1912; "Thorpe as Santa Claus," *Arrow*, January 19, 1912.

166 "What's the use of bothering": Warner, "Red Menaces," *Colliers*, October 31, 1931, 17.

166 "Oh, all right then": Crawford, *All American*, 118.

166 "I trained as I never trained": Buford, *Native American Son*, 113.

166 Thorpe's Olympic trial: "Indian Athlete Wins Pentathlon Tryout," *New York Sun*, May 19, 1912.

167 "When do we start": Steiger and Thorpe, *Thorpe's Gold*, 167.

167 "He did everything wrong": Steiger and Thorpe, *Thorpe's Gold*, 167.

169 Leaving for Sweden: "America's Pride off to Conquer the World," *New York Sun*, June 15, 1912.

169 "Please send me $100" and agent's response: Newcombe, *The Best of the Athletic Boys*, 182.

## Stockholm

171 Training aboard the *Finland*: "US Athletes Training at Sea," *New York Evening Observer* (NY), June 15, 1912; "Olympic Men Keeping Fit," *New York Sun*, June 16, 1912.

171 "What are you doing": Rice, *The Tumult and the Shouting*, 228.

171 "deadly in earnest": Buford, *Native American Son*, 124.

172 Kiviat relates his *Titanic* worries: Holst, *American Men of Olympic Track and Field*, 79.

172 "We were pretty nervous": Steiger and Thorpe, *Thorpe's Gold*, 173.

174 Thorpe's performance in the pentathlon is described in "Americans Capture First Olympic Race—Pentathlon Is Also Ours," *New York Times*, July 8, 1912; Steiger and Thorpe, *Thorpe's Gold*, 175–177; Anderson, *Carlisle vs. Army*, 236–239.

174 "The Scandinavians couldn't believe": Steiger and Thorpe, *Thorpe's Gold*, 176.

174 "It is a complete answer": "Americans Capture First Olympic Race—Pentathlon Is Also Ours," *New York Times*, July 8, 1912.

175 Louis Tewanima background and Olympic experience: Gilbert, "Marathoner Louis Tewanima and the Continuity of Hopi Running, 1908–1912," *The Western Historical Quarterly*, Autumn 2012, 325–341; Crawford, *All American*, 71–72; Warner, "Red Menaces," *Colliers*, October 31, 1931, 16–17.

175 "He had nothing": Holst, *American Men of Olympic Track and Field*, 80.

176 "It seemed they were disappointed": Thorpe recounted this story in an autobiographical sketch titled "Red Son of Carlisle," prepared for the 1951 film, *Jim Thorpe—All American*.

176 "I had trained well": Steiger and Thorpe, *Thorpe's Gold*, 182.

176 Details of Thorpe's decathlon victory: Steiger and Thorpe, *Thorpe's Gold*, 179–183; Wheeler, *Jim Thorpe*, 107–109; "Thorpe, a Real American, Wins," *New York Tribune*, July 16, 1912; "James Thorpe, Greatest All-Round Athlete in History of Sports," *New York World*, July 17, 1912.

178 "There was a great burst": "America First as Olympics End," *New York Times*, July 16, 1912.

178 "Sir, you are the greatest": Newcombe, *The Best of the Athletic Boys*, 186.

## One More Year

179 "You have set a high standard": Taft's letter printed in the *Arrow*, September 13, 1912.

179 "You have shown us": "Carlisle Honors Her Olympic Victors," *Arrow*, September 13, 1912; more on ceremonies in Carlisle in "Honor Indian Athletes: 10,000 Persons at Reception to Thorpe and Tewanima at Carlisle," *New York Times*, August 17, 1912.

180 New York City parade: "Olympic Champions Cheered and Dined," *New York Times*, August 25, 1912; "Pop Warner, the Man Who Discovered Thorpe and Tewanima," *Arrow*, September 13, 1912.

180 "The fact that I was able": *Philadelphia Inquirer*, quoted in Buford, 137.

181 "I'm glad you're back": Buford, *Native American Son*, 136.

181 "the finest all-around athlete": "America First as Olympics End," *New York Times*, July 16, 1912.

181 "the greatest all-around": "James Thorpe, Greatest All-Round Athlete in History of Sports," *New York World*, July 17, 1912.

181 "Goliath and some fabled": "Sac and Fox Indian a Marvelous Man in Many Forms of Sport," *New York Times*, July 21, 1912.

181 "hustlers with their own": Bynum, *Pop Warner*, 142.

182 Eisenhower background and football tryout: Ambrose, *Eisenhower*, 26–27; Perret, *Eisenhower*, 13–14.

## Into the Whirlwind

184 "Keep your eye on him": McVeigh, "Jim Thorpe at School," *Literary Digest*, October 5, 1912, 593.

184 Descriptions of the 1912 Carlisle-Dickinson game: "World's Greatest Athlete—Plus Ten Other Parts of a Powerful Machine—Defeat Us," *Dickinsonian*, September 30, 1912; Steckbeck, *Fabulous Redmen*, 93.

185 New rules for 1912: "Plenty of Scoring Under New Rules," *New York Times*, September 1, 1912; Newcombe, *The Best of the Athletic Boys*, 194–195.

186 Carlisle 1912 roster and game-by-game results: Steckbeck, *Fabulous Redmen*, 92–97.

186 "He was my idol": Crawford, *All American*, 181.

187 "It brought me lots": "Belle Story Gives Thorpe Rabbit's Foot for Luck," *Harrisburg Telegraph*, October 3, 1912.

187 Descriptions of the 1912 Carlisle-W&J game: "Carlisle Team Is Tied by Washington and Jefferson," *Washington Post*, October 6, 1912; "Athletics," *Arrow*, October 11, 1912.

187 "The team's play-calling": Bynum, *Pop Warner*, 137.

188 Warner's version of postgame scuffle with Thorpe: Bynum, *Pop Warner*, 137–138; newspaper accounts include "Thorpe and Warner in Fight After Game," *Scranton*

188 "Thorpe, you've got to behave": Bynum, *Pop Warner*, 139.

189 "one of the most promising": *New York Times*, quoted in Ambrose, *Eisenhower*, 49.

189 "Ike was the first cadet": Davis, *Soldier of Democracy*, 135.

189 Descriptions of the 1912 Carlisle-Syracuse game: "Captain Jim Thorpe Is Star of Game in Which Carlisle Indians Beat Syracuse, 33 to 0," *Syracuse Herald*, October 13, 1912; "Athletics," *Arrow*, October 18, 1912.

190 "Where's your sense": Crawford, *All American*, 184.

190 "Had the field not been soft": "Captain Jim Thorpe Is Star of Game in Which Carlisle Indians Beat Syracuse, 33 to 0," *Syracuse Herald*, October 13, 1912.

190 "Thorpe will never run through": Crawford, *All American*, 185.

190 "We did everything we could": Wheeler, *Jim Thorpe*, 119.

190 Descriptions of the 1912 Carlisle-Pitt game: "Indians Administer Beating,"

*Pittsburgh Daily Post*, October 20, 1912; "Same Old Story: Thorpe," *New York Sun*, October 20, 1912.

191 "It was worth one's life": "Enthusiastic Crowd Sees Carlisle Beat Georgetown," *Washington Post*, October 27, 1912.

191–192 "Break up that interference" and "had not been called upon": "Georgetown Crushed in First Half," *Washington Herald*, October 27, 1912.

192 Descriptions of the 1912 Carlisle-Toronto game: "Carlisle Went over on the Kick-Off," *Ottawa Journal*, October 29, 1912; "Carlisle Indians Defeat Toronto Eleven, Score 49–1," *Harrisburg Daily Independent*, October 29, 1912; for a quick explanatoin of rugby rules and how Toronto scored a single point, see "Difference in Style" *Pittsburgh Post-Gazette*, October 29, 1912.

## Football Evolution

193 The extreme security measures Warner typically took before games in 1912: "Indians After Quakers' Scalps," *New York Times*, November 11, 1912.

193 Warner's single-wing formation: Bynum, *Pop Warner*, 29; Benjey, *Oklahoma's Carlisle Indian School Immortals*, 8.

194 "Which team do you boys": Hall, *Go, Indians!*, 79.

194 "There is my idea": Cohane, *Gridiron Grenadiers*, 73.

194 "Pot was a supreme proponent": Cohane, *Gridiron Grenadiers*, 74.

194 "I want to see blood!": Cohane, *Gridiron Grenadiers*, 73.

194 "They are a wall of bone": "For Honor of the Service, West Point's Football Warriors Battle," *Washington Herald*, October 27, 1912.

195 "Our coaches told us": from recording of Eisenhower used in *Jim Thorpe: The World's Greatest Athlete*, a Moira Productions film, 2009.

195 "He started weaving his way": Wheeler, *Jim Thorpe*, 127.

195 Descriptions of the 1912 Carlisle-Lehigh game: "Thorpe Was Thorn in Lehigh's Side," *Philadelphia Inquirer*, November 3, 1912; "Lehigh Puts Up Game Fight, but Carlisle Wins," *Washington Herald*, November 3, 1912.

196 "Introverted is not the way": Buford, *Native American Son*, 71.

196 "What about going around" and Garlow quote: Crichton, "Good King Jim," *Colliers*, November 14, 1942, 56.

196 "When Indian outbreaks": "Indians to Battle with Soldiers," *New York Times*, November 9, 1912.

197 "It was not that they felt": Warner, "The Indian Massacres," *Colliers*, November 17, 1931, 7.

197 "Indians to Battle with Soldiers," *New York Times*, November 9, 1912; "Indian Attack Feared," *Philadelphia Inquirer*, November 8, 1912; "Indians Out to Scalp the Cadets," *Brooklyn Eagle*, November 9, 1912.

197 "Coach Warner fully appreciates": "Indians Halt Scrimmage," *Washington Post*, November 6, 1912.

198 "Captain Thorpe barely feels": "Indians Aim for Cadets," *Scranton Republican*, November 6, 1912.

198 "The soldiers expect": "Devore Will Play," *Washington Times*, November 5, 1912.

198 "Carlisle may have a good team": "Army's Willing," *Washington Times*, November 9, 1912.

198 "Neither Warner nor Captain Thorpe": "Indians to Battle with Soldiers" *New York Times*, November 9, 1912; additional pregame coverage in "Indians Warned Are Working Hard," *Harrisburg Telegraph*, November 7, 1912; "Practice with Wet Ball," *Washington Post*, November 8, 1912; "Army-Carlisle," *New York Sun*, November 9, 1912; "Indians in Fine Fettle," *Washington Post*, November 9, 1912.

198 "We were confident": Thorpe, "This Is My Story," *Sports World*, September 1949, 70.

## Carlisle vs. Army

199 "the key to America": Reeder, *The West Point Story*, 9; geographic details: Walker, *Engineers of Independence*, 203.

199 "Carry the fight": Cohane, *Gridiron Grenadiers*, 74.

200 "I shouldn't have to prepare": Adams, "More Than a Game," *The Western Historical Quarterly*, Spring 2001, 47; more on players' recollections of pregame scene in the locker room in Wheeler, *Jim Thorpe*, 128; Crawford, *All American*, 189.

201 "I didn't think we had": Wheeler, *Jim Thorpe*, 128.

201 "He was primed": Paddock, "Chief Bright Path," *Colliers*, October 19, 1929, 48.

201 Descriptions of the 1912 Carlisle-Army game: "Thorpe's Indians Crush West Point," *New York Times*, November 10, 1912; "Army Put to Rout by Indian Team," *New York Sun*, November 10, 1912; "Army Is Massacred by Carlisle Braves," *Brooklyn Eagle*, November 10, 1912; "Indians Wage Bloody Battle with Cadets," *Pittsburgh Post-Gazette*, November 10, 1912; "Cadets Are Routed by Carlisle Band," *Pittsburgh Daily Post*, November 10, 1912; "Army Eleven in a Rout," *New York Tribune*, November 10, 1912.

201 "The cadets had never seen": Bynum, *Pop Warner*, 141.

201 "The shifting, puzzling": "Army Eleven in a Rout," *New York Tribune*, November 10, 1912.

202 "it was a crowd made": "Thorpe's Indians Crush West Point," *New York Times*, November 10, 1912.

202 "Hell's bells, Mr. Referee": Anderson, *Carlisle vs. Army*, 280.

203 "Then Mr. Thorpe": "Army Put to Rout by Indian Team," *New York Sun*, November 10, 1912.

203 "Thorpe runs too fast": Buford, *Native American Son*, 147.

203 "His catch and his start": "Thorpe's Indians Crush West Point," *New York Times*, November 10, 1912.

204 "the rattling of the bones": Jenkins, *The Real All Americans*, 286.

204 "I was thoroughly enjoying": Wheeler, *Jim Thorpe*, 133.

205 "The West Pointers were smeared": "Army Put to Rout by Indian Team," *New York Sun*, November 10, 1912.

205 "We played as one": Buford, *Native American Son*, 146.

205 "We knew Thorpe would": Davis, *Soldier of Democracy*, 137.

205 "We were sure we'd": Davis, *Soldier of Democracy*, 137.

206 "When we got up": Buford, *Native American Son*, 147.

206 "More than once": "Army Eleven in a Rout," *New York Tribune*, November 10, 1912.

206 "The cadets had been": "Thorpe's Indians Crush West Point," *New York Times*, November 10, 1912.

207 "very quiet and kind": Buford, *Native American Son*, 149.

207 "That Indian is the greatest": Wheeler, *Jim Thorpe*, 132.

## Last Games

208 "At Yale we don't play": Wheeler, *Jim Thorpe*, 132.

208 "Mr. Camp": Newcombe, *The Best of the Athletic Boys*, 202.

209 "It was 2:25 pm": "Story in Detail of Penn's Victory," *Philadelphia Inquirer*, November 17, 1912.

209 Descriptions of the 1912 Carlisle-Penn game: "Fumbles Cost Indians Game," *Washington Post*, November 17, 1912; "Pennsylvania Wins Sensational Game: Indians' Misplays Help to Cause Their Downfall," *New York Times*, November 17, 1912; "Penn Was Quick to Seize Fumbles," *Philadelphia Inquirer*, November 17, 1912; "Story in Detail of Penn's Victory," *Philadelphia Inquirer*, November 17, 1912; "Indians Fall Before Penn: Quakers Sensational in Their Play," *Boston Globe*, November 17, 1912; "First Defeat of the Season," *Arrow*, November 22, 1912.

210 "He was fatigued": "Thorpe Sure of Success in Baseball," *El Paso Herald*, February 17, 1913.

210 "Penn played and waited": "Story in Detail of Penn's Victory," *Philadelphia Inquirer*, November 17, 1912.

210 "I never thought the receiver": Warner recalls the scene in Bynum, *Pop Warner*, 139–140.

211 "Why, I know that guy": Newcombe, *The Best of the Athletic Boys*, 204.

211 "I was losing something": Buford, *Native American Son*, 150.

212 "The team realizes": "Brown Preparing to Repel Indians," *Boston Journal*, November 26, 1912.

212 "He eluded the outstretched": *Providence Journal*, quoted in Newcombe, *The Best of the Athletic Boys*, 206; "He plunged, dodged, ducked": "Thorpe, Thorpe, Thorpe, Thorpe, Thorpe, Thorpe: This Being the Story of How Carlisle Beat Brown, 32–0," *Boston Journal*, November 29, 1912; more game details in "Carlisle Beats Brown," *Springfield Daily News* (Springfield, MA), November 29, 1912.

212 "in a blaze of glory": many papers used this phrase to describe Thorpe's final performance, including "Indians Badly Defeat Brown," *Washington Post*, November 29, 1912;

"Thorpe Ends in a Blaze of Glory," *Charlotte Observer* (Charlotte, NC), November 29, 1912.

## Brutal Business

213 Thorpe and Carlisle stats: Steckbeck, *Fabulous Redmen*, 96–97; Newcombe, *The Best of the Athletic Boys*, 206–207; Buford, *Native American Son*, 151.

213 "Whenever I see": Warner, "The Indian Massacres," *Colliers*, November 17, 1931, 63.

214 "The Indians are very proud": "Jim Thorpe Hero in His Own Town," *Wichita Beacon*, January 1, 1913.

214 "Thorpe with Professional": Crawford, *All American*, 198–199.

214 "Is Thorpe a Pro?," *Wilkes-Barre Record*, January 24, 1913.

214 "Jim Thorpe Vindicated," *Indianapolis News*, January 25, 1913.

215 "Case Against Jim Thorpe Seems to Be Fully Proved," *Washington Post*, January 26, 1913.

215 "I don't understand, Pop": Buford, *Native American Son*, 160.

215 "I never made any secret": Wheeler, *Jim Thorpe*, 151.

215 "All I know about the charges": "Thorpe Not Professional," *New York Times*, January 25, 1913.

215 "The faculty and athletic director": Newcombe, *The Best of the Athletic Boys*, 209.

215 "I played baseball": "Olympic Prizes Lost; Thorpe No Amateur," *New York Times*, January 28, 1913; text of letter reprinted in entirety in Wheeler, *Jim Thorpe*, 144–145.

216 "hard and cruel" Thorpe, *Red Son of Carlisle*, 64.

216 "Thorpe Confesses to His Errors," *Harrisburg Telegraph*, January 28, 1913; "Olympic Hero, Carlisle Football Marvel, Is Branded a Professional," *Washington Herald*, January 28, 1913; "All Indian's Olympiad Prizes Will Have to Be Returned," *San Francisco Call*, January 28, 1913.

218 "a brutal business": Warner, "Red Menaces," *Colliers*, October 31, 1931, 51.

218 "Mr. Warner is a good": "Carlisle Indian School Hearings," Joint Commission of the Congress of the United States, Sixty-Third Congress, Second Session, to Investigate Indian Affairs, February 6, 7, 8, and March 25, 1914, 1341.

218 "Glenn Warner must have": *The Sporting News*, quoted in Buford, *Native American Son*, 165.

218 "There are any number": "Expressions of Sympathy for Jim Thorpe, Carlisle Indian, Heard on Every Side Today," *Washington Times*, January 28, 1913.

218 "There is no reason": *London Daily Citizen* quoted in *Chicago Day Book*, January 29, 1913.

218 "Objections to qualifications": Crawford, *All American*, 209.

219 "I don't know what": Buford, *Native American Son*, 167.

## Undefeated

220 "He has received": "Jim Thorpe Refused Offers of Thousands," *Houston Post*, Associated Press report, January 28, 1913; offers also described in "Ball Clubs Want Thorpe," *York Daily* (York, PA), January 29, 1913; "Jim Thorpe Will Be Asked to Become Big 'Red Hope,'" *New York World*, January 30, 1913.

221 Thorpe signing contract: "Thorpe Signs His New York Contract," *New York Sun*, February 2, 1913; "Thorpe Meets McGraw and Signs Contracts," *New York Tribune*, February 2, 1913; "Jim Thorpe Is Now a Giant," *Washington Herald*, February 2, 1913.

221 "I haven't any doubt": "Thorpe Signs His New York Contract," *New York Sun*, February 2, 1913.

221–222 "I am pleased to get" and "No one knows how sorry": "Thorpe Signs Giant Contract for a Year," *New York Times*, February 2, 1913.

222 "Our greatest glory": "Annual Banquet," *Red Man*, January 1898.

222 "They tell me": "Thorpe Is Big Drawing Card," *Courier-Journal* (Louisville, KY), February 23, 1913; beginning of spring training also described in "Jim Thorpe's Playing in Opening Workout of Giants Pleases McGraw," *New York World*, February 20, 1913; "James Thorpe Does Well in His Work-Outs at Marlin," *Washington Post*, February 24, 1913.

## Epilogue: Back on Top

223 "You know, Chief": Ritter, *The Glory of Their Times*, 183.

223 The Thorpe-Miller wedding: "Wedding of James Thorpe and Miss Margaret Iva Miller," *Harrisburg Telegraph*, October 14, 1913; "James Thorpe, World's Greatest Athlete, Weds," *Harrisburg Daily Independent*, October 14, 1913.

224 For the entire record of the congressional investigation, see: "Carlisle Indian School Hearings," Joint Commission of the Congress of the United States, Sixty-Third Congress, Second Session, to Investigate Indian Affairs, February 6, 7, 8, and March 25, 1914.

224 Warner's career records: Bynum, *Pop Warner*, 321–322.

225 "After thirty-six years": Warner, "The Indian Massacres," *Colliers*, November 17, 1931, 7.

226 "I have done my best": Benjey, *Wisconsin's Carlisle Indian School Immortals*, 256.

226 "It's the same old story": "A Great Character," *Richmond Times Dispatch*, February 1, 1970.

226 Welch details: "Athletic Career of Gus Welch," *Richmond Times Dispatch*, February 12, 1928; "Thorpe Teammate at Carlisle Dies," *Evening Times* (Trenton, NJ), January 30, 1970; "Gus Welch Dies; Played with Thorpe," *Richmond Times Dispatch*, January 30, 1970.

226 Carlisle cemetery described: Fear-Segal, *White Man's Club*, 231–232; I also visited this site during my research.

226 Carlisle closes, and legacy: Witmer, *The Indian Industrial School*, 88–90; Fear-Segal, *White Man's Club*, 276, 281.

227 Census data from "The American Indian and Alaska Native Population, 2010," US Census Bureau, 2012.

227 "I kept the language" and other quotes from Standing Bear's essay: Standing Bear, "What the Indian Means to America," in *Voices of the American Indian Experience, Volume 1,* ed. James E. Seelye and Steven A. Littleton, 508–512.

228 Death of Thorpe's son, including "Jim was never the same" and "He was broken-hearted": Buford, *Native American Son,* 214–215.

229 "Thorpe, by sheer strength": *Canton Daily News,* quoted in Buford, *Native American Son,* 205; Thorpe describes his career in pro football in Thorpe, "This Is My Story," *Sports World,* September 1949, 71.

230 "White people thought": Deloria, *Indians in Unexpected Places,* 130; for an entire book on the Oorang Indians, see Whitman, *Jim Thorpe and the Oorang Indians.*

230 "It represents honor": "Daniel Snyder on the Redskins Name Controversy," *Washington Post,* September 3, 2014.

230 *"Redskins* is defined": "What's in a Name?," *Time for Kids,* November 18, 2013.

230 "I'm not your mascot": "Levi Stadium Protestors Urge Washington Redskins to Change Name," *San Francisco Chronicle,* November 23, 2014.

231 "I never heard anything": Crawford, *All American,* 235.

231 "The people that he trusted": interview with Jack Thorpe, conducted by Joseph Bruchac for *Jim Thorpe: The World's Greatest Athlete,* a Moira Productions film, 2009.

231 "I can't decide": Steiger and Thorpe, *Thorpe's Gold,* 224.

231 Mid-century polls described: "Greatest Gridder of All, Thorpe Likes Sports Talk," *Miami Daily News-Record* (Miami, OK), January 25, 1950; "Jim Thorpe, Voted Greatest Grid Player, Recalls Former Exploits," *Corvallis Gazette-Times* (Corvallis, OR), January 25, 1950; "Jim Thorpe Acclaimed as America's Greatest Gridder," *Syracuse Post-Standard,* January 25, 1950.

231 Thorpe visit to Carlisle: "Carlisle Honors Big Jim Thorpe," *Hanover Evening Sun* (Hanover, PA), January 26, 1950; "Jim Thorpe Returns to Scene of Earliest Triumphs to Be Honored," *York Gazette and Daily* (York, PA), January 27, 1950.

232 "It was great to see": "Carlisle Honors Big Jim Thorpe," *Hanover Evening Sun* (Hanover, PA), January 26, 1950.

233 "One of the most wonderful": Jenkins, *The Real All Americans,* 312.

233 "I will not quit": Steiger and Thorpe, *Thorpe's Gold,* 237; Charlotte Thorpe documents her decades-long efforts in this book.

233 "My dad's life": "Jim Thorpe's Name Rises to Top Again," *Santa Cruz Sentinel* (Santa Cruz, CA), January 19, 1983.

233 "It's about time": "Thorpe's Gold Medals Finally Returned to His Family," *San Bernardino County Sun* (San Bernardino, CA), January 19, 1983.

# WORKS CITED

## Books, Magazines, and Documentaries

Abbott, Karen. "Score One for Roosevelt." *Smithsonian.com*, September 20, 2011.

Adams, David Wallace. *Education for Extinction: American Indians and the Boarding School Experience, 1875–1928*. Lawrence, KS: University Press of Kansas, 1995.

Adams, David Wallace. "More Than a Game: The Carlisle Indians Take to the Gridiron, 1893–1917." *The Western Historical Quarterly*, Spring, 2001, 25–53.

Ambrose, Stephen. *Eisenhower: Soldier, General of the Army, President-Elect, 1890–1952*. New York: Simon and Schuster, 1983.

Anderson, Lars. *Carlisle vs. Army: Jim Thorpe, Dwight Eisenhower, Pop Warner, and the Forgotten Story of Football's Greatest Battle*. New York: Random House, 2007.

Ball, Eve. *Indeh, An Apache Odyssey*. Norman, OK: University of Oklahoma Press, 1980.

Bell, Genevieve. *Telling Stories Out of School: Remembering the Carlisle Indian Industrial School, 1879–1918*. Dissertation, Stanford University, 1998.

Benjey, Tom. *Doctors, Lawyers, Indian Chiefs: Jim Thorpe & Pop Warner's Carlisle Indian School Football Immortals*. Carlisle, PA: Tuxedo Press, 2008.

Benjey, Tom. *Oklahoma's Carlisle Indian School Immortals*. Carlisle, PA: Tuxedo Press, 2010.

Benjey, Tom. *Wisconsin's Carlisle Indian School Immortals*. Carlisle, PA: Tuxedo Press, 2011.

Benson, Michael. *Winning Words: Classic Quotes from the World of Sports*. Lanham, MD: Taylor Trade Publishing, 2008.

Bigelow, Bill and Bob Peterson, editors. *Rethinking Columbus*. Milwaukee: Rethinking Schools, 1998.

Bloom, John. *To Show What an Indian Can Do: Sports at Native American Boarding Schools*. Minneapolis: University of Minnesota Press, 2000.

Brooks, Philip L. *Forward Pass: The Play That Saved Football*. Yardley, PA: Westholme Publishing, 2014.

Brown, Dee. *Bury My Heart at Wounded Knee: An Indian History of the American West*. New York: Holt, Rinehart, and Winston, 1970.

Bruchac, Joe, and Tom Weidlinger. *Jim Thorpe: The World's Greatest Athlete*, a Moira Productions film, 2009.

Buford, Kate. *Native American Son: The Life and Sporting Legend of Jim Thorpe*. Lincoln, NE: University of Nebraska Press, 2010.

Bynum, Mike, editor. *Pop Warner, Football's Greatest Teacher: The Epic Autobiography of Major College Football's Winningest Coach*. Langhorne, PA: Gridiron Football Properties, 1993.

Cantwell, Robert. "The Poet, the Bums, and the Legendary Redmen." *Sports Illustrated*, February 15, 1960, 74–84.

Carlson, Lewis H., and John J. Fogarty. *Tales of Gold: An Oral History of the Summer Olympic Games Told by America's Gold Medal Winners*. Chicago: Contemporary Books, 1987.

Child, Brenda J. *Boarding School Seasons: American Indian Families, 1900–1940*. Lincoln, NE: University of Nebraska Press, 1988.

Cohane, Tim. *Gridiron Grenadiers: The Story of West Point Football*. New York: G.P. Putnam's Sons, 1948.

Cohane, Tim. *The Yale Football Story*. New York: G. P. Putnam's Sons, 1951.

Cooper, Michael L. *Indian School: Teaching the White Man's Way*. New York: Clarion Books, 1999.

Corbett, Bernard, and Paul Simpson. "When Men Were Men and Football Was Brutal." *Yale Alumni Magazine*, November 2004, 59–62.

Crawford, Bill. *All American: The Rise and Fall of Jim Thorpe*. New York: John Wiley & Sons, 2005.

Crichton, Kyle. "Good King Jim." *Colliers*, November 14, 1942, 42, 56.

Daly, Dan. *The National Forgotten League: Entertaining Stories and Observations from Pro Football's First Fifty Years*. Lincoln, NE: University of Nebraska Press, 2012.

Danzig, Allison. *Oh, How They Played the Game: The Early Days of Football and the Heroes Who Made It Great*. New York: The Macmillan Company, 1971.

Davis, Kenneth. *Soldier of Democracy: A Biography of Dwight Eisenhower*. Garden City, NY: Doubleday, Doran & Company, 1945.

Deloria, Philip J. *Indians in Unexpected Places*. Lawrence, KS: University Press of Kansas, 2004.

Dunbar-Ortiz, Roxanne. *An Indigenous People's History of the United States*. Boston: Beacon Press, 2014.

Eastman, Elaine Goodale. *Pratt: The Red Man's Moses*. Norman, OK: The University of Oklahoma Press, 1935.

Edwards, William H. *Football Days: Memories of the Game and of the Men Behind the Ball*. New York: Moffat, Yard and Company, 1916.

Fear-Segal, Jacqueline. *White Man's Club: Schools, Race, and the Struggle of Indian Acculturation*. Lincoln, NE: University of Nebraska Press, 2007.

"Football in 1911." *Outing*, January 1912, 506–512.

"Football in 1912." *Outing*, January 1913, 506–512.

Gansworth, Howard. "My First Days at the Carlisle Indian School." *Pennsylvania History*, October 1, 2004, 479–493.

Gilbert, Matthew Sakiestewa. "Marathoner Louis Tewanima and the Continuity of Hopi Running, 1908–1912." *The Western Historical Quarterly*, Autumn 2012, 325–346.

Gilstrap, Harriet Patrick. "Memoirs of a Pioneer Teacher." *The Chronicles of Oklahoma*, Spring 1960, 20–34.

Hall, Moss. *Go, Indians! Stories of the Great Indian Athletes of the Carlisle School*. Los Angeles: Ward Ritchie Press, 1971.

Holst, Don, and Marcia S. Popp. *American Men of Olympic Track and Field: Interviews with Athletes and Coaches*. Jefferson, NC: McFarland, 2005.

Jenkins, Sally. *The Real All Americans: The Team That Changed a Game, a People, a Nation*. New York: Broadway Books, 2007.

Johnson, John L. "Albert Andrew Exendine: Carlisle Football Coach." *The Chronicles of Oklahoma*, Autumn 1965, 319–331.

Jordan, Edward. "Buying Football Victories." *Colliers*, November 25, 1905, 21–24.

King, Gilbert. "Geronimo's Appeal to Theodore Roosevelt." *Smithsonian.com*, November 9, 2012.

Knox, William F. "The New Football." *Harper's Weekly*, December 7, 1907, 1766.

McVeigh, Thomas, Jr. "Jim Thorpe at School." *Literary Digest*, October 5, 1912, 593–596.

Miller, John J. *The Big Scrum: How Teddy Roosevelt Saved Football*. New York: Harper-Collins, 2011.

Moore, John Hammond. "Football's Ugly Decades, 1893–1913." *Smithsonian Journal of History*, Fall 1967, 49–68.

Morrison, Jim. "The Early History of Football's Forward Pass." *Smithsonian.com*, December 28, 2010.

Needham, Henry Beach. "The College Athlete." *McClure's*, July 1905, 260–272.

Nelson, David M. *The Anatomy of a Game: Football, the Rules, and the Men Who Made the Game*. Newark, DE: University of Delaware Press, 1994.

Newcombe, Jack. *The Best of the Athletic Boys: The White Man's Impact on Jim Thorpe*. New York: Doubleday, 1975.

Paddock, Charley. "Chief Bright Path." *Colliers*, October 5, 1929, 16–17; October 12, 1929, 40, 80–81; October 19, 1929, 30, 48; October 26, 1929, 30, 56.

Perret, Geoffrey. *Eisenhower*. New York: Random House, 2000.

Pope, Edwin. *Football's Greatest Coaches and the Story of the Players and Plays That Made Them Famous*. Atlanta: Tupper and Love, Inc. 1955.

Pratt, Richard Henry, edited by Robert M. Utley. *Battlefield and Classroom: An Autobiography of Richard Henry Pratt*. New Haven, CT: Yale University Press, 1964.

Prucha, Francis Paul, editor. *Americanizing the American Indians: Writings by the "Friends of the Indian," 1880–1900*. Cambridge, MA: Harvard University Press, 1973.

Reeder, Colonel Red and Nardi Reeder Campion. *The West Point Story*. New York: Random House, 1956.

Reid, Bill. *Big-Time Football at Harvard, 1905: The Diary of Coach Bill Reid*. Edited by Ronald A. Smith. Urbana, IL: University of Illinois Press, 1994.

Revsine, Dave. *The Opening Kickoff: The Tumultuous Birth of a Football Nation*. Guilford, CT: Lyons Press, 2014.

Rice, Grantland. *The Tumult and the Shouting: My Life in Sport*. New York: A.S. Barnes & Company, 1954.

Ritter, Lawrence S. *The Glory of Their Times: The Story of the Early Days of Baseball Told by the Men Who Played It*. New York: William Morrow, 1984.

Ryan, Carmelita S. *The Carlisle Indian Industrial School*. Dissertation, Georgetown University, 1962.

Stamp, Jimmy. "How the Football Field Was Designed, from Hash Marks to Goal Posts." *Smithsonian.com*, September 24, 2012.

Standing Bear, Luther. *My People the Sioux*. Boston: Houghton Mifflin Company, 1928.

Standing Bear, Luther. "What the Indian Means to America." In *Voices of the American Indian Experience, Volume 1*, edited by James E. Seelye and Steven A. Littleton, 508–512. Santa Barbara, CA: Greenwood, 2013.

Steckbeck, John S. *Fabulous Redmen: The Carlisle Indians and Their Famous Football Teams*. Harrisburg, PA: J. Horace McFarland Company, 1951.

Steiger, Brad, and Charlotte Thorpe. *Thorpe's Gold: The Inspiring Untold True Story of Jim Thorpe—World's Greatest Athlete*. New York: Dell Publishing, 1984.

Sullivan, James E. "What Happened at Stockholm." *Outing*, October 1912, 21–31.

Thorpe, Grace. "The Jim Thorpe Family, Part II." *The Chronicles of Oklahoma*, Summer 1981, 179–199.

Thorpe, Jim, with Russell J. Birdwell. *The Red Son of Carlisle*, Warner Brothers Archive, University of Southern California.

Thorpe, Jim. "This Is My Story." *Sports World*, September 1949, 42–45, 68–71.

Vuckovic, Myriam. *Voices from Haskell: Indian Students Between Two Worlds, 1884–1928*. Lawrence, KS: University Press of Kansas, 2008.

Walker, Paul K. *Engineers of Independence: A Documentary History of American Engineers in the American Revolution, 1775–1783*. Honolulu: University Press of the Pacific, 1981.

Ward, Geoffrey C. *The West: An Illustrated History*. Boston: Little, Brown and Company, 1996.

Warner, Glenn S. *A Course in Football for Players and Coaches*. Carlisle, PA: 1912.

Warner, Glenn S. "Athletics at the Carlisle Indian School." *The Indian Craftsman*, March 1909, 9–11.

Warner, Glenn S. "Battles of Brawn." *Colliers*, November 7, 1931, 10, 45–47.

Warner, Glenn S. "Heap Big Run-Most-Fast." *Colliers*, October 24, 1931, 18–19, 46.

Warner, Glenn S. "Here Come the Giants." *Colliers*, November 21, 1931, 20, 34.

Warner, Glenn S. "Red Menaces." *Colliers*, October 31, 1931, 16–17, 51.

Warner, Glenn S. "Review of the Football Season of 1908." *Outing*, January 1909, 511–516.

Warner, Glenn S. "The Indian Massacres." *Colliers*, November 17, 1931, 7–8, 61–63.

Warner, Glenn S. "What's the Matter with Football?" *Colliers*, November 14, 1931, 26, 57–58.

Watterson, John S. *College Football: History, Spectacle, Controversy*. Baltimore: The Johns Hopkins University Press, 2000.

Watterson, John S. "Political Football: Theodore Roosevelt, Woodrow Wilson, and the Gridiron Reform Movement." *Presidential Studies Quarterly*, Summer 1995, 555–564.

Watterson, John S. "The Gridiron Crisis of 1905: Was It Really a Crisis?" *Journal of Sport History*, Summer 2000, 291–298.

Weyand, Alexander M. *The Saga of American Football*. New York: The Macmillan Company, 1955.

Wheeler, Robert W. *Jim Thorpe: World's Greatest Athlete*. Norman, OK: University of Oklahoma Press, 1975.

Whelan, Mack. "Football Coaches—Drivers and Diplomats." *Outing*, October 1913, 193–198.

Whitman, Robert L. *Jim Thorpe: Athlete of the Century*. Defiance, OH: The Hubbard Company, 2002.

Whitman, Robert. *Jim Thorpe and the Oorang Indians: N.F.L.'s Most Colorful Franchise*. Mount Vernon, IN: Windmill Publications, 1984.

Whitney, Caspar. "Amateur Sport." *Harper's Weekly*, November 14, 1896.

Whitney, Caspar. "The View-Point." *Outing*, January 1908, 495–498.

Witmer, Linda F. *The Indian Industrial School, Carlisle, Pennsylvania, 1879–1918*. Carlisle, PA: Cumberland County Historical Society, 2000.

## Newspapers

Many of the best and most detailed descriptions of Carlisle's games come from the sportswriters who witnessed and reported on the games. I consulted many hundreds of articles from the following newspapers:

*Altoona Tribune*
*Atlanta Constitution*
*Bedford (VA) Bulletin*
*Boston Globe*
*Boston Herald*
*Boston Journal*
*Boston Post*
*Brooklyn Eagle*
*Carrol (IA) Sentinel*
*Charlotte Observer*
*Chicago Day Book*
*Chicago Inter-Ocean*
*Chicago Sentinel*
*Chicago Tribune*
*Cornell Daily Sun*
*Corvallis (OR) Gazette-Times*
*Courier-Journal (Louisville, KY)*

*Daily Princetonian*
*Dickinsonian*
*El Paso Herald*
*Evening Times (Trenton, NJ)*
*Great Bend (KS) Tribune*
*Hanover (PA) Evening Sun*
*Harrisburg Daily Independent*
*Harrisburg Telegraph*
*Harvard Crimson*
*Houston Post*
*Indianapolis News*
*Kansas City Star*
*Miami (OK) Daily News-Record*
*Minneapolis Journal*
*Muskogee (OK) Daily Phoenix*
*New York Daily Tribune*
*New York Evening Observer*
*New York Herald*
*New York Journal*
*New York Sun*
*New York Telegram*
*New York Times*
*New York Tribune*
*New York World*
*Ottawa Journal*
*Pennsylvanian*
*Philadelphia Inquirer*
*Philadelphia Press*
*Philadelphia Times*
*Pittsburgh Daily Post*
*Pittsburgh Post-Gazette*
*Raleigh News and Observer*
*Reading (PA) Times*
*Richmond Times Dispatch*
*Rome (GA) Tribune*
*San Bernardino County Sun*
*San Francisco Call*
*San Francisco Chronicle*
*San Francisco Examiner*
*Santa Cruz Sentinel*
*Scranton Truth*

*Springfield (MA) Daily News*
*Sunday Gazette (York, PA)*
*Syracuse Daily Orange*
*Syracuse Herald*
*Syracuse Post-Standard*
*Washington Herald*
*Washington Post*
*Washington Times*
*Wichita Beacon*
*Wilkes-Barre Record*
*Yale Daily News*
*York (PA) Daily*
*York (PA) Gazette and Daily*

## Carlisle School publications

Carlisle students helped produce a series of newspapers and magazines over the years, often featuring stories of the football team, as well as other details about life at the school.

*The Indian Helper, 1885–1900*
*The Red Man, 1888–1900*
*The Red Man and Helper, 1900–1904*
*The Arrow, 1904–1908*
*The Carlisle Arrow, 1908–1917*
*The Red Man, 1910–1917*

## Additional Sources

Carlisle Indian School student files—many of these files have been digitized and are available online at the Carlisle Indian School Digital Resource Center.

"Carlisle Indian School Hearings," Joint Commission of the Congress of the United States, Sixty-Third Congress, Second Session, to Investigate Indian Affairs, February 6, 7, 8, and March 25, 1914.

Oral histories of Albert Exendine, Henry Roberts, and Rose Roberts, Oklahoma Historical Society.

Oral histories of Warner's assistant Arthur Martin, Cumberland County Historical Association.

Websites of the American Indian Athletic Hall of Fame, American Indian Center, Cherokee Nation, College Football Hall of Fame, Sac and Fox Nation.

# ACKNOWLEDGMENTS

The rise of Jim Thorpe and the Carlisle Indian football team is one of the most inspiring stories I've ever written about—and one of the most heartbreaking. While working on this book, I really struggled to find some kind of balance between stories about this thrilling team and all they overcame, and the harsh realities behind the stories. I expressed this concern to Barbara Landis at the Cumberland County Historical Society, who has spent many years studying the history of the Carlisle School and its students, and she said something very wise:

"You can't balance it. You just have to tell the stories."

That's what I've tried to do.

Thanks to Barbara, who gave me a personal tour of the Carlisle campus (now the Army War College), and to everyone at the Cumberland County Historical Society for their help finding research materials and photographs. Barbara also shared digital copies of every issue of all the newspapers and magazines published at the Carlisle School over thirty-two years. This was a great resource for football stories, but, as Barbara cautioned, less useful for finding out what life was really like at Carlisle. Though many of the articles were written by students, they were clearly edited by administrators, and no criticism of Pratt or Carlisle appears. Wherever possible, I have sought out and used interviews with and writings by Jim Thorpe and the other football players, and others who were students at Carlisle.

An enormous thank you to Joseph Bruchac, the great writer and storyteller, who has written and made films about Jim Thorpe, and knows as much about the story as anyone. When I went to visit Joe, I left carrying a box packed with books and other research materials he has collected over the years. He generously continued to answer questions and offer advice throughout the process of writing and revising this book.

Thanks also to Jim Gerencser and the entire Archives and Special

Collections staff at Dickinson College for welcoming me to their archive of material from the Carlisle School. They've also set up an amazing website, the Carlisle Indian School Digital Resource Center, which has scans of student files, photos, and much more. For game details and oral histories, I relied on materials from many other archives as well, and offer my thanks to the librarians and archivists at the University of Tulsa, Oklahoma Historical Society, Concord Historical Society (in Pop Warner's hometown of Springville, New York), the University of Southern California, Syracuse University, and the New York Public Library.

A big thank you to Tom Benjey, who has written some of the most exhaustively researched books about Carlisle's great players and teams, for generously sharing hard-to-find articles from his files. And thanks to Karen Blumenthal, nonfiction master and fellow football fan, for reading a draft of this book and offering insightful suggestions.

I'm so grateful to Simon Boughton at Roaring Brook for his continued support—he grew up thinking football was played with a round ball and nets, but saw merit in this story anyway. It's been a pleasure to work with Connie Hsu, an amazing editor (kind of like a great football coach, but without the cursing), and with Anne Diebel, and the entire Roaring Brook/Macmillan team, including Jill Freshney, Megan Abbate, Johanna Kirby, Morgan Dubin, Lucy Del Priore, Katie Halata, and John Nora. Thanks also to Susan Cohen, Amy Berkower, and everyone at Writers House for being such great teammates over the years.

And speaking of teams, no one could ask for a more supportive crew than my wife, Rachel, and our kids, Anna and David. Thanks for visiting Harvard Stadium with me, and for helping to reenact Carlisle's legendary hidden ball trick in our local park (Carlisle did it better). Thank you to Rachel, for believing in this writing thing long before there was any good reason to, and, as always, for those countless work-in-progress conversations that always leave me feeling better about what to do next.

# PHOTO CREDITS

# INDEX

Numbers in **bold** indicate pages with illustrations

Carlisle football games (*continued*)

1899 games, 77–84; 1899 season record, 84; 1900 games, 91; 1900 season record, 91; 1902 season record, 92; 1903 games, 92–95; 1907 games, 114–118, 120–131; 1907 season record, 131; 1908 games, 131–132, 134; 1909 games, 137–138; 1910 games, 139; 1911 games, 144–148, 152–165; 1911 season record, 165; 1912 Army game, 182, 199–207; 1912 games, 181–182, 184–188, 189–194, 195–213; 1912 games, average points scored during, 186; 1912 season record, 213

Carlisle football team: abilities and drive of, 75–77, 114–116, 118; all-time greatest and top-ranking teams, inclusion in, 84, 131, 213; athletic quarters and kitchen for, 110, 138, 144; attention brought to school by, 54, 56, 73; ban on playing, 24, 40–41; beginning of, 24–26; blocking and tackling practices, 2–3, 77, 119–120, **119**; camaraderie and pranking among players, 128, 138; changes to game play by, 24, 120–123, 126, 131, 185, 213, 224; coaching to improve, need for, 68; conduct of players and clean play by, 65, 91–92, 118; decision to not return to, 137–138; duty to team, Warner talk to Jim about, 166; expense accounts for, 132, **133**; facilities built on campus from money made by, 132; fairness of officiating in games played by, 54, 71; favors and special privileges for, 132, **133**, 227; feelings of team toward Jim, 157, 160; field for, 49, 65, 231; first winning season of, 68; forward pass use by, 115–116, **115**, 120–123, 131, 231; fun-loving approach to game, 195–196; Haskell visit by, 85–86; Hickok coaching of, 52, 56; hidden ball play, 92–95; hope and inspiration from, 45; last game of Jim with, 211–212; McCormick coaching of, 43–45, 52; meaning behind game with Army, 182, 196–197, 200; money made by, 131–132; motivation for beating teams, 153–154, 156; new path, forging after a defeat, 222; newspaper stories about, 50, 52; Oklahoma meetings with Jim about

returning to school, 137–138, 139–140; perfect football machine, 1907 team as, 118; performance and achievements of, 6; photos and footballs from big wins, display of, 98–99; practices of, 50, 74–75, 151, 193–194, 197–198, 209; Pratt feelings about, 25–26, 40; prejudices toward and racial comments about, 42, 92, 118, 123; pride and prestige in playing and winning, 154, 161–162, 197, 209; punt, Jim catching own in Pitt game, 147–148; quality of football played by, 65, 131, 139, 146, 185–186, **185**, 198, 207–208; quitting when going gets tough, stereotype about, 75, 125; resuming play by, meeting about and conditions for, 41–43; reverse play, 77–78, 81–82; road games and schedule of and player fatigue, 6, 65, 123–124, 125, 131, 163, 165, 187, 192, 209–211, 213; Rough Riders comparison to, 81; scoring by, 185–186; scouting and game plan for next opponent, 118–119; scouting of practices and games by future opponents, 146–147, 148, 193, 194; single-wing formation, 193–194, **193**, 201; size of players, 75–76, **75**, 92, 93, 115, 200–201; speed of play and hurry-up offense of, 81–83; suggestions for beating, sharing of by teams, 124; swearing and verbal abuse by Warner, 74, 151, 224; team colors, 52; teamwork of, powerful weapon of, 205; ticket sales, share of for, 73; tricky players, warning about by Army coach, 195; tryout for, 1–3, **2**, 6, 101, 110–111, 114; undefeated team and rising after every fall, 222; Warner coaching of, 6, 108; whirlwind football playing by, 120–123, 129–130, 146–147, 159, 195; White House visit by, 90–91

Carlisle Indian Industrial School: athletic abilities of women students, 99, **99**; buildings for, 29, 36; buildings for, return of to War Department, 226; cemetery at, 38, 226; clothing for students, 35, 98, **98**, 144; control over students at, 26, 38–40, 62–64; daily life and routine at, 38–40, **39**, **40**, 62–64, 98–101, 138, 144, 165, 224; death of students at, 38,